Norton Utilities 8 For

MW00387701

Commands-At-A-Glance

When You Need To	Try	Command	Read About It
Find files	File Find	FILEFIND	Chapter 5
			UnErase
UNERASE	Chapter 14		
	File Locate	FL	Chapter 33
Test system	Norton Diagnostics	NDIAGS	Chapter 25
			Disk Doctor
NDD	Chapter 26		
	Calibrate	CALIBRAT	Chapter 17
	System Watcher	Windows	Chapter 18
	System Info	SYSINFO	Chapter 13
Format a disk	Safe Format	SFORMAT	Chapter 11
Prepare for a disaster	Rescue Disk	RESCUE	Chapter 15
	Image	Image	Chapter 16
	Tracker	Windows	Chapter 19
Disaster recovery	Disk Doctor	NDD	Chapter 26
	Rescue Disk	RESCUE	Chapter 15
	UnErase	UNERASE	Chapter 14
	UnFormat	UNFORMAT	Chapter 27
Change display in DOS	Norton Control Center	NCC	Chapter 10
Change display Windows	INI tools	Windows	Chapter 20
Change display in NU	Norton Configuration	NUCONFIG	Chapter 2
Get Help	Norton Advisor		Chapter 43
	INI Advisor		Chapter 20
Speed up system	Norton Cache	NCACHE2	Chapter 8
	Speed Disk	SPEEDISK	Chapter 12

Symantec Corporation
(manufacturer of Norton Utilities)

Technical Support: Fax Retrieval System:
Voice: 503-334-7470   800-554-4403
Fax: 503-334-7470

                          Symantec Corp.
                          10201 Torre Avenue
Customer Service: Cupertino, CA 95014
800-441-7234

... For Dummies: #1 Computer Book Series for Beginners

Norton Utilities 8 For Dummies

Cheat Sheet

COMPUTER BOOK SERIES FROM IDG

DOS Reminder: Filenames

Filenames can have up to eight letters, a period, and up to three more letters (those last three letters are called the *extension*). Acceptable filenames: REPORT.DOC, 1.SEP, BALLOON. Unacceptable filename: BIG.STORM

DOS Reminder: Wildcards

Wildcards are helpful when looking for files — for example: FILEFIND *.DOC finds all files ending with DOC. The wildcard — * — is a placeholder for other characters (more on wildcards in Chapter 1)

Ten-Second Vocabulary

Directory	Place on hard disk where files reside
Current Drive	The letter at the system prompt (example: C:\>)
Switch	A DOS or Norton command is altered by using a switch (example: DIR /P)
Background	In Windows, a program working invisibly while another is in use

Error Messages

When you see `Bad Command or File Name`, you've either typed a command incorrectly or a program isn't on the computer.

When you see `Non-DOS disk`, you left a floppy disk in the drive when you turned on the computer. More about error messages and troubleshooting in Chapter 21.

If you can't remember anything...

Type **NORTON** and press Enter *or* double-click the Norton Integrator icon in Windows. Either action gets you into the Norton Utilities program, where there is plenty of help standing by. (See Chapter 38, "Ten Ways to Fake Your Way Through Norton Utilities," or Chapter 43, "Ten Free (Mostly) Ways to Get Help with Norton Utilities 8.")

Important Words To Live By

"Do or do not. There is no try." — Yoda, *The Empire Strikes Back*
"No matter where you go, there you are." — Buckaroo Bonzai

... For Dummies: #1 Computer Book Series for Beginners

NORTON
UTILITIES 8
FOR
DUMMIES™

NORTON UTILITIES 8 FOR DUMMIES™

by **Beth Slick**

Foreword by Steven E. de Souza

IDG BOOKS

IDG Books Worldwide, Inc.
An International Data Group Company

San Mateo, California ♦ Indianapolis, Indiana ♦ Boston, Massachusetts

Norton Utilities 8 For Dummies

Published by
IDG Books Worldwide, Inc.
An International Data Group Company
155 Bovet Road, Suite 310
San Mateo, CA 94402

Library of Congress Catalog Card No.: 94-75907

ISBN 1-56884-166-3

Printed in the United States of America

10 9 8 7 6 5 4 3 2 1

1B/QU/RZ/ZU

Distributed in the United States by IDG Books Worldwide, Inc.

Distributed in Canada by Macmillan of Canada, a Division of Canada Publishing Corporation; by Computer and Technical Books in Miami, Florida, for South America and the Caribbean; by Longman Singapore in Singapore, Malaysia, Thailand, and Korea; by Toppan Co. Ltd. in Japan; by Asia Computerworld in Hong Kong; by Woodslane Pty. Ltd. in Australia and New Zealand; and by Transword Publishers Ltd. in the U.K. and Europe.

For general information on IDG Books in the U.S., including information on discounts and premiums, contact IDG Books at 800-762-2974 or 415-312-0650.

For information on where to purchase IDG Books outside the U.S., contact Christina Turner at 415-312-0633.

For information on translations, contact Marc Jeffrey Mikulich, Foreign Rights Manager, at IDG Books Worldwide; FAX NUMBER 415-358-1260.

For sales inquiries and special prices for bulk quantities, write to the address above or call IDG Books Worldwide at 415-312-0650.

is a registered trademark of IDG Books Worldwide, Inc.

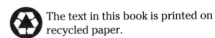

The text in this book is printed on recycled paper.

About the Author

Beth Slick joined the computer revolution in 1982 when she bought her first computer — which eventually lead to a seven-year stint as a manager of a computer store where she was also in charge of training and phone support to the clients there.

Even while she was running the computer store, Beth was writing articles for computer magazines as well as writing two other computer books for IDG Books.

Of course, living in Venice, California, Beth Slick spends her spare time crafting the great American screenplay — with the assistance of her cat, Yoda. While working on that perfect screenplay, Beth has also written two episodes of *Star Trek: The Next Generation,* as well as a few other TV shows.

About IDG Books Worldwide

Welcome to the world of IDG Books Worldwide.

IDG Books Worldwide, Inc., is a subsidiary of International Data Group, the world's largest publisher of computer-related information and the leading global provider of information services on information technology. International Data Group publishes over 195 computer publications in 62 countries. Forty million people read one or more International Data Group publications each month.

If you use personal computers, IDG Books is committed to publishing quality books that meet your needs. We rely on our extensive network of publications, including such leading periodicals as *Macworld, InfoWorld, PC World, Computerworld, Publish, Network World*, and *SunWorld*, to help us make informed and timely decisions in creating useful computer books that meet your needs.

Every IDG book strives to bring extra value and skill-building instructions to the reader. Our books are written by experts, with the backing of IDG periodicals, and with careful thought devoted to issues such as audience, interior design, use of icons, and illustrations. Our editorial staff is a careful mix of high-tech journalists and experienced book people. Our close contact with the makers of computer products helps ensure accuracy and thorough coverage. Our heavy use of personal computers at every step in production means we can deliver books in the most timely manner.

We are delivering books of high quality at competitive prices on topics customers want. At IDG, we believe in quality, and we have been delivering quality for over 25 years. You'll find no better book on a subject than an IDG book.

John Kilcullen
President and CEO
IDG Books Worldwide, Inc.

IDG Books Worldwide, Inc. is a subsidiary of International Data Group. The officers are Patrick J. McGovern, Founder and Board Chairman; Walter Boyd, President. International Data Group's publications include: **ARGENTINA'S** Computerworld Argentina, Infoworld Argentina; **ASIA'S** Computerworld Hong Kong, PC World Hong Kong, Computerworld Southeast Asia, PC World Singapore, Computerworld Malaysia, PC World Malaysia; **AUSTRALIA'S** Computerworld Australia, Australian PC World, Australian Macworld, Network World, Mobile Business Australia, Reseller, IDG Sources; **AUSTRIA'S** Computerwelt Oesterreich, PC Test; **BRAZIL'S** Computerworld, Gamepro, Game Power, Mundo IBM, Mundo Unix, PC World, Super Game; **BELGIUM'S** Data News (CW) **BULGARIA'S** Computerworld Bulgaria, Ediworld, PC & Mac World Bulgaria, Network World Bulgaria; **CANADA'S** CIO Canada, Computerworld Canada, Graduate Computerworld, InfoCanada, Network World Canada; **CHILE'S** Computerworld Chile, Informatica; **COLOMBIA'S** Computerworld Colombia; **CZECH REPUBLIC'S** Computerworld, Elektronika, PC World; **DENMARK'S** CAD/CAM WORLD, Communications World, Computerworld Danmark, LOTUS World, Macintosh Produktkatalog, Macworld Danmark, PC World Danmark, PC World Produktguide, Windows World; **ECUADOR'S** PC World Ecuador; **EGYPT'S** Computerworld (CW) Middle East, PC World Middle East; **FINLAND'S** MikroPC, Tietoviikko, Tietoverkko; **FRANCE'S** Distributique, GOLDEN MAC, InfoPC, Languages & Systems, Le Guide du Monde Informatique, Le Monde Informatique, Telecoms & Reseaux; **GERMANY'S** Computerwoche, Computerwoche Focus, Computerwoche Extra, Computerwoche Karriere, Information Management, Macwelt, Netzwelt, PC Welt, PC Woche, Publish, Unit; **GREECE'S** Infoworld, PC Games; **HUNGARY'S** Computerworld SZT, PC World; **INDIA'S** Computers & Communications; **IRELAND'S** Computerscope; **ISRAEL'S** Computerworld Israel, PC World Israel; **ITALY'S** Computerworld Italia, Lotus Magazine, Macworld Italia, Networking Italia, PC Shopping Italy, PC World Italia; **JAPAN'S** Computerworld Today, Information Systems World, Macworld Japan, Nikkei Personal Computing, SunWorld Japan, Windows World; **KENYA'S** East African Computer News; **KOREA'S** Computerworld Korea, Macworld Korea, PC World Korea; **MEXICO'S** Compu Edicion, Compu Manufactura, Computacion/ Punto de Venta, Computerworld Mexico, MacWorld, Mundo Unix, PC World, Windows; **THE NETHERLANDS'** Computer! Totaal, Computable (CW), LAN Magazine, MacWorld, Totaal "Windows"; **NEW ZEALAND'S** Computer Listings, Computerworld New Zealand, New Zealand PC World; **NIGERIA'S** PC World Africa; **NORWAY'S** Computerworld Norge, C/World, Lotusworld Norge, Macworld Norge, Networld, PC World Ekspress, PC World Norge, PC World's Produktguide, Publish& Multimedia World, Student Data, Unix World, Windowsworld; IDG Direct Response; **PANAMA'S** PC World Panama; **PERU'S** Computerworld Peru, PC World; **PEOPLE'S REPUBLIC OF CHINA'S** China Computerworld, China Infoworld, PC World China, Electronics International, Electronic Product World, China Network World; IDG HIGH TECH BEIJING'S New Product World; IDG SHENZHEN'S Computer News Digest; **PHILIPPINES'** Computerworld Philippines, PC Digest (PCW); **POLAND'S** Computerworld Poland, PC World/Komputer; **PORTUGAL'S** Cerebro/PC World, Correio Informatico/ Computerworld, MacIn; **ROMANIA'S** Computerworld, PC World; **RUSSIA'S** Computerworld-Moscow, Mir - PC, Sety; **SLOVENIA'S** Monitor Magazine; **SOUTH AFRICA'S** Computer Mail (CIO),Computing S.A.,Network World S.A.; **SPAIN'S** Amiga World, Computerworld Espana, Communicaciones World, Macworld Espana, NeXTWORLD, Super Juegos Magazine (GamePro), PC World Espana, Publish, Sunworld; **SWEDEN'S** Attack, ComputerSweden, Corporate Computing, Lokala Natverk/LAN, Lotus World, MAC&PC, Macworld, Mikrodatorn, PC World, Publishing & Design (CAP), Datalngenjoren, Maxi Data,Windows World; **SWITZERLAND'S** Computerworld Schweiz, Macworld Schweiz, Macworld Schweiz, PC Katalog, PC & Workstation; **TAIWAN'S** Computerworld Taiwan, Global Computer Express, PC World Taiwan; **THAILAND'S** Thai Computerworld; **TURKEY'S** Computerworld Monitor, Macworld Turkiye, PC World Turkiye; **UKRAINE'S** Computerworld; **UNITED KINGDOM'S** Computing /Computerworld, Connexion/Network World, Lotus Magazine, Macworld, Open Computing/Sunworld); **UNITED STATES'** AmigaWorld, Cable in the Classroom, CD Review, CIO, Computerworld, Desktop Video World, DOS Resource Guide, Electronic Entertainment Magazine, Federal Computer Week, Federal Integrator, GamePro, IDG Books, Infoworld, Infoworld Direct, Laser Event, Macworld, Multimedia World, Network World, NeXTWORLD, PC Letter, PC World, PlayRight, Power PC World, Publish, SunWorld, SWATPro, Video Event; **VENEZUELA'S** Computerworld Venezuela, MicroComputerworld Venezuela; **VIETNAM'S** PC World Vietnam

Acknowledgments

I would like to thank, from IDG Books, John Kilcullen, David Solomon, Mary Bednarek, Janna Custer, Megg Bonar, and Tracy Barr.

Also, thanks to my editor, Greg Robertson for his invaluable help.

There were a number of people at Symantec Corporation who gave generously of their time, including Vicki Routs, Frank Arjasbi, Valerie Rice, and Brett Smith. Particular thanks goes to Richard Yim for acting as my technical editor and Wes Stantee for writing "The Ten Most Commonly Asked Questions."

Finally, of course, I'd like to acknowledge the generosity of Steven E. de Souza and Larry Gelbart for their kind words.

(The publisher would like to give special thanks to Patrick J. McGovern, without whom this book would not have been possible.)

Credits

VP & Publisher
David Solomon

Managing Editor
Mary Bednarek

Acquisitions Editor
Janna Custer

Production Director
Beth Jenkins

Senior Editors
Tracy L. Barr
Sandra Blackthorn
Diane Graves Steele

Production Coordinator
Cindy L. Phipps

Acquisitions Assistant
Megg Bonar

Editorial Assistant
Darlene Cunningham

Project Editor
Gregory R. Robertson

Technical Reviewer
Richard Yim

Production Staff
Tony Augsburger
Valery Bourke
Mary Breidenbach
Chris Collins
Sherry Gomoll
Drew R. Moore
Kathie Schnorr
Gina Scott

Proofreader
Betty Kish

Indexer
Sharon Hilgenberg

Book Design
University Graphics

Cover Design
Kavish + Kavish

Contents at a Glance

Cartoons at a Glance
By Rich Tennant

page 182

page 137

page 245

page 56

page 193

page 104

page 288

page 307

page 27

page 7

Table of Contents

Foreword

I am one of those benighted fools who immediately runs out to buy the latest piece of computer equipment the minute it becomes available. 386, 486, Mini-Data, DAT, Double, Triple, Quadruple CD — whatever it is, at the moment the first models are still on the trucks from the factory, I'm already waiting outside the store like a concert fan getting the jump at TicketMasters.

Of course, two, three, four weeks after I rush home with my purchase, head swelling with the notion that I alone am only He Who On My Block Hath This Freshly Minted Widget, the competition comes out with their (cheaper) version of it, or my manufacturer recalls it for radiation leakage, or the Pentium makes it all obsolete before I've even disposed of the Styrofoam peanuts. (The Computer Industry, I have recently learned, has a name for consumers like me: "Early Adapters." This is a decided improvement over my wife's name for consumers like me: "Idiots.")

But that's not the point: The point is, for those few brief Days of Summer when my purchase marks the ever-shifting Cutting Edge, I am the Chuck Yeager of the Desk Top. For I, alone, have The Right Stuff.

Except that I don't have the first idea of how to use it, let alone install it.

And that's when I call in Beth Slick, the Sacajewea of Cyberspace, who has been my guide and guru since my days of a 256K double floppy 8088. She is unflappable, even when I tell her that I have taken my machine apart to switch modem ports and can't get it back together, and by the way, a studio messenger is coming by to pick up a script in 20 minutes. She is somehow capable of fixing my book problems while at the same time letting me try out my latest dialogue on her, and she can be a handy wetware reference if you have confused Fred Pohl and Fred Saberhagen. I am firmly convinced that she worked out her book on XTree while she was teaching me that program, but I don't begrudge her the royalties now that I am getting my moment in print. You tired, you poor, you wretched refuse on the Cyber Shore, look no further than these pages: You have found your Lady with the Lamp.

Steven E. de Souza, Screenwriter

Beverly Hills Cop III
Die Hard
Die Hard 2
48 Hrs.

Introduction

*E*ven if you always thought that the Norton Utilities were something that belonged to Ralph Kramden's best pal, Ed, this book is for you. And for Ed.

This book, as with all *...For Dummies* books, is for normal people who use computers in their lives — not for people whose computers *are* their lives.

One Norton Utilities myth I'd like to explode right now is the notion that you have to know all about computers and hard disks to use Norton Utilities effectively.

False. You can get virtually 90% of the benefit of Norton Utilities while operating the programs in a passive mode — by just pressing Enter now and again to confirm that you don't want to do anything special. That's what this book is for — it tells you when to press Enter — and when not to.

It's true that in order to use these programs to their utmost capacity, you have to be a *nerd plus ultra* — but it's also true that nerds can get themselves into far more trouble than non-nerds and they need fancier solutions to extract themselves from the muck.

About This Book

What you'll find in this book are step-by-step details on the most useful aspects of Norton Utilities and clearly marked trails to sidestep the program's land mines.

What you won't find in this book are pictures of "our friend, the hard disk." If you really care about the anatomy of a hard drive and exactly how Norton does what it does, the Disk Companion stuff in the Norton manual is chock-full of that kind of information — the folks at Norton love to wax poetic on sectors, tracks, clusters, heads, seeks, and the rest. My assumption is that you just want to know what button to press in the most concise, understandable way possible.

I Say Potato — You Type Potahto

Since this book is a step-by-step guide, there are lots of places in this book with a bunch of instructions with steps in them. You know, type this, press that, do the Hokey Pokey and turn yourself around — or do you turn yourself about? — and then press Enter. That kind of stuff.

What we like to use here are all-purpose instructions that can be used by people with mice or without.

For example:

- Press Alt+File ⇨ **Options**.

   With a mouse, this means to click the File menu at the top of the screen and select — from the drop-down menu that appears once you click **File** — **O**ptions.

   With keyboarders, you hold down the Alt key and press the letter F. Then press the letter O. The basic idea is that whatever is boldfaced, you type.

Another example:

- Type **EDIT AUTOEXEC.BAT** and press Enter.

   Not everything can be done with a mouse. In this case, you simply must type the word **EDIT**, press the spacebar, type **AUTOEXEC.BAT**, and then press the Enter key.

Final example (I promise):

- When Norton says `Are you sure`, press Enter or click **OK**.

   First of all, whenever you see type `that looks like this`, it means that someplace on your computer screen — if you're following along at home — you'll see that exact message from Norton Utilities. Don't move to the next step until you see the message. Once you do see that message, you can press Enter to continue. Or, if you're a mouse person, click the OK button. Or, if you've got a phobia about pressing Enter, you can hold down the Alt key and press the letter O. See how it took this whole paragraph to verbalize that simple little sentence?

We'll be talking a lot about how to look at and understand Norton Utilities *dialog boxes* in the first chapter.

What to Ignore

This book is intended to make it easy for you to find and instantly put to use the particular Norton Utility of your desire. Each chapter covers a single utility — and you needn't read the rest of the book to use that one chapter.

And while we're at it, most people don't use all the Norton Utilities. Neither will you. It's not that they're too hard to learn — it's simply that some of the programs fix problems you don't care about or fill needs that you don't have.

Just treat this book like a jump rope — jump in and out at any point.

Mad about You

This is where I tell you what I think about you, so you can decide whether I'm on your wavelength and can fulfill your needs. First of all, let me say that my first impression of you is that you're simply marvelous — good-looking, witty, and you are obviously kind to children and animals.

I also think you use a computer — probably for work, possibly against your will — and you'd like to get a little more control over what your computer's doing. I'm also assuming you own Norton Utilities version 8. It's also possible you've owned a previous version of Norton Utilities, but never ventured much beyond File Find and UnErase.

Was I close?

Preview of Coming Attractions

Each chapter starts out with an explanation of what that Utility does, why it was created, and then how to use it — as in "press this button" — with minimal effort required on your part. Each succeeding section of the chapter details some of the options you may be interested in. Finally, in some cases, we chronicle the shortcut way to perform the same task if you prefer typing cryptic command lines over pointing and clicking in interactive dialog boxes.

Part I — How Norton Thinks

This covers the commands and the so-called user interface that is common to all Norton Utilities. It also brings you up to speed on stuff that Norton assumes you already know about your computer and how it operates.

Part II — Norton Lite

The dirty dozen essential Norton Utilities that you'll use on a daily basis to simplify your life are covered in this part.

Part III — An Ounce of Prevention

These are the programs that make recovering from a disaster a whole lot easier. Many of them are automatic — as long you as press the "go" button.

Part IV — Rescue Me!

Now you've done it. Or maybe, now it's done it *to* you! Either way, this section is about how to get out of trouble whether you've prepared for it or not.

Part V — The Norton Grab Bag

You know the bit about one man's meat is another man's poison — or is it the other way around? Anyway, the grab bag programs are those that are a little on the arcane side, or have been replaced by other Norton Utilities but are being kept around for sentimental reasons. I've separated these out from the others because if you've only got a limited amount of time to spend learning Norton Utilities, these aren't the ones to start with.

Part VI — Part of Tens

Quick lists of various items, ranging from "Ten Ways to Fake Your Way Through Norton" to the "Ten Most Commonly Asked Technical Support Questions."

Icons Used in This Book

Throughout this book are *icons* — little pictures — to emphasize situations that require some kind of special attention.

A little suggestion that will save time and trouble.

Let's call a spade a spade — it's techno-babble. If you read the paragraph next to this little guy, you're about to step into a muddle-puddle of jargon. You can either jump over it or play in it.

Something to bear in mind as you move to the next step in the instructions.

Sort of a *yellow alert* — you're not in grave danger, but you've entered the Neutral Zone and things could get bad quickly. Stay frosty.

If you don't follow this instruction, bad things will happen. Not bad things will *maybe* happen — bad things *will* happen.

To the Moon, Alice

Norton Utilities *looks* complicated and full of technical stuff. But that's only because it *is* complicated and full of technical stuff. Fortunately, though, Norton Utilities is on your side. Even if you don't understand all the complicated technical stuff, you can still do complicated and technical things like fix your hard drive, retrieve files from certain death, and make the world safe for. . . are we still concerned about making the world safe for democracy these days?

Anyway — the day you use Norton Utilities to recover from a disaster, you won't need Ralph Kramden to send you to the moon! You'll have done it for yourself.

Part I
How Norton Thinks

In this part...

In addition to learning how Norton Utilities thinks, we also have to deal with what Mr. Peter Norton, progenitor of the Norton Utilities, *thinks* you already know about computers. Since Mr. Norton and his buddies sit around all day talking tech, he assumes that you also are fluent in computer jargon and have a considerable understanding of how a computer works. Ahem. So, in case you've made the mistake of having a life outside the world of computers, this section is also devoted to divulging just enough jargon and computer stuff to let you make Norton Utilities bend to your will. Don't worry, though, nothing is covered in this part unless you will really put it to use — many times — throughout this book.

And, just to show Norton who's boss — we'll fiddle around a bit with the setup until you get it just the way you like it.

Chapter 1
Laws of the Jungle

● ●

In This Chapter

▶ The Zen of Norton

▶ Yakking with a dialog box

▶ DOS Boot Camp

▶ A map to my computer

● ●

*Y*ou know that part in the Oscars where they have Frick and Frack from Price-Waterhouse come out and explain how the balloting works and who gets to vote and how their accounting firm tallied the ballots and swore to take cyanide rather than reveal the results of the balloting? It's the guaranteed boring part of the evening — but if they didn't have rules and vote, there would *be* no evening.

So maybe rules and procedures are important. Although talking about *operating systems* — your computer's disk operating system (DOS), and the way Norton Utilities operates its system — is a bit dry, it's key to understanding how everything works.

And I promise, this is the incredibly condensed version of the facts of computer life. Whatever is covered here is used in the rest of the book. There are no wasted moments here.

I'll make this as quick as possible.

The Zen of Norton

What is the Zen of Norton? I guess the penny said it best — E Pluribus Unum. Out of many, one. Even though Norton Utilities is composed of more than three dozen separate utilities, these programs have common characteristics. Buddha says, therefore, that if you become familiar with these common characteristics, you'll be able to kick some righteous Norton butt. Because no matter where you go, there you are. And he's right. Buddha, that is.

So before we start doing the yellow brick road thing, let's see whether we can come up with a grand unified theory that works with Norton Utilities.

Getting in

There are two major ways to start Norton Utilities because there are, in essence, two major parts of Norton Utilities. Don't you love symmetry?

Norton for DOS

The most common way into the DOS version of Norton Utilities is just to type **NORTON** and press Enter. You'll get Figure 1-1.

The main features in this Norton Utilities menu are:

✔ The Control menu box in the upper left corner.

✔ A System and Menu configuration menu bar. Also, don't forget to take advantage of the comprehensive Help system that provides help for DOS as well as Norton Utilities.

✔ Underneath, the menu bar program names are listed on the left — point to one with a mouse or keyboard, and the description and usage suggestions for that program — albeit in Norton-ese — appears on the right. Press Enter when the correct program has been highlighted and options typed in. (What options to use and how they apply is what this whole book is about... so you'll have to read the chapter pertaining to the program you're interested in.)

✔ The dotted line at the bottom works just like the C:\> on your computer. It's where you type in a command.

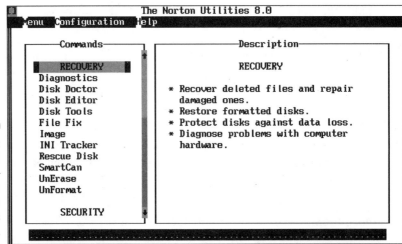

Figure 1-1:
Your friend and mine — The Basic Norton Utilities Menu.

Norton for Windows

The second way to access the various Norton Utilities programs is via Windows. During the setup, Norton Utilities automatically creates two Windows groups, as in Figure 1-2.

Figure 1-2:
The Norton
Utilities now
appearing in
Peeping
Toms'
favorite
program —
Windows.

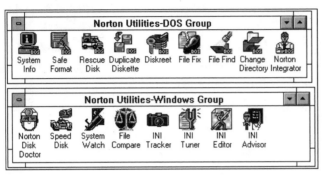

✔ All the normal Windows rules apply, including sizing and expanding the window.

✔ Double-click any icon to activate that program.

✔ If you double-click the Norton Integrator in the DOS group, you end up in Figure 1-1.

✔ Double-clicking items in the Windows group starts the corresponding Windows-specific program.

Yakking with a dialog box

In almost every situation, giving the command to start a Norton Utilities operation results in Norton asking you to supply more information. It's embarrassing to report that the Norton Utilities programmers apparently have yet to figure out how to make the program read your mind. So when Norton wants to know more, up pops a *dialog box*. Since Norton for DOS was designed to look like a Windows program, the dialog box from both sides of the fence work pretty much the same.

Figure 1-3 shows off a dialog box with an inquiring mind — each part of the box has been labeled.

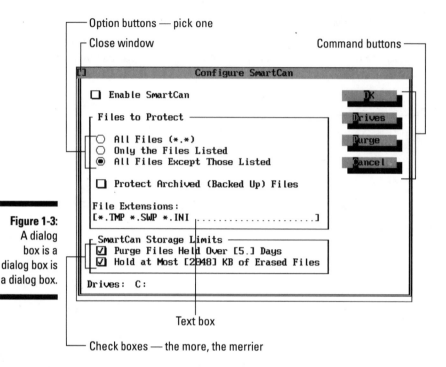

Option buttons — pick one

Close window

Command buttons

Figure 1-3:
A dialog
box is a
dialog box is
a dialog box.

Text box

Check boxes — the more, the merrier

Pressing the Tab key moves you through the major options in all dialog boxes. Pressing the spacebar selects an option button or check box. Pressing spacebar on a selected item deselects it. Pressing Esc always takes you out of the box without saving any changes.

Control menu

In the upper left corner of every dialog box are two square brackets. This is the Control menu. If you double-click on it, the window closes.

Other ways to exit a window:

✔ Press Esc.

✔ Press Alt+F4.

Command buttons

Usually on the right or on the bottom of a dialog box are command buttons. You can click them with a mouse to kick an action into gear.

Other ways to activate command buttons:

✔ Press Alt and the highlighted letter.

✔ Pressing Enter means OK.

✔ Press Tab until you reach the desired button, and then press Enter.

Option buttons

Option buttons are the small circles. Usually, they come in mutually exclusive groups: If you pick one, you can't pick another. You can click a button to select that option.

Another way to select an option button:

✔ Press Tab until you get to the general area you want to change, and then press the spacebar until the desired option is selected.

Text box

A text box is where you type text — of any reasonable length. Press Backspace to erase errors.

Check boxes

Square check mark boxes allow you to select or deselect items. Even though check mark boxes travel in packs, they can show up by themselves some times.

Another way to make a selection:

✔ Press Tab until you get to the general area you want to change, and then press spacebar until the desired option is selected.

Stop in the name of <Your name here>

You can always stop Norton from carrying out a command by:

✔ Pressing Esc.

✔ Selecting a command button labeled Cancel or Quit.

✔ Pressing Alt+F4 to close a dialog box.

Menus

Many of the Norton Utilities have a menu bar that can be accessed by using the mouse or by pressing Alt and the highlighted letter. Once a menu item has been accessed, there may be some items in parentheses. These items are *not active*. If you're disappointed to find your favorite option off the active-duty list, it's directly attributable to either the configuration of your system or what your cursor was highlighting before the menu was accessed. We'll see this in action later, but I just thought I'd put it out there while we are dealing with all the bookkeeping stuff.

You talking to me?

So far, all we've done is talk about dialog boxes. There is a way to run Norton Utilities for DOS without using the interactive dialog boxes. The alternative method is called the *command-line method*.

A command line is the system prompt. The *system prompt* is the C:\> thing you see after turning on your computer. So the command-line method is when you type your order while at the system prompt.

Okay, let's say you wanted to use a Norton Utilities program called SmartCan. In the interactive approach, you could call up the Norton Utilities menu, find SmartCan in the list of programs, highlight Smartcan, and press Enter. Or, using the command-line method, you can simply type **SMARTCAN** and press Enter without once looking at the incredibly cool Norton Utilities menu.

The command line is the streamline approach to Norton Utilities. The only catch is that you really have to know, in advance, all your options. That's why mostly you won't use it. But it's there if you need it.

Using a switch

When working with the Norton Utilities command line, there's one term that you have to learn — *switch*.

A switch in computers is basically *an option* that alters a main choice. Let me put it this way. You go to a restaurant and order a hamburger */w fries*. You know what that means, right? "A hamburger with fries." In this case, the fries is a switch. It's the same thing with computers.

When you type the DOS command **DIR**, for example, adding **/P** means "with pause." So **DIR /P** means "give me a directory, with a pause after every screen."

An example of a Norton Utilities switch is something like **NCC /CURSOR**, which invokes the CURSOR command in the Norton Control Center. The idea is that switches are an option.

A helpful switch for anyone new to Norton is the **/?** switch, which displays all the other switches of a given program. For example, typing **FILEFIND /?** asks for all the File Find options.

Someone's in the Kitchen with *Dyhana*

Dyhana, as you all know, is the original Sanskrit term that the Chinese pronounced as "Zen." And, according to my Funk & Wagnall's, Zen is a way of seeing the world exactly as it is — without injecting our own feelings and opinions. And that, of course, is our goal with Norton Utilities — to perceive it, understand it, comprehend it without commingling our own anxieties. However, an-other part of the Zen philosophy believes that the nature of the world cannot be described or de-fined by any fixed system. As the author of this book, I must protest that Norton Utilities can, in fact, be described and defined. And I have other questions: What's the result of one file being File Compared? And if a hard disk crashes with noth-ing on it, is any damage done? Let us meditate.

DOS Boot Camp

One of the charming aspects of the Norton Utilities is that it assumes we know lots about our computer's own disk operating system, or DOS. Well, you know what they say about assuming . . .

All in all, there are a few concepts and vocabulary words that you at least need to have an acquaintance with to get the most out of Norton.

So c'mon people, let's just power on through these words and concepts! There's no test at the end of the chapter. What will happen is that by the end of the book, you'll have seen these ideas in use so often they'll become second nature.

Well, maybe not second nature, exactly — but at least you won't shrink in horror the next time someone brings them up.

Files

What you do all day — day in and day out — is create data files on your computer. A *file* is the receptacle of your work. There are all sorts of rules about files that you have to be aware of. The more you know about these rules, the more you'll be able to use them to help yourself rather than be baffled by them.

Filenames

A filename has to conform to a certain look. Think of it as a school uniform — everyone has to conform. A file can be up to eight characters long, contain a period, and then have up to three more characters tacked on. You can't use spaces, and certain kinds of punctuation, in a filename.

A typical file name is REPORT.DOC — which is six letters, a period, and three more letters. Then there's 100494.XLS, which is an October 4 spreadsheet file. The pattern here is simple: eight characters, a period, and three more characters. You don't have to use all eight, you don't have to have a period, and you don't have to have the three more. You just can't have *more* than that.

File extensions

The last three letters of a filename (the "three more characters") are called the *extension*. The extension of a file is kind of like the file's last name in that it helps identify a file as belonging to a certain group. For example, a file that ends with EXE is a program. If you were to see WP.EXE, you would know it's a program. A file that ends in BAK is a duplicate backup file — and can probably be deleted. A file that ends in DOC is probably a document file created by your word processor.

Directory

A directory is a place on a disk that contains files. If you think of files as letters, then the directory is a Pendaflex folder.

Wildcards

A *wildcard* is a symbol — usually an asterisk (*) — that means, literally, *everything*. It is used to group a bunch of files together for the purpose of issuing a command. For example, if you want to copy a dozen files that all have a DOC extension, you can use a wildcard symbol to say "all those files that end in DOC" by typing **COPY *.DOC**. Or all those files that end in BAK are designated by ***.BAK**. Or all files that begin with the letter R are designated by **R*.***.

In Norton Utilities, you find yourself using the wildcard often when you don't know exactly what it is you're looking for. For example — did you lose the JOHNSON.RPT or JOHNSON.DOC? It doesn't make any difference if you search for **JOHNSON.*** — which means "anything that starts out JOHNSON, but I don't care where it ends."

ASCII or text file

There's a special breed of file called an ASCII file — also known as a text file — that has the characteristic of containing only letters or numbers. Most other documents created by word processors or big-time applications also contain, unbeknownst to us until now, invisible codes and commands.

The humble ASCII file contains no secrets — just letters and numbers.

The only thing about ASCII files is that we have to be careful when editing them to make sure that invisible codes are not added back in with our word processor. That's why we use DOS's EDIT program to make changes to ASCII files. DOS's EDIT program doesn't stick invisible junk in the file.

It is possible to edit an ASCII file using your regular word processor as long as you save the file as a text or ASCII file.

Otherwise, you get to learn a bit more about DOS's EDIT program. Goody.

Vocabulary words

Here are a few words that you'll be running into later. Right now, we just introduce them in a little get-acquainted moment.

- ✔ Batch files. A small file that lists a series of commands that the computer then carries out, or *executes*. It's a shortcut. It's sort of a speed dial for your computer.

- ✔ Boot. Another word for "turn on the computer." A series of three special files must be available to the computer when it's first turned on in order for the machine to actually start working. Any disk that contains those three files — known as *system files* — is considered to be a bootable disk.

- ✔ Clean boot disk. This is a floppy disk with little more than the capability to boot the computer.

- ✔ Reset and Reboot. Both terms mean to turn the computer off and then back on again. Usually, you do this after the computer freezes or starts ignoring you completely. Now, if only we could reset people who don't pay attention . . .

- ✔ Background. This term is associated with Windows, which allows more than one program to be functioning at the same time. The program running in the background is the one that's not on top.

- ✔ Case sensitive. This has to do with how commands are typed. In other words, it doesn't make any difference in DOS or in Norton Utilities whether the commands are typed in uppercase, lowercase, or any other case.

- ✔ Error messages. These are little hints, tips, and clues from DOS that help you figure out what you did wrong. A basic understanding of error messages makes it a lot easier to correct mistakes.

A Map to My Computer

It's not a map to my computer — it's a map to *your* computer. Here's a blank chart that you may want to spend a few minutes filling in. You don't have to if you don't want to, but it might be a good exercise to help you start looking at your computer a whole new way. The best way to do this is to get into an application as you normally do. Then go to the File Open command and stop, look, and listen. Yes, right there is the full name of the directory where your files are stored. *That's* the information you want to make note of.

After all, if you don't know where your files are supposed to be, how can you tell whether they're lost? Even little kids know their own addresses, right?

What it is	*Where it is*
The Root	C:\
My Norton Utilities files	C:\NU
My DOS Files	C:\DOS
My word processor	
My spreadsheet	
My Windows	
Other programs:	

Chapter 2

Cruising Through the Configuration Choices

. . . .

In This Chapter

▶ Launching the configuration menus

▶ Configuring the system

▶ Changing the menu system

. . . .

Do you like to tinker, tune, and tweak? Do you like to have designer things nobody else has? Well, that's what the Norton Utilities *configuration* software is all about.

When you configure software, it means that you're changing various aspects of how a program works. That's right: You can actually change how Norton Utilities works. Now, if even the mere suggestion of going behind the scenes with Norton gets you a little jittery, please don't worry. You don't *have* to change anything if you don't want to. Skip this chapter if you like. Once Norton is set up, it's ready to go and you don't have to change a thing.

If, however, you want a different screen color, or if the idea of completely rewriting the main Norton Utilities menu has you intrigued — perhaps a little excited — then stick with us. There's lots of flexibility in the Norton Utilities system, and once you're finished with your alterations, you'll have an exclusive one-of-a-kind original — custom-built just for you — Norton Utilities system. And all your friends will be envious of your system and your obvious genius at being able to set it up.

If you're new to Norton Utilities, you may want to use the program for a little while before changing the configuration — just so you have a better notion of what you want more or less of. However, if you're an inveterate tinkerer, go for it. You can always change things back to the way they were. No harm done.

Launching the Configuration Menus

Because one of the hallmarks of Norton Utilities is providing a plethora of ways to accomplish every little task, there are also many ways into the configuration portion of the program.

Norton Utilities menus

The option that takes the least effort on your part is to use the menus in the regular Norton Utilities menu, as in Figure 2-1 and 2-2. If you use the Norton Utilities menu to access all your Norton Utilities anyway, configuring the program from there requires no extra effort.

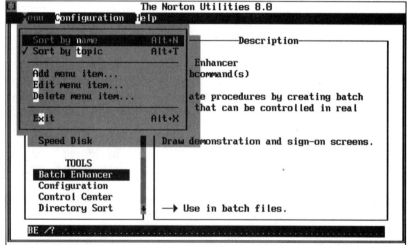

Figure 2-1:
The Norton
Utilities
menu, uh,
Menu —
let's you
alter the
menu.

1. To get to either the Norton Utilities Menu menu or the Norton Utilities Configuration menu, do one of the following:

    • From a system prompt, type **NORTON** and press Enter, or

    • From Windows, in the Norton Utilities - DOS programs, click the Norton Integrator icon.

2. Press Alt+**M**enu to get to Figure 2-1 or Alt+**C**onfiguration to achieve Figure 2-2.

Now you're poised to explore all your incredible configuration options.

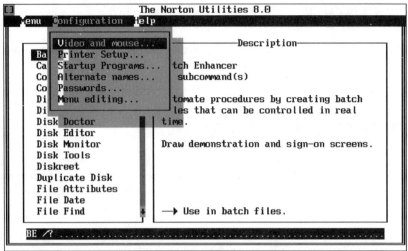

Figure 2-2:
The Norton
Utilities
menu
configuration
menu —
where the
operation of
the whole
Norton
Utilities
program
can be fine-
tuned.

Introducing NuConfig

And in this corner... NuConfig, which provides all the options of the other
method except the capability to edit the menu (see Figure 2-3).

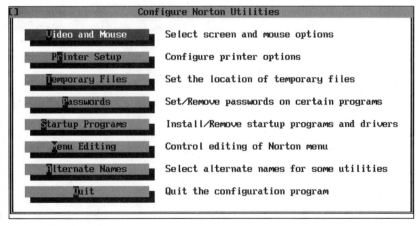

Figure 2-3:
NuConfig —
a program
dedicated to
change.

To get into the NuConfig program, just type **NUCONFIG** at the system prompt
and press Enter.

One thing that's kind of nice about NuConfig is that if you make changes that
require rebooting to be put into effect, it'll offer to do that — reboot the
computer — for you.

On the minus side, however, NuConfig doesn't let you edit the menu. I know there's a command button that says Menu Editing in Figure 2-3, but that only grants *permission* to edit the menu — it doesn't actually let you edit the menu. Gosh, this is confusing. Let's just use the Norton Utilities menu and keep everything simple.

Configuring the System

There are half a dozen Configuration options — each hiding at least another dozen options. You can go visit each of the options — just to see what can be adjusted. In fact, you could probably use up an entire afternoon on this stuff alone:

✔ Video and Mouse (see Figure 2-4). The Screen Options let you change the look of the Norton Utilities menus, from the amount of fancy graphics to the use of color. The Mouse Options allow fine-tuning of the mouse cursor. There's an interesting sort of miscellaneous option, called Enter Moves Focus, that, when selected, changes how the Enter key works in a dialog box. Most of the time Enter is the same as OK — in other words, pressing Enter closes a dialog box. If you select Enter Moves Focus, then Enter only moves you to the next portion of the screen — it requires an actual OK to finish up the dialog box.

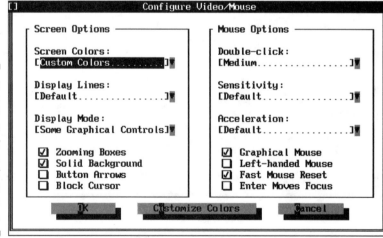

Figure 2-4: Configure Video and Mouse lets you apply your own color scheme to the Norton Utilities.

✓ **Printer Setup.** Throughout Norton are plenty of places to print riveting reports on the status of your system and the contents of your important setup files. If you plan to print using Norton Utilities, then you want to make sure that it knows what printer you're using. Norton can accommodate just about any kind of printer — and you can even print sideways if you want.

✓ **Startup Programs.** The use of the Startup Programs options will be explained as we get to each of the programs to be started up. Basically, this is the option that automatically installs and uninstalls programs in your AUTOEXEC.BAT and CONFIG.SYS files for you.

✓ **Alternate Names.** A program by any other name would still smell as sweet? Well, not exactly. But the Alternate Names option lets you cut a few keystrokes off your command line by renaming often-used programs with shorter names (see Figure 2-5). Just click on the down-arrow to see the optional shorter names. You can, for example, rename FILEFIND to FF.

Figure 2-5: In the old days, all the Norton programs had short, two-letter names. Later, names were made longer so that they'd be easier to remember.

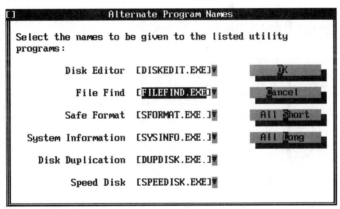

✓ **Passwords.** As Figure 2-6 so eloquently explains, you can select a password and then assign it to all or a few of those programs that have the potential to do damage to the hard disk. If no one is using the computer except you, this option won't be very important.

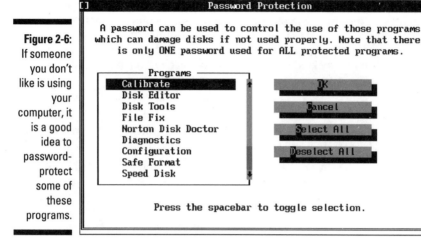

Figure 2-6:
If someone
you don't
like is using
your
computer, it
is a good
idea to
password-
protect
some of
these
programs.

 ✔ Menu Editing. Another security option, Menu Editing enables you to
   remove the right to edit the menu. You don't actually edit here — you just
   say that you could edit, if you wanted to.

Changing the Menu System

The Norton Utilities menu is completely at your mercy. It can be reorganized,
edited, and rewritten.

Reorganizing

The programs in the Norton Utilities menu can be organized either alphabetically or grouped together by such riveting topics as Recover, Security, Tools,
and so on.

To change modes, press Alt+Menu⇨Sort by Name or Alt+Menu⇨Sort by Topic.
Or Alt+N or Alt+T, for short. Flipping back and forth by topic or name is impressive and easy. Though, to be honest, I think most people select one mode and
kind of stick with it.

Creating a new menu

Well, you can't *exactly* create a menu, but you can delete current menu items,
add new menu items — even non-Norton items — add topics, and edit the
description (the box on the right) to make it more meaningful to you. I feel like
that Amazing Discoveries guy — "Hey, isn't this just great!" You *do* spend every
Sunday watching those infomercials, don't you? Well, don't you?

Okay, here's how to change the menu:

1. Highlight the menu item to be changed.

   Just in case you didn't know, you cannot only adjust all menu items, but all menu *topics* as well. If you don't like the word Recovery, change it to Regeneration or anything else that makes more sense to you than Norton's choice. The point is to make it your own.

2. Press Alt+**M**enu, to see Figure 2-1.

   Once the drop-down menu has dropped down, you can see your menu editing powers unfold — you got your basic **A**dd menu item, **E**dit menu item, and **D**elete menu item.

If the menu editing commands are dimmed, it may be because the Alt+**C**onfiguration⇨Menu Editing has been disabled. Or it may mean that you missed the target by highlighting a topic rather than an actual program name before activating the Configuration menu. Just press Esc and start again.

✔ If you elect to edit a menu item, you end up with something like Figure 2-7, where I've decided to Edit Norton Diagnostics. Anything in the Description box may be edited, deleted — whatever you want. If you don't believe me, just look at Figure 2-8. It's possible to add a bit of pizzazz to your Description text by pressing F2 to turn on *text attributes* — fancy-talk for boldface and underline. Just press Tab until you get a look you want to know better. When you're finished editing, press OK.

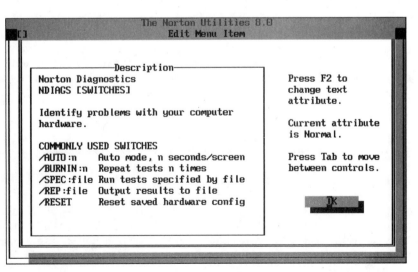

Figure 2-7:
Edit any description — adding your own notes or often-used commands in place of the bizarre incantations presented by Norton Utilities.

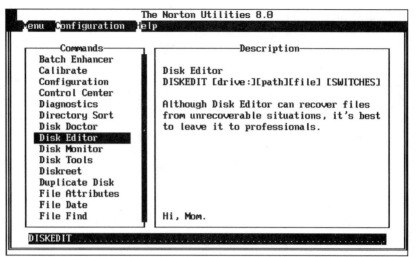

Figure 2-8:
Here's a
Disk Editor
Description
that's been
edited —
probably by
a football
player.

✔ If you prefer to eliminate never-used programs, just highlight the program by pressing Alt+**M**enu and then selecting **D**elete Menu Item. You probably will be asked whether you "really want to remove" the menu item. You know what to do.

✔ Finally, you can add items to the menu if you want to be able to launch other programs from inside the Norton Utilities menu. When you use the Alt+**M**enu⇨**A**dd Menu Item, you are asked if you want to add a Command or a Topic. In either case, you are asked for names and specifics.

You may want to add DOS's EDIT command to the Norton Utilities menu. Press Alt+**M**enu⇨**A**dd Menu Item from the Norton Utilities menu. When asked, tell Norton you want to add a Command. In the Name in menu box, type **EDIT**. In the DOS command text box, type **EDIT** again. Select a topic under which Edit will appear — Tools makes the most sense to me. Press Alt+**O**K or Enter to finish the job. Now you can uses DOS's EDIT command from the Norton Utilities menu!

A change of menu

It may seem strange to be able to change the Norton Utilities menu so much. After all, you're certainly not able to redesign your spreadsheet menu. The reason we've got so much menu technology going here is because Norton has borrowed a bit from another piece of software they invented called the Norton Commander. Its logo is a captain's hat. It's very cute. So don't be shy about changing things if you need to.

Part II
Norton Lite

The 5th Wave — By Rich Tennant

"UNFORTUNATELY, THE SYSTEM'S NOT VERY FAULT-TOLERANT."

In this part...

*U*sing the word "Lite" to name this part doesn't violate any new FDA truth-in-advertising regulations governing products containing the word "light" or any variations thereof (we had our lawyer check). First of all, we don't try to teach you any heavy-duty, anti-insomnia facts about your computer. In fact, the Lite utilities lift you up by locating lost files, protecting you while formatting floppy disks, magically restoring accidentally erased files, and even making your computer run faster — and longer — and lots more. Second, as with all Lite products, using them often will keep you in good shape.

Chapter 3

Directory Sort

● ●

In This Chapter

▶ Viewing your files in order

▶ Making the new order permanent

▶ Airing DOS's DIRty secrets

● ●

*G*etting the computer to list all the files in the current directory — although not terribly exciting — is fairly simple using the boring DIR command: At the system prompt, type **DIR**, press Enter, and watch as the list appears and then immediately scrolls off the screen at a pace that would frustrate even gold-medal speed readers. Thanks a lot, Mr. Computer. And even if you *could* read the list of files as they zip by, they are in an order that makes sense only to the computer.

Directory Sort's simple mission — should you decide to accept it — is to bring order to your list of filenames. With Directory Sort, you have the option of putting the filenames in alphabetical order — or sorting by date and time or even by size. Directory Sort doesn't replace DIR, it simply makes DIR more useful.

Sorting with Help from Norton

To get to the Directory Sort dialog box shown in Figure 3-1, either:

✔ From the Norton Utilities menu, highlight Directory Sort and press Enter

✔ From a system prompt, type **DS** and press Enter

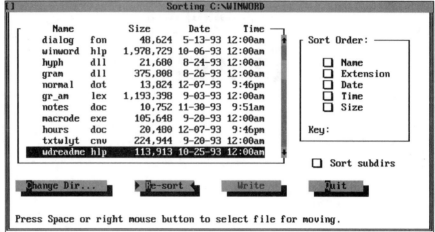

Figure 3-1:
What sort of
fool am I? —
the
Directory
Sort, of
course.

Figure 3-1 shows a typical list of unsuspecting scrambled files, brought to you
by your computer's brilliant operating system.

Getting to the right place

Once you've roused the Directory Sort dialog box, look at the top of the dialog
box to make sure that you're in the right directory. The "right" directory is
simply the directory containing the files you want to sort. Generally speaking,
you are automatically in the right directory without doing anything special.
That's because Directory Sort assumes that you want to sort the directory you
were in when you summoned the program. In Figure 3-1, I happen to be in the
WINWORD directory on drive C — you could be anywhere. Only you can decide
what's right for you (kinda New Age, huh?).

If — and only if — you need to change to another directory, here's how:

1. Press Alt+Change Dir.

   After you click Change Dir, you'll find yourself in the Change Directory
   dialog box (see Figure 3-2).

2. If you want to impress others, just type the path name of the directory you
   want to go to. An easier way is to point — via either mouse or arrow keys
   — to the path name in the box underneath and press Enter. If the path
   name you want doesn't seem to be in the box, it may be because you're on
   the wrong subdirectory level. Select the backslash (\) to travel up to the
   top of the system and start your search afresh.

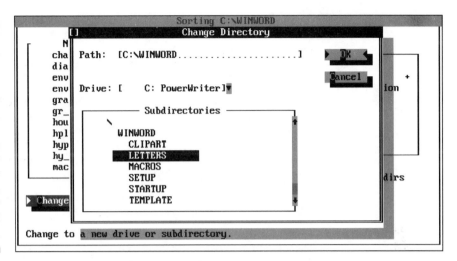

Figure 3-2:
Directory
Sort's
Change
Directory
button
allows you
the freedom
to scurry
through your
system,
looking for
unsorted
directories.

This returns you to something like Figure 3-1, with your new directory listed at the top of the screen and the files in that directory now listed in the little window.

✔ While in the Change Directory zone, you also can change to another drive if you want, including a floppy drive. Yes, you can sort files on a floppy drive — both an excellent work-avoidance tactic and a way to organize floppies so that you can organize things alphabetically or by date.

Selecting a sort order

Okay, you've already done the hardest part of the program — getting in the right directory. This rest of this is simple.

1. Using the mouse or the arrow keys, move over to the Sort Order box and tell Norton how you want the files organized by selecting the appropriate box (use the spacebar if you're mouseless) — or boxes.

   The sort order options include: **N**ame (alphabetical), **E**xtension (which groups files together by the last three letters of the filename), **D**ate, **T**ime, and **S**ize.

   • If you want a simple alphabetical list, choose **N**ame, and a check mark appears in the box — a number also appears to the left of the box and a plus sign on the right, but more about those in a moment.

• If you want to sort alphabetically first and, within the alphabet, by date, select the **D**ate box after selecting **N**ame. That's right, mix or match boxes as needed. As you select each box, a number appears to the left, indicating that particular criterion's position in the sort's pecking order. The box labeled number one is the primary sort box.

• To get a list in reverse order — newest to oldest, Z to A, big to little — you need to change the little plus sign on the right of the check box into a minus. Plus means ascending order — minus means, well, descending order. To toggle between plus and minus, click on the plus sign next to the item you want to change (keyboarders must be on the item they want to change before typing the minus sign).

• To deselect an item, select the selected item again (so that the check mark in the box disappears).

• Finally, there's even an option to have the sort ripple through to *all the subdirectories* underneath the current directory — if you need to. To try it out, just select the Sort Subdirs box. If we were to use that command while in the WINWORD directory, as in the previous example, the sort would now include all its subdirectories — you can see the subdirectories listed in Figure 3-2. Going to the root directory (\) of the computer and issuing the Sort subdirs command would sort the entire hard drive.

2. Press Alt+**R**e-Sort.

   When you choose **R**e-Sort, Norton does its thing and, as in Figure 3-3, all file names are alphabetized and you can scroll through the list.

Figure 3-3:
The directory listing is now sorted alphabetically — which is how DOS should've done it in the first place!

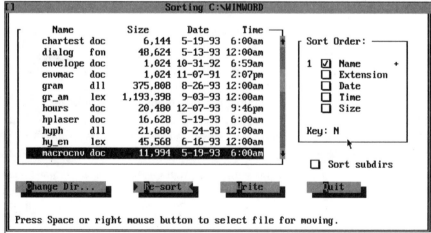

Saving the sort

So far, all you've done is to sort a list of file names *on the screen*, and that may be enough. However, Directory Sort has the power to make your computer reindex the files on the disk to match the order you've created on-screen. By doing this, the files appear in sequence when using other applications — including DIR the Pathetic.

To save the new list order:

1. Click the **W**rite button.

   Now relax a moment while the hard drive whirs and the File Allocation Table (FAT) — which is where the directory index is maintained — is updated. Okay, vacation's over — back to work.

2. Choose **Q**uit.

✔ If you leave the Directory Sort program without reindexing your disk, you are warned — see Figure 3-4 — as you would be by any application that noticed you were quitting without saving. In Figure 3-4, choose **Y**es to save or **N**o to exit without saving. Cancel leaves you in the Directory Sort program.

✔ Whether you want to save the sort order or not is strictly up to you. However, if you want DIR to produce a sorted list, you have to *save* — which Norton calls *write*.

Figure 3-4:
Is it wrong to "Write?" Hardly — it's how Directory Sort gets the computer to save your sorting efforts for use by other applications.

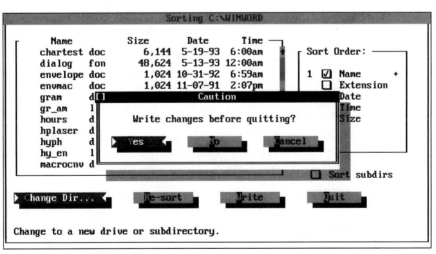

At any time you can press Esc to exit. If you don't like — or need — the sort order you've produced, just choose **No** when asked if you want to `Write changes before quitting?`

Sorting Shortcut

You may have noticed in Figure 3-3 that once Name was selected in the Sort Order box, the letter N appeared at the bottom of the Sort Order box near the word `Key`. (If you didn't notice it, notice it now, please.) If you also select **T** (for Time), the Key would read `NT`. It's obvious a pattern is developing, but what's it mean? Well, if you're interested in using the quickest way to sort a directory listing, the Key is the key.

Here's how the letter in the Key works if an alphabetical list is the goal:

At the system prompt type, **DS N** and press Enter. Directory Sort will — almost instantly — sort the files by Name and automatically reindex the files in the new order. In short, you bypass the dialog box experience. Once the sort is completed, type **DIR** and press Enter to see the alphabetized list.

As another example, let's say you're looking for the newest file in the directory. Simply type **DS D** (for Date) and press Enter. Then, after the directory is sorted, type **DIR** and press Enter.

It is simply the fastest, easiest-to-remember way to whup your files into shape.

- ✔ To get a list in reverse (descending) order, put a minus sign after the command. For example, **DS N-** puts the files beginning with Z at the top and the ones beginning with A at the bottom.

- ✔ If you want to sort the current directory *and all the subdirectories underneath*, add a /S to the command — for example, **DS N/S** and Enter.

If you want to use the shortcut method, but can't remember the key commands, call up the Norton Utilities menu and highlight Directory Sort — the commands are listed on the right. Type what you need and press Enter.

Neither the shortcut nor dialog box method of Directory Sort will save sorted lists on network or virtual drives. If you don't know what those things are, you probably don't have one. However, if Directory Sort won't save on your system, then you probably do have one of those things after all.

Airing DOS's DIRty secrets

To prevent filenames from quickly scrolling off the screen when using DOS's DIR command, use a twist on DIR — DIR/P. The /P forces the computer to pause — stop, actually — after every screenful of filenames so that you can read the filenames at your leisure. When you're ready to see another screen of filenames, just press any key.

Another way to keep files from scrolling away is to use DIR/W. The /W makes the presentation of filenames go wide — into four columns on the screen instead of one. Four columns of filenames allow a lot more files on the screen at a time, which may keep them from scrolling into the ether. Of course, with the four columns, you have to give up the date and time information. After all, there's no free lunch.

If you really, really, really have a lot of files, you can even combine the two with DIR/W/P. However, if you've got that many files in one directory, you should consider doing a little housekeeping.

Another way to stop the quick scrolling of filenames requires lots of hand-eye coordination. As the filenames scroll by, press Ctrl+S (or simply press the Pause key on your keyboard) to stop the list — you have to be quick. To continue a stopped scroll, press any other key on the keyboard — like the Enter key, for example. To terminate the scrolling in mid-scrawl, press Ctrl+C.

When you add new files to the directory, you must sort the directory again to integrate the new files into the list.

Chapter 4
Duplicate Disk

· ·

· ·

*D*id you know that you can make a copy of a floppy disk — a virtual clone even if your system has only one disk drive? Pretty amazing.

When you need to have an exact duplicate of a floppy disk, Norton's Duplicate Disk command is a lot nicer to use than DOS's crummy old DISKCOPY command. Why? Well, Duplicate Disk is more safety-conscious, easier to run, and works faster. What else could you want? The only thing that'd better would be if they came out with a program called Duplicate Money.

Setting Up

What you need to get started is:

1. A floppy disk to be copied.

   The original floppy disk is referred to by Duplicate Disk as the *Source diskette* — as in "let the Source be with you."

2. A floppy disk to be turned into a duplicate of the original.

   This floppy disk is referred to as the *Target diskette*. You can't just pick any disk to be the Target disk, though. It has to meet the following Food and Game Commission requirements:

   ✔ The Target disk must be the same size — 3 1/2 or 5 1/4 inches — as the Source and have the same capacity — either High Density or Double Density — as the Source diskette.

   ✔ The Target disk must be blank, unformatted, or contain data that you don't want any more.

TIP

Help! I don't know what kind of floppy disks I have!

As mentioned elsewhere, Duplicate Disk works only between two diskettes that are the same size. It doesn't take a rocket scientist to determine whether the diskettes are the same physical size — either 3 1/2 or 5 1/4 inches square.

Much more difficult to determine is a disk's *capacity* — how much data it will hold. The two kinds of capacity are called "high density" and "double density" (also known as "low density"). When you go to buy more disks, the store clerk will ask whether you need high density or low density disks.

Manufacturers of most blank disks will thoughtfully print HD or DD on the disks themselves, which takes the guesswork out of the equation. Plus, high-density 3 1/2-inch disks have two retangular holes in them, one in each of two corners. Most software manufacturers aren't that helpful when creating Source disks. So, here's one way to determine the density of a floppy disk.

1. Put the suspect disk in the floppy drive.

2. At the system prompt, type **CHKDSK A:** and press Enter.

3. After a few seconds, you see lots of numbers, with the top one being *bytes total disk space.* That's your capacity.

✔ For 3 1/2 disks, if it's more than 1,400,000 — it's high density. If it's less, it's double density.

✔ For 5 1/4 disks, if it's more than 1,200,000 — it's high density. If it's less, it's double density.

✔ Even if you use two nonmatching disks by accident, nothing bad will happen. Eventually, Duplicate Disk will tell you that the Target diskette doesn't match the Source. It'll even offer to format the "nonmatching disk," but it won't do any good. The bottom line is that you'll be asked to stick another disk in the drive. One that matches.

✔ Oh, and when you ran CHKDSK, if the computer gave you a message saying your floppy drive was failing, don't worry. There really isn't anything wrong with your drive — that's just DOS's subtle way of letting you know the disk you're testing isn't *formatted* yet. Either format the disk and try again or test another disk. If you don't know how to format a disk, skip on over to Chapter 12 for the latest scoop on what *formatting* is and how to do it.

Making Duplicate Disks

To get to the Duplicate Disk dialog box shown in Figure 4-1, use one of the following methods:

✔ From the Norton Utilities menu, highlight Duplicate Disk and press Enter, or

✔ From a system prompt, type **DUPDISK** and press Enter, or

 ✔ From Windows, in the Norton Utilities DOS group, click the Duplicate Disk icon.

Figure 4-1:
The
Duplicate
Disk
command
helps clone
a floppy disk
even if your
system has
only one
disk drive.

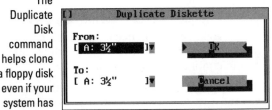

If typing DUPDISK produces a complaint from the computer rather than the charming dialog box in Figure 4-1, it may be because you — or someone you know — has mutated the program's name via Norton's **Configuration** ⇨ **Alternate names** option covered in Chapter 2. Try typing **DISKCOPY** and pressing Enter or **DD** and pressing Enter instead.

1. Tell Duplicate Disk which floppy drive you plan to use for copying.

   If your drive A is a 3 1/2-inch drive, you're all set. If you want to use drive B, click the down-arrow and make your selection.

2. Choose **OK**.

   Or, if you want to call the whole thing off, choose Cancel.

3. When prompted, put the Source diskette into the drive and press Enter.

4. Do nothing for a little while as Figure 4-2 appears on the screen and Duplicate Disk starts memorizing what's on the Source diskette.

5. Eventually, you'll be told to put the Target diskette in the drive and press Enter. Do it.

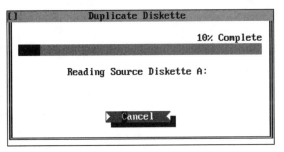

Figure 4-2:
Duplicate
Disk reads
— or
memorizes
— the
original disk.

Yes, that means take out the Source disk — Duplicate Disk has it all memorized and doesn't need it anymore — and insert the Target disk. Don't forget to press Enter after inserting the Target disk.

- If your Target disk isn't blank, Duplicate Disk pops up a screen like the one in Figure 4-3, giving you one last chance to examine the filenames on the Target disk to approve, once and for all, their total annihilation. Choose **Yes** to continue with this disk.

- If you don't want to use this Target disk after all, choose **No** and put a different Target disk in the drive instead. Then, of course, press Enter.

Figure 4-3: Duplicate Disk's safety feature makes sure that you really want to say, "Hasta la vista, baby" to the files on the Target disk.

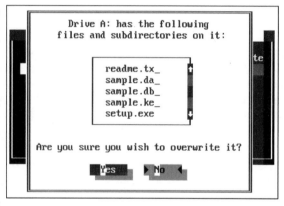

6. This is another step where you just sit there.

   A message similar to Figure 4-2 pops up — this time telling you that Duplicate Disk is regurgitating the information from the Source disk to the Target disk. When the cycle is complete, you see Figure 4-4.

7. Choose **Yes** to make another copy of the Source disk on a second Target disk — or **No** to end the Duplicate Disk program.

   - If you choose **Yes**, you'll be taken back to Step 5.

   - If you choose **No**, you'll be whisked away from Duplicate Disk.

Figure 4-4:
Look ma, no
swapping! It's
easy to make
lots of copies
of a Source
disk by
continuing to
feed Duplicate
Disk more
Target disks.

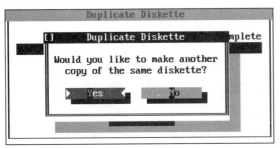

The X-Copy files

Although XCOPY isn't exactly a top government secret like Hangar 18 (where they keep the UFOs), they've done the next best thing to keep XCOPY a secret — they made it a DOS command.

As mentioned earlier, Duplicate Disk can't clone disks of one size or capacity onto a disk with a different size or capacity. That's immutable. However, by using DOS's XCOPY command, we can achieve a similar effect — almost. To copy the contents of a disk in drive A to a disk in drive B — perhaps a 5 1/4-inch disk onto a 3 1/2-inch disk — do this:

1. Place both disks in their drives.

2. If the Source disk is in drive A and the Target disk is in drive B, type **XCOPY A: B: /E** and press Enter.

   This command tells DOS to copy everything — even duplicate all subdirectories no matter what. By the way, if this command seems arcane — it is. That's why there's a little tech icon at the beginning of this section and that's why Duplicate Disk was needed. You really start to appreciate Duplicate Disk once you starting moseying about in DOS-land.

✔ If your Source is in drive B and the Target in drive A, you'd use **XCOPY B: A: /E** and press Enter.

✔ If you need to copy a disk but your computer has only one floppy drive, then use that first command anyway. DOS pretends that there's a drive B — you'll swap Source and Target disks from the one drive.

✔ *Really important* — make sure that the destination disk is blank or has enough free space to hold the material being copied. You wouldn't expect a gallon of water to fit in an eight-ounce cup — so don't expect a 3 1/2-inch disk crammed with 1.4MB of data to fit into a 5 1/4-inch floppy disk with 1.2MB of capacity. It just ain't gonna happen.

✔ XCOPY does not copy those pesky hidden files, including system files — the files that give a floppy disk the power to start up the computer. You can copy system files with Disk Tools (see Chapter 22). As for the other hidden files — well, if you know enough to have discovered that your original disk has invisible files, you also know enough to copy them.

Chapter 5

File Find

. . . .

In This Chapter

▶ Finding files

▶ Finding text

▶ Printing a list of files found

▶ Using File Find to copy, delete, and otherwise dispose of your files

. . . .

*I*f finding a file on your hard disk has become a high-stakes, high-tech version of "Where's Waldo?" then it's time you found File Find. File Find is one of the most oft-used utilities in the Norton pack — mostly because losing files is one of the most oft-experienced computer screw-ups.

From now on, when something isn't where you expected it to be, tell File Find to go fetch. Like an obedient puppy, File Find sifts through everything on your entire system and reports back with the location of your missing stuff. Finding files, however, is just the beginning of what File Find can do — as you'll see in this chapter.

By the way, if you managed to stay alert during DOS Boot Camp (way back in Chapter 1), here's your chance to dazzle the world with what you learned about filenames and wildcards. Even if you dozed off during DOS Boot Camp, all you *really* need to know is the name of your missing file. Armed with that information, you can still perform a basic search.

Finding Files — The Basics

To get to the File Find dialog box shown in Figure 5-1, use one of the following:

✔ From the Norton Utilities menu, highlight File Find and press Enter, or

✔ From a system prompt, type **FILEFIND** and press Enter, or

 ✔ From Windows, in the Norton DOS Utilities group, click the File Find icon

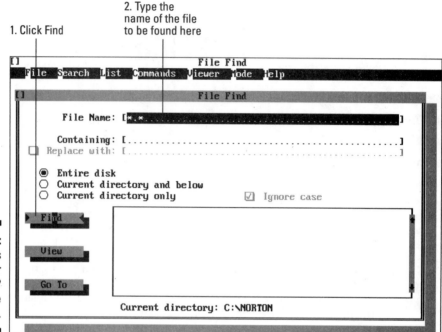

1. Click Find

2. Type the
name of the file
to be found here

Figure 5-1:
Who knows
where your
files lurk?
Only File
Find knows.

If typing **FILEFIND** and pressing Enter produces an error message instead of the riveting Figure 5-1, it may be because you have availed yourself of the opportunity to change File Find's name with Norton's Configuration ⇨ Alternate names feature, which is covered in Chapter 2. Try typing **FF** and pressing Enter instead.

In the simplest terms, this is how to find a file once you have the File Find dialog box open as in Figure 5-1:

1. Type the name of the file to be found in the File Name text box.

2. Click on the Find button.

   • While the search is on, File Find provides a thrilling commentary at the bottom of the screen, detailing the directories and drives it's searching through and how many files it's found so far.

   • You can call off the search by pressing Esc or clicking on the Stop button (which replaces the Find button during the search) at any time. If you notice that File Find has found the file you need or you realize you've made a typo in the File Name box, it's okay to stop the process. You can always start it up again later.

3. After a few seconds, a message appears, telling you either `Search Com-plete` or `No Files Found`. The response in either case is to press Enter — or, if you prefer, click OK.

- If you're lucky enough to get the Search Complete message, the file or files that match your lost filename are listed in the "Found box" in the lower right part of the screen. Figure 5-2 shows the results of a search for a file named EXPENSE1.DOC — which was found in the \WORD\MKT directory.

Found box ──

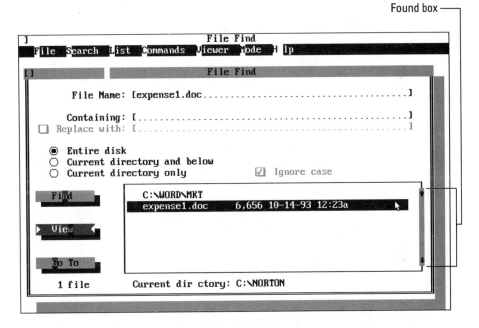

Figure 5-2:
Faster than
you can say
"Unsolved
Mysteries,"
File Find
locates your
missing files
and, ever
the
overachiever,
displays
their size
and the date
and time
they were
last saved.

- If you get a `No Files Found` message, that means File Find couldn't find the file you asked for. All is not lost, though. There are more things to try. First of all, make sure that the lost filename was typed properly in the first place — maybe you sent File Find off on a wild goose chase. If the filename was incorrect, fix it and try to find it again. If you still have no luck, try a *fuzzy* search, as described later in this chapter. If you're still drawing dust, read "When File Find Can't Find It" — also later in this chapter.

Viewing found files

Once File Find has a file listed in the Found box, it's possible to peek inside the file by using the View button. Viewing a file is almost like opening a file. View lets you *see* the contents of the file, but you can't change it in any way.

View is especially helpful when you end up with several files in the Found box, and you need to figure out which file is *the* file.

> ✔ View works only on files you've created. If you try to view program files, you'll just get a bunch of garbage and happy faces on the screen, but it won't hurt anything.

> ✔ Viewing is just a helpful option. If you don't need to view the file, there's no law that says you have to.

To view a file in the Found box:

1. Highlight the name of the file you want to view.

   Be sure to aim the mouse or arrow key properly — it's the filename you want, not the directory name. Figure 5-2 has the filename highlighted as an example.

2. Once the filename is highlighted, click on the View button (or press Enter).

   In Figure 5-3 we're viewing the EXPENSE1.DOC file — which looks like it was formatted by a two-year-old. Although View can expose what's in a file, text-wise, it doesn't show the file in its fully formatted glory. The sole purpose of View is to let you answer the question "Is this the file I was looking for?" Once you open it in your program, it'll look just fine.

   • If File Find listed several files in the Found box, you can automatically shuffle through all of them by using the Next File button at the bottom of the screen.

3. When you've finished viewing the file, either click Close or just press Esc. You'll be back to the File Find dialog box in no time flat.

Going to where the files are

Once it's been established that the found file is, indeed, the little rascal that's been evading you — what next? You have two options. For instance, you can make note of where the file is, shut down File Find by pressing Esc, and then use the CD command to go to where the file is. But that wouldn't be elegant.

File Find has already assumed that you may want to beam on over to the directory where the file was found and even offers to escort you there by hand. And they say chivalry is dead.

1. Highlight the name of the *directory* that contains the file you want to go to.

2. Click on Go To button (or press Enter), and you're there.

Name of file being viewed

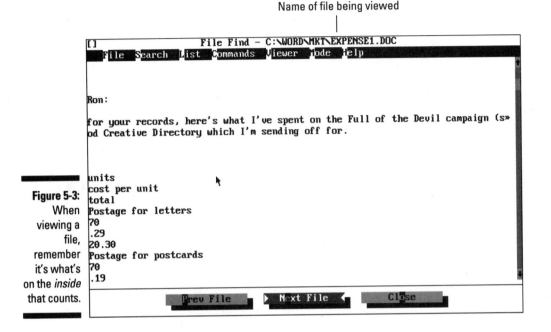

Figure 5-3:
When
viewing a
file,
remember
it's what's
on the *inside*
that counts.

> ✔ If you got into File Find via the Norton Utilities menu, you need to press Esc one more time to exit the menu.

Taking File Find Shortcuts

At the system prompt, type **FILEFIND** and the name of the file you're looking for, and then press Enter. For example, if you're looking for EXPENSE1.DOC — and who isn't — you type **FILEFIND EXPENSE1.DOC** and press Enter. The File Find dialog box pops up and immediately starts searching for the file you asked for.

Save a few more keystrokes by using Configuration ⇨ Alternate Names, covered in Chapter 2, to change the FILEFIND command to just **FF**. Then all you have to type is **FF EXPENSE1.DOC** and press Enter. This not only saves a whopping six keystrokes, but also keeps carpal tunnel syndrome at bay a while longer. Amazing the things that software can do these days.

Finding Files — The Next Generation

Thirsty for more? Hold onto your hats, because there are lots more ways to find files. More, in fact, than you probably want to know about. As you move through this section, each successive method of searching is more arcane than the preceding one. Basically, I've placed all the good stuff up front.

Using wildcards — the fuzzy search

The fuzzy search doesn't refer to the condition of your brain. Rather, it's the kind of search to employ when you're not exactly sure what it is you're looking for. After all, who can be expected to remember every little bit of every single filename — right? There's another use for the fuzzy search, but we'll save that as a surprise.

Be warned that this is where the stuff from DOS Boot Camp kicks in. If you skimmed or skipped it, go back to Chapter 2 now and refresh your memory. If you don't want anything to do with DOS, then you'll have to forget about fuzzy searches.

Playing charades with File Find

It sounds like... Well, you can't *exactly* play charades with File Find, but it seems like it. If, for example, you can't remember whether that certain file was named ROBOT.DOC or ROB.DOC — you can type **ROB*.DOC** in the File Find blank so that File Find will list every file that starts with ROB and ends in DOC. If you're really fuzzy, then searching for R*.DOC will find everything that's even thinking of starting with the letter R.

Gathering the flock

The other use for a fuzzy search is when you'd like a list of a certain *group* of files. For example, let's pretend you'd like to find all the DOC files on your hard disk — or even all your XLS files. Typing ***.DOC** (or ***.XLS**) in the File Find blank and then clicking on Find (or pressing Enter) will give you such a list.

Use fuzzy searches even when you know the whole filename, to save yourself a few keystrokes. Who wants to type **REP1_791.XLS** when a simple **REP1*.*** can do the job well enough?

Looking for the right word

File Find, in its infinite genius, can also look through files on the hard disk in search of a particular turn of phrase. If there's a file — someplace on the hard disk — that contains the word "Spock," for example, File Find can locate it for you. Here's an example of how this sort of magic is accomplished:

1. Get to the File Find dialog box by using one of the methods described at the beginning of this chapter (like typing **FILEFIND** and pressing Enter).

2. If you know anything at all about the filename that contains the search word, then type that into the File Name text box.

   In this example, I know the text is in a document file, so I'd type ***.DOC.** You don't have to limit the search in any way. If you can limit the search, though, it'll save you a little time.

3. Next, in the Containing text box, type the text you're looking for.

   In this example, I'd type **Spock**. I'm looking for a file that ends with DOC and contains the word "Spock." You, of course, need to enter the word or words you're looking for.

4. Click the Find button (or press Enter).

   The search will take a little longer than a normal File Find, but it will end up in something like Figure 5-4. In that example, two files satisfied the current search criteria. Who'd have ever thought you'd have search criteria?

   ✔ To take the matter one step further, when you View a Found file, the program automatically highlights the text you're searching for.

   ✔ If you've conducted a fuzzy search and turned up 50 documents, applying a text search to those files is a good way to separate the good files from the bad and the ugly.

File Find also has the capability to search and replace words in found documents. My recommendation is, if possible, to perform search-and-replace missions with the application that created the file. If, however, you're some kind of techno-type with an assignment to update or change a bunch of AUTOEXEC.BAT or CONFIG.SYS files on a network, it's an easy way to handle an otherwise tedious operation.

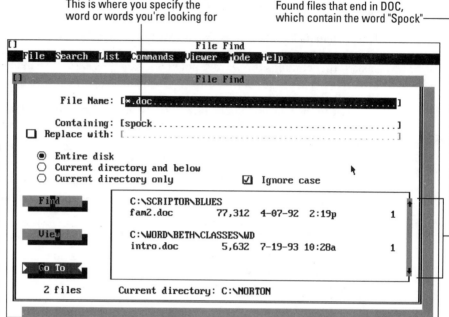

This is where you specify the
word or words you're looking for

Found files that end in DOC,
which contain the word "Spock"

Figure 5-4:
File Find's x-
ray vision
can locate
files that
contain the
words or
phrases
you're
looking for.

Searching in all the right places

Normally, File Find searches through the files on the current hard drive.
Generally, that's drive C. And, generally, that's just fine. However, lots of people
have D and E and F drives. You can add them to the search by doing the following:

1. Choose Alt+**Search** ➪ **Search Drives.**

   You'll get the Drives to Search dialog box (see Figure 5-5).

2. Check off the drive letter you want to search.

   In Figure 5-5, you see that I have a drive D. I'm not adding that to my
   search, however, because it's a CD-ROM drive. The files on that drive are
   never going to contain things I'm looking for. You probably won't want to
   add a CD-ROM drive to the search, either.

3. Once you have selected all drives you want, choose either Save, to make
   this selection the new default — or choose OK to move back to the File
   Find screen and use the new selection until you exit the program.

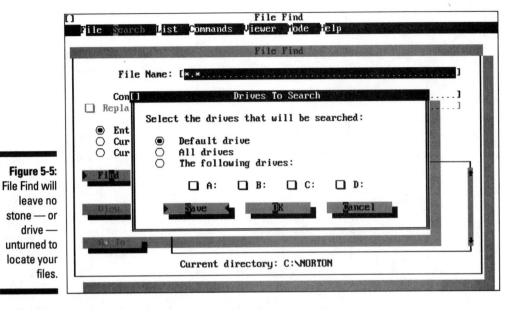

Figure 5-5:
File Find will
leave no
stone — or
drive —
unturned to
locate your
files.

Going Beyond Finding Files

Are you exhausted from seeing what File Find can do? Don't take a nap quite yet, because there's more. But *this* bunch of File Find tools has the unique property of having nothing to do with finding files. Computers make so much sense, don't they?

Printing a list

Sometimes, when a list of files has been placed in the Found box, it can suddenly hit you how convenient it would be to have a hard copy of the list. File Find can accommodate your desires, if you ask politely.

Assuming you've already conducted a search and have files in the Found box, do this:

1. Choose Alt+List ⇨ Print List.

2. In the Print List dialog box, select the Printer radio button to print the file.

3. Click OK — or press Enter — to print the list.

You can see in Figure 5-6 that File Find is willing to print either a list jam-packed with information or a bare-bones skeleton, depending on your selection. Most of the choices are self-explanatory.

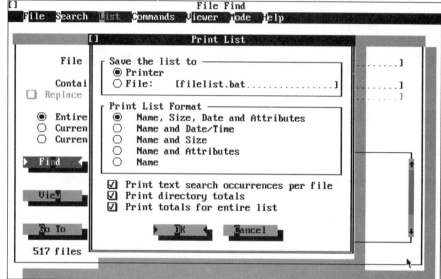

Figure 5-6:
File Find can
print out —
or save to a
file — the
files listed in
the Found
box so that
you'll
always have
a memento
of the
occasion.

Copying, deleting, and more with File Find

How does a program that finds files also manage to copy and delete (and more)? It's a little kinky, but if you're an adult you should be able to handle this without giggling.

Okay, start with the fact that File Find has the capability to create a file containing a list of the files it has found, as you now know. Add to that the human element — that's you — to insert a command or two in the list. And, finally, when the list is saved with a BAT extension, the list magically becomes a miniprogram called a *batch file*.

Printing with Norton

If you have a laser printer, printing in Norton can be a little weird. Basically, unlike every other program you own, Norton doesn't automatically push the last page out of the laser printer. I'm sure there's some really great techno-weenie reason that this is a "good thing" — but I don't like it. Anyway, once you've "printed" something, it may seem as though nothing at all has happened or

that the last page is missing. Notice, however, that your printer's Form Feed light is on. That's your clue that something's inside the printer, dying to get out. To push the paper out, press the On Line button — then the Form Feed button. The paper should come out. Be sure to put the printer back On Line after the page comes out.

Don't roll your eyes. Hang in there with me during this example before you decide it's too much.

Let's say you know that you want to delete all the BAK files on your system. As you may know, files that end with BAK are automatically created by your word processing software as a safety measure. However, they tend to multiply like rabbits, and sometimes it's a good idea to nuke 'em. Unfortunately, you'll discover that BAK files spread throughout all the directories of your hard drive. Does that mean you're forced to go to every directory and issue the delete command? I guess you'd have to if you didn't have File Find. Here's how to make the job of deleting all the BAK files simple.

1. Get to the File Find dialog box.

2. In the File Find blank, type ***.BAK** and click on Find.

   Remember, ***.BAK** means "everything that ends in BAK," or, all the BAK files.

3. Once the Search Complete message comes up, click OK.

4. Now choose **List** ⇨ **Create Batch**.

   This is where things are taking a new twist. You should now be looking at something like Figure 5-7.

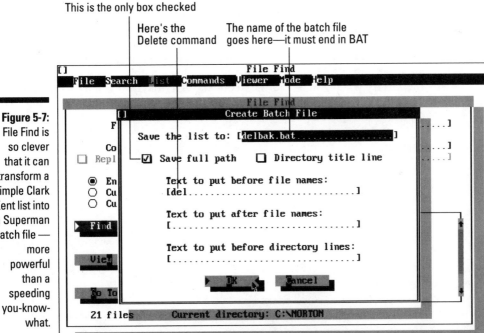

This is the only box checked

Here's the Delete command

The name of the batch file goes here—it must end in BAT

Figure 5-7: File Find is so clever that it can transform a simple Clark Kent list into a Superman batch file — more powerful than a speeding you-know-what.

5. The first item in the Create Batch File dialog box is `Save the list to:` — typical Norton jargon for "what do you want to name the batch file?" In the example, I used DELBAK.BAT — for "delete BAK files." You can call your file whatever works for you as long as it ends in .BAT.

   Whatever name you do use, remember it. It's the last step in the process.

6. Deselect the box to the left of `Directory title line`.

   We don't need fancy titles in the batch file. All that's necessary is directions to where all the files are located on the hard drive.

7. In the blank underneath `Text To Put Before File Names`: type **DEL**.

   DEL is the command for delete. By putting DEL in front of each file name in the list, it will be as if you issued the DOS command: DEL FILENAME.BAK — which is what is needed to delete a file.

8. Click OK to close the dialog box.

9. Press Esc to exit File Find.

10. Type the name of the batch file — without the BAT — that you chose in Step 5 and press Enter. Since my file name was DELBAK.BAT, I'd type **DELBAK** and then press Enter.

Another way you can use this capability is to copy a group of files. By putting **COPY** in Step 7 (in the `Before file names` text box) and **A:** in the `Text to put after file names` text box, you can create a batch file that copies all the files to drive A.

If you followed all the way to this point, congratulate yourself. After all, this was a section with a technical icon. Maybe creating a batch file is something you want to try when you're snowed in one day. Or, maybe if you try this, it'll be just the motivation you need to mow the lawn. No matter, once you "get" what this does, it's quite a powerful and helpful tool.

When File Find can't find it

You *swear* the file was saved. And yet, even File Find turns up empty. Now what? Don't give up yet — change course and try another tack.

The first step is to forget searching for the file by its name. Face the possibility that the file has been *accidentally renamed*. How's that possible? Easy. In many programs, part of the file-saving process involves viewing the name of the file to be saved. And, in many programs, tapping any key on the keyboard while that highlighted filename is on-screen replaces the filename with whatever was just typed. I've even seen files called '.DOC, because the Apostrophe key — very close to the Enter key on most keyboards — was pressed and the user didn't notice that the filename had become ' before pressing Enter. The other top filename in the miss-parade is Y.DOC — created by pressing Y to continue in the wrong spot. As usual, timing is everything.

Another way a file's name can change is if the system froze while you were working on that file and the file was saved in some temporary file someplace with a really, really weird name.

The point is, things happen. And here's what you can do about it:

1. Search for *text* in the file (as explained in this chapter).

2. Use Directory Sort (covered in Chapter 3) to list all files on the computer by date and time. If you know when the file disappeared, it may be possible to track it down by a process of elimination with the date and time.

3. Try using UnErase (explained in Chapter 14). The file may have been deleted, and it may be possible to bring it back from the dead.

Chapter 6

File Size

I'll admit this right up front, File Size doesn't do much. On the other hand, it doesn't ask much from you, so it all kind of evens out. Since File Size is a leftover from earlier versions of Norton Utilities, it doesn't even rate its own dialog box. However, File Size does have a purpose.

Basically, File Size is useful when you need something a bit better than DIR, but not as complex as Directory Sort (explained Chapter 3) to list files. On the plus side, File Size does math. It can calculate whether this group of files over here is going to fit on that floppy disk over there. But I'm getting ahead of myself. Where are my manners? Everyone, meet File Size.

Replacing DIR — Almost

Since File Size doesn't have a dialog box to coach you along, you kind of have to know what you want before you kick File Size into action. The one way around that is to use the Norton Utilities menu to get to File Size, as shown in Figure 6-1, which places all the options before you.

If you fall in love with File Size, though, it's best to use it from the *command line* — the system prompt — you know, this thing: C : \>

Norton's helpful hints on the File size command

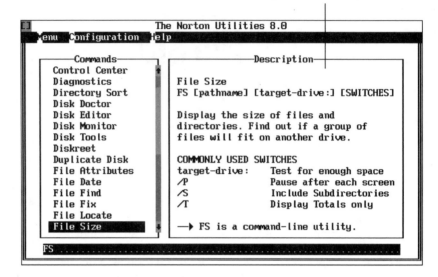

Figure 6-1:
If you get to the File Size command via the Norton Utilities menu, you receive a typically cryptic reminder of what the program can do.

Beginning File Size

At its most basic, using File Size is a matter of:

1. Getting to a system prompt

2. Typing **FS** and pressing Enter

You'll get something like Figure 6-2, where File Size provides the stats on the "bottom line." As you can see, File Size not only tells you how much space you have left, but it also provides the depressing news that DOS is squandering some of your disk space — which, of course, you can't do anything about.

Getting tricky with File Size

We talked about *switches* back in Chapter 1. If you'll recall, switches are, basically, a way to vary how a program operates. File Size has several options, but one of the more useful is the /P option. This works a lot like DIR's /P option — it makes the list you see in Figure 6-2 pause after a screenful so that you can actually read the filenames (a radical concept). Here's how:

This is the size of the files in the current directory

```
    sdenginb.dll           120,688 bytes
    nuconfig.exe           208,729 bytes
    iniadvsr.hlp         1,233,702 bytes
    ndiags.exe             236,747 bytes
    symgui3.dll            273,648 bytes
    speedisk.exe           196,676 bytes
    nlib200.rtl            200,683 bytes
    nddwbmps.dll           533,040 bytes
    nddw.exe               276,976 bytes
    ftrackrd.exe           375,406 bytes
    instdos.inf              2,326 bytes
    norton.cmd              13,119 bytes
    ndos.ini                   346 bytes
    ncache.ini                 198 bytes
    diskreet.ini               854 bytes
    copydoc.bat             18,486 bytes

    7,395,931 total bytes in 112 files
    7,913,472 bytes disk space occupied, 6% slack

Drive usage
  342,466,560 bytes available on drive C:
   85,688,320 bytes unused on drive C:, 25% unused

C:\NORTON >
```

Figure 6-2:
File Size tells you how much disk space is left on the drive.

This is what you've got left over

This is the total size of the current drive

1. Get to the system prompt.

2. Type **FS /P** and press Enter.

   You'll get something like Figure 6-3, where the screen has paused — giving you a chance to see what you've got.

   ✔ Once in Pause, pressing the spacebar advances a whole screenful, and pressing Enter (or any other key) scrolls the listing forward one line at a time — which is kind of nice. Finally, pressing Esc will get you back to the system prompt.

   ✔ You can use wildcards with File Size just like you do in DIR. So if you want to list only those files ending in DOC — with a pause after every screen — you type **FS *.DOC /P** and press Enter.

Your files are listed here

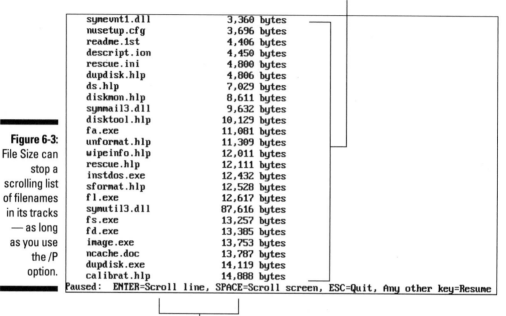

symevnt1.dll	3,360 bytes
nusetup.cfg	3,696 bytes
readme.1st	4,406 bytes
descript.ion	4,450 bytes
rescue.ini	4,800 bytes
dupdisk.hlp	4,806 bytes
ds.hlp	7,029 bytes
diskmon.hlp	8,611 bytes
symmail3.dll	9,632 bytes
disktool.hlp	10,129 bytes
fa.exe	11,081 bytes
unformat.hlp	11,309 bytes
wipeinfo.hlp	12,011 bytes
rescue.hlp	12,111 bytes
instdos.exe	12,432 bytes
sformat.hlp	12,528 bytes
fl.exe	12,617 bytes
symutil3.dll	87,616 bytes
fs.exe	13,257 bytes
fd.exe	13,385 bytes
image.exe	13,753 bytes
ncache.doc	13,787 bytes
dupdisk.exe	14,119 bytes
calibrat.hlp	14,888 bytes

Paused: ENTER=Scroll line, SPACE=Scroll screen, ESC=Quit, Any other key=Resume

Figure 6-3:
File Size can stop a scrolling list of filenames in its tracks — as long as you use the /P option.

Instructions on how to advance the list are here

Sometimes you don't really need a list of files. Sometimes all you really want to know is "how much space is being used here." You can ask File Size to just give you the bottom line with a /T (for "totals") switch at the end of the command, just like so:

1. Get to the system prompt.

2. Type **FS /T** and press Enter.

   This produces just the bottom part of Figure 6-2.

Determining Whether the Files Fit the Floppy

One cute trick File Size performs at all the birthday parties and that is always a big hit with the relatives is looking at one group of files and predicting whether they'll all fit on a particular floppy disk. This lets you avoid the stigma of receiving an insufficient disk space error message while copying files.

To do this — avoid the error message, that is — add a *destination* (where you want the files to go) to the File Size command. In almost-English, that would be like "File Size these files *to drive A.*" Drive A is the destination. It's a weird command. I'll walk you through it and then you'll see.

In this example, pretend that you want to copy all the DOC files from the current directory to drive A. Before you do the copying, you need to know whether they'll all fit on the disk currently in drive A. The tension mounts.

1. Get to the system prompt.

2. Type **FS *.DOC A:/T** and press Enter.

   This asks Files Size (FS) whether all the DOC files (*.DOC) will fit on drive A (A:) and tells it to give you the totals only, please (/T). You'll end up with something like Figure 6-4.

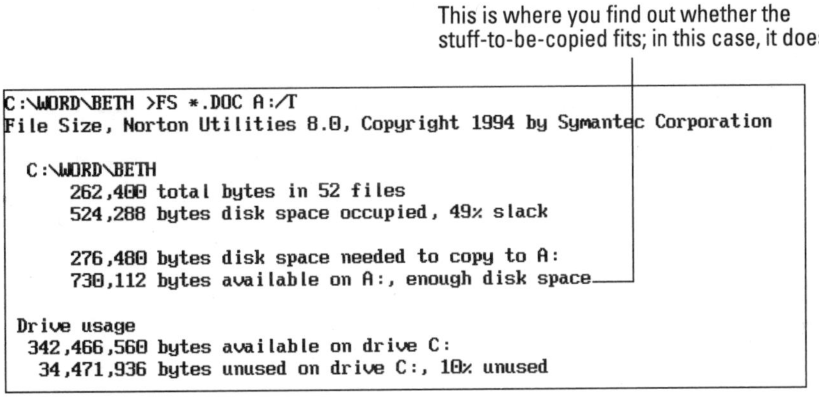

This is where you find out whether the stuff-to-be-copied fits; in this case, it does

Figure 6-4:
File Size
solves the
eternal
mystery of
whether
these files
can fit on
the disk in
drive A.

```
C:\WORD\BETH >FS *.DOC A:/T
File Size, Norton Utilities 8.0, Copyright 1994 by Symantec Corporation

  C:\WORD\BETH
      262,400 total bytes in 52 files
      524,288 bytes disk space occupied, 49% slack

      276,480 bytes disk space needed to copy to A:
      730,112 bytes available on A:, enough disk space

Drive usage
  342,466,560 bytes available on drive C:
   34,471,936 bytes unused on drive C:, 10% unused
```

   ✔ If you intend to copy files from one floppy drive to another, File Size will tell you in advance whether that's a good plan if you ask: Type **FS A: B:/T** and press Enter.

Picking up the slack

One of the problems with Norton — in general — is that it tells you things you'd be happy remaining ignorant about.

If you've looked carefully at the figures in this chapter, you may have noticed that there appears to be a difference between the *size of the files* and the *disk space occupied*. In Figure 6-4, the 52 files are 262,400 bytes big, but take up 524,288 bytes on the disk? And, to make matters worse — those same files will take up 276,480 bytes on the disk in drive A. Is Norton tripping or what?

Even though it doesn't make sense, Norton is actually right — on all counts.

The reason for the discrepancy — without getting too boring and technical — can be blamed on the way DOS distributes space on the disk and the way the disks are formatted (blame it on the cluster size). Anyway, it's just another one of those alternate reality things. The bottom line is that, for all practical purposes, you don't ever have to worry about it. After all, you've gone this far without even knowing there was a difference. So, why worry about it now?

At least now you know to take advantage of File Size when copying to a floppy to get the most out of your disks.

Chapter 7
File Compare for Windows

I don't think Shakespeare had computers in mind when he started thinking about comparing thee to a summer's day in one of his sonnets. Besides, it doesn't really take a computer — or even a rocket scientist — to realize that there are major differences between a human being and a random day between June and August.

However, it may take a computer and File Compare to spot the differences between two text files.

The purpose of File Compare is to throw two text files up on the screen and — as we had to do in history exams — "compare and contrast" the differences between the two files. Specifically, the idea is to compare two INI files or two AUTOEXEC.BAT files or even two CONFIG.SYS files.

We've talked a bit about AUTOEXEC.BAT and CONFIG.SYS files — which are necessary to the proper operation of your computer. INI files are sort of the same idea — but they work for Windows. Every piece of software has its own *initialization* file to tell Windows what its wants and needs are.

Just as with AUTOEXEC.BAT and CONFIG.SYS, the INI files are subjected to seemingly random changes when new software is installed or if you make changes to a program's setup. And although I know *you* would never do this, sometimes people with too much time on their hands experiment with these files and get themselves in a mell of a hess and it's helpful to be able to see what was before and what is now.

File Compare works with ASCII files only. It was not designed to compare the document you wrote yesterday in Word for Windows with the edited version you got back from a colleague.

File Compare — Part of a system

File Compare is just one of the building blocks in the suite of Windows-management software provided by Norton Utilities. The other pieces of the puzzle are Tracker (covered in Chapter 19) and INI Advisor, INI Editor, and INI Tuner (all discussed in Chapter 20). You can pop back and forth between these programs from inside one of them. You'll find File Compare as an option inside Tracker, where, for example, you'll be able to compare not only files, but changes to directories by comparing Tracker snapshots of a directroy "before" and "after."

If you don't understand why anyone would want to use File Compare, then don't worry about it. Skip it. After all, there's no denying that comparing two files like this has a certain techy ring to it. File Compare's the kind of program that you either wonder where it's been all your life or you don't get why it's here at all.

One of the features of File Compare is Edit. Which means you can, in fact, change the files you're comparing. If you use File Compare as a look-don't-touch program, it is harmless. On the other hand, once in Edit mode, you've got the opportunity to change things you shouldn't — because you didn't realize they were important. You may want to take a snapshot of the files you're going to compare if you plan to do any editing (see Chapter 19).

INI Meeny Miney Moe — Comparing Two INI Files

One final warning before we get to it: this chapter is not about the rules governing INI files and when to — or not to — edit them. For that kind of information, please consult a book like *Windows For Dummies* — which is probably offered for sale in the back of this book. We're just going to explore what File Compare does. The rest is, as they say, up to you.

1. Get into Windows (probably by typing **WIN** and pressing Enter).

2. In the Norton Utilities Windows programs, click the File Compare icon. You see Figure 7-1.

3. When asked, supply the first filename you want to compare and choose OK.

Type name of file to compare   It doesn't *have* to be an INI file

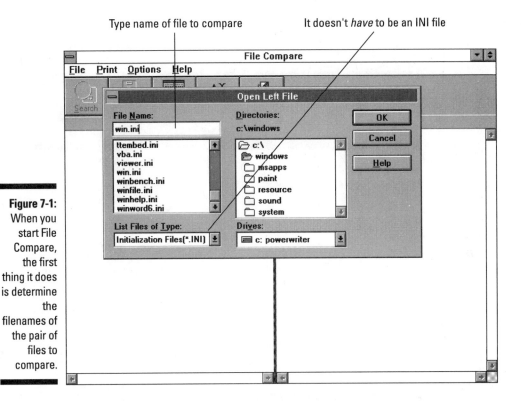

Figure 7-1:
When you
start File
Compare,
the first
thing it does
is determine
the
filenames of
the pair of
files to
compare.

In this example, I used the infamous WIN.INI file, which contains the changes created when I installed Norton Utilities version 8.

4. Next, File Compare wants the name of the second file in the combo. After providing that information, choose OK.

In this example, I used WIN.NU8 — which was my file before Norton Utilities got into it. After you supply the second filename, you get something like Figure 7-2.

Once you're comparing two files, as in Figure 7-2

✔ The scroll bar on the right scrolls both files simultaneously — with the differences between the two highlighted in a color of your choosing. In Figure 7-2, you can see that there are differences between lines 31 and 33.

✔ Since both files are cut off on the right — so that they'll fit side-by-side on-screen — horizontal scroll bars have been installed at the bottom so that you can scooch a file to the right.

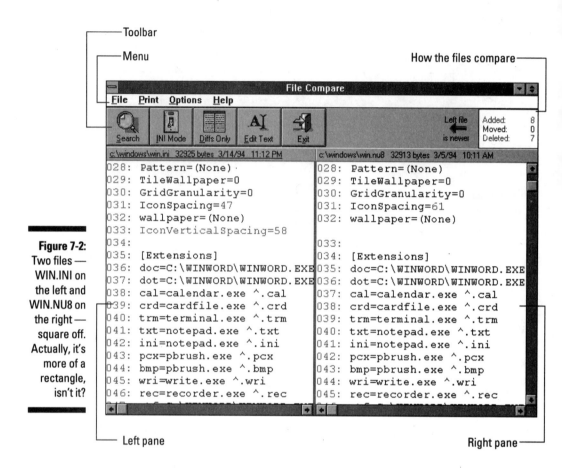

Figure 7-2: Two files — WIN.INI on the left and WIN.NU8 on the right — square off. Actually, it's more of a rectangle, isn't it?

✔ In the upper right portion of the window, you can see a summary of differences in terms of lines that have been added, moved, or deleted. That way, you can determine at a glance how much of a difference there is between the files.

Toolbar options

As in all Windows programs, the Toolbar at the top provides instant-click access to the most-used options in the program.

✔ Search. This option activates a search dialog experience, as in Figure 7-3, that lets you ask to see the sections that are the same between the two files or the sections that are different between the two files. Of course, you also can search for text.

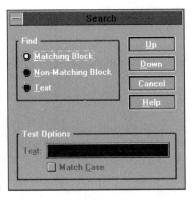

Figure 7-3:
A Search
dialog box
lets you
quickly jump
to the place
the two files
don't match.

✔ INI Mode. If you're examining an INI file, turn the light switch on to have Norton filter out comments and organize the files by groups alphabetically.

✔ Differences Only. The ultimate filter shows only what is different between the two files.

✔ Edit Text. This option lets you make changes to either file. Selecting this option requires you to choose which file to edit — door number one or door number two — but after that, it's like using Notepad or any of the other simple editing programs.

✔ Exit. This is the "Beam Me Outta Here, Scotty" command. Leave the program.

Menu options

✔ File. If you get tired of the two files you started with, you can use Alt+File Open Left Pane (or Right Pane) to load new files for comparison.

✔ Print. As you might suspect, this allows you to print either the left pane or the right pane. It also prints out a comparison of the two files — so you'll have something to read in bed while falling asleep.

✔ Options. This menu enables you to Customize the display some, in terms of colors and fonts (see Figure 7-4).

If there are certain sections of the INI files you don't want to see, highlight the section in the left pane and press Alt+**Options** ⇨ Exclude to get them out of your face. If you change your mind, press Alt+**Options** ⇨ Edit Exclusions.

✔ Help. Remember, Norton has an excellent and extensive help system. If you don't know what the heck is going on . . . or just want to use the three or four main features of the program, use Help and QuickHelp, respectively, to shift into high gear. After all, asking for help is nothing to be ashamed of.

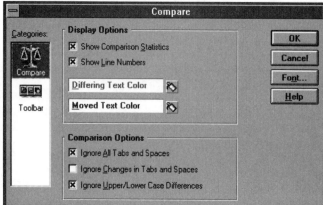

Figure 7-4:
The Options
you
configure in
File
Compare
are —
beyond
compare!

Comparing other files

Although File Compare assumes that you want to work with INI files, you also can compare and edit other files, like AUTOEXEC.BAT and CONFIG.SYS. Sometimes, when you're installing a new program, it'll tell you something like "I'm changing your AUTOEXEC.BAT file and saving the old version as AUTOEXEC.OLD." Well, you can use File Compare to look at AUTOEXEC.BAT in one of the panes and AUTOEXEC.OLD in the other and see what, exactly, was changed. And, of course, you can change it back or do whatever you want.

Chapter 8
Norton Cache

● ●

In This Chapter

▶ Making your computer run faster and jump higher

● ●

*H*ave you seen the psychic friends 900 phone services advertised on TV —
you know, they'll predict your future for $3.99 a minute? If you want a
psychic, you have only to turn to the Norton Cache (pronounced "cash") — the
psychic for your computer. Norton Cache may not be able to pick a winning
lotto number, but it can predict what commands you'll be using as you work
and will have them loaded and ready to go when needed. This means you don't
have to wait while the computer goes and looks something up.

The cache program is one of those programs that works in the background —
invisibly doing its thing while you do yours. You don't see it working, but it's there.

A simple example of how a cache works is with the DIR command. If you type
DIR and press Enter at a system prompt, the computer runs to the hard drive,
quickly compiles a list of files, and then reports back to you. If you need that list
a second time, the cache — if it's installed — has already memorized the list
from the first time and doesn't have to go back to the hard drive for the information — it just instantly shoots it out to you.

The cache works with applications, too. If you're using certain commands or
documents a lot, they are kept loaded and ready so that the computer doesn't
have to keep dipping back into the hard drive for instructions.

You'd think that this would be the way it normally works — but, hey, when did
computers ever make sense?

Although getting a winning lotto number from a psychic friend may be more
enticing, cache's predictions are far more likely to actually pay off in increased
speed and reduced exercising of the hard drive — which means the drive will
last longer. Also, the cache doesn't leave you $39.90 poorer after ten minutes.

Cache Wars

Norton's cache program isn't the only one on the planet. In fact, it probably isn't even the only one on your hard disk. If you have Windows, its own caching program — SMARTDRV — was automatically installed as part of the Windows setup routine.

If that's the case, you may not want to bother switching to Norton's Cache — especially if you haven't had any difficulties with Windows freezing up and pleasantries like that.

However, according to Norton, *their* caching program is better — more stable, smarter, and so forth.

If you don't have any other cache program installed, you'll definitely want to give Norton Cache a tryout. Also, the cache program speeds up access to floppy disks by half. So if you use floppy disks a lot, you'll see a big difference there.

Making Cache

You don't have to be Donald Trump to make a cache. You don't even have to be Marla.

Because the cache works in the background and is always there, you need to install the program so that it's launched every time the computer is turned on. Sounds like a job for AUTOEXEC.BAT or CONFIG.SYS, doesn't it? (If you don't remember what AUTOEXEC.BAT or CONFIG.SYS is, go back to DOS Boot Camp in Chapter 1).

Here's how to install the cache:

1. At the system prompt, type **NORTON** and press Enter to get into the Norton Utilities menu.

2. Press Alt+Configuration ➪ **Startup Programs.**

   You arrive at Figure 8-1, the Startup Programs dialog box.

   If there's already a check mark next to Start Norton Cache, **then the cache is already installed. You don't have to do anything else at this point except press Esc and celebrate.**

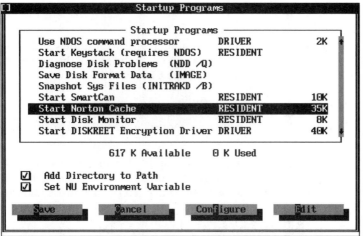

Figure 8-1:
The Startup
Programs
dialog box
lets you
choose the
programs
you want to
be activated
when you
first start
your
computer.

3. As in Figure 8-1, highlight Start Norton Cache.

4. Press Alt+Configure to get to Figure 8-2.

5. Choose the configuration options you want to use — in this case, just match the choices in Figure 8-2.

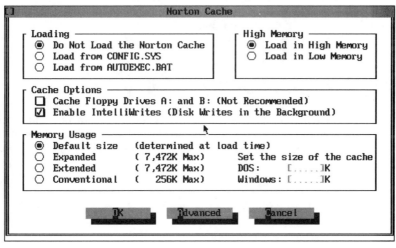

Figure 8-2:
Although
Norton
provides
many
investment
options for
your cache,
you can
leave all the
tough
choices to
Norton.

- Loading — the "start Norton Cache" command — may be placed in either the CONFIG.SYS or AUTOEXEC.BAT files. Conventional wisdom suggests CONFIG.SYS is the best place. However, if you need to uninstall the cache when using memory-hungry programs, put the cache program in the AUTOEXEC.BAT file. Either way, you can always change your mind later.

- Memory Usage can be left at Default Size — which lets Norton make the choice. This is a nice, safe, and easy option.

- If you have an older computer with no Windows and only 640K of memory, then you'll need to limit the size of the cache. In the Set the Size of the Cache area, type **64** in the DOS box.

6. When finished, press Alt+OK.

7. When you're back in Figure 8-1, press Alt+**S**ave, and Norton updates your files to make the cache run.

- When Norton has finished updating your files, a little note reminds you that the job's not quite done. To switch the cache on, the computer must be turned off and on — just press Enter to make the note disappear.

8. Reboot the computer by pressing Ctrl+Alt+Del — or press the reset button, if you have one, on the front of your computer.

✔ You may have noticed in Figure 8-2 that there are Advanced cache settings. We're not worrying about the advanced options at this point. The defaults will do the job. All you have to know is that the system is set up to go as quickly as possible. If you're filled with a desire to tweak the settings — and there are a couple dozen options at least — then you're in the wrong book. Go look in the manual.

✔ If you had been using SMARTDRV before installing Norton's Cache, Norton automatically disables SMARTDRV for you. Norton handles everything. Convenient, don't you think?

Is Your Cache Working for You?

You've installed the Cache, rebooted the computer, started using your programs and, by golly, things are running faster! Norton Cache is hard at work in the background. If you're from Missouri and need some kind of "show me" proof that Norton's on the job, you can request an audit so that you can see a strict accounting of your cache.

To see how hard your cache is working

1. Get to the system prompt.

2. Type **NCACHE2 /REPORT** and press Enter.

   You'll get something like Figure 8-3.

✔ If your report shows 0.0% in the Disk Reads area, then Norton Cache is not working on your system. Did you reboot?

Figure 8-3:
NCACHE2
/REPORT
shows you
how many
times the
cache
saved the
hard disk
from being
accessed
— sort of
like those
billboards
that show
how many
dollars in
long
distance
fees have
been saved.

```
┌─────────────────────────────────────────────────────────────────────┐
│   Conventional memory:         0K cache     0K management    595K free │
│   High DOS memory:             0K cache    28K management     20K free │
│   Expanded (EMS) memory:       0K cache     0K management   2704K free │
│   Extended (XMS) memory:    4096K cache    16K management   2688K free │
│                                                                        │
│        Total cache size is 4096.0K - Currently using 3001.0K  (73.2%)  │
│                                                                        │
│ DOS = 0K                BLOCK = 8192    USEHIGH  = ON     DELAY = 1.00  │
│ EXP = 0K, 0K            READ  = 8K      USEHMA   = ON     QUICK = ON    │
│ EXT = 4096K, 2048K      WRITE = 8K      OPTIMIZE = SPEED  MULTI = OFF   │
│                                                                        │
│         A  C  I  W  P     R     G      Cache Hits / Disk Reads         │
│ A:      -  +  -  +  -     D8   128             0 / 0           (0.0%)   │
│ B:      -  +  -  +  -     D8   128             0 / 0           (0.0%)   │
│ C:      +  +  +  +  -     D8   128        — 5862 / 10685       (54.8%)  │
└─────────────────────────────────────────────────────────────────────┘
```

└─ Only the hard drive should be cached

Norton uses cache info half the
time, speeding things up a lot!

> ✔ If you're trying to save keystrokes — and who isn't in these ecology-
> minded times? — you can actually get the report by typing the abbreviated
> **NCACHE2/R** and pressing Enter.

Caching in Your Chips

If you decide that you don't want Norton Cache after all, you can remove it
without fear of penalty for early withdrawal. In fact, you'll find that removing
the cache is almost exactly the same process as putting it in.

1. At the system prompt, type **NORTON** and press Enter to get into the
   Norton Utilities menu.

2. Press Alt+**C**onfiguration ⇨ **S**tartup Programs.

3. As in Figure 8-1, highlight Start Norton Cache.

4. Press Alt+**C**onfigure to get to Figure 8-2.

5. Choose Do Not Load the Norton Cache in the Loading options portion of
   the dialog box.

6. When finished, press Alt+OK.

7. When you're back in Figure 8-1, press Alt+**S**ave.

Faster than you can say "Mr. Drysdale," the cache is removed from your system and a little note appears, telling you to reboot the computer to finish the job.

8. Reboot the computer to finish the job.

If you had been using SMARTDRV before, Norton is not so gallant as to reactivate it for you. That you have to do on your own.

1. At the system prompt, type **EDIT \AUTOEXEC.BAT** and press Enter.

   • If your DOS Edit command isn't working, create the file by using your own word processor, but pay careful attention to the saving instructions in Step 4.

2. Somewhere in the file is a line that starts with `REM By NU8:` and contains the word `SMARTDRV`.

3. Delete the `REM By NU8:` part of the line.

4. Save the file and exit.

   If you're using the DOS EDIT command, that means pressing Alt+**F**ile ⇨ **S**ave, and then Alt+**F**ile ⇨ Exit. If you're using a word processing program, make sure that you save it as a text or ASCII file, or, in WordPerfect, use the Text Out function.

5. Reboot the computer.

   Press the reset button on the front of your computer or press Ctrl+Alt+Del on your keyboard.

Mem'ries

Just to make sure that you don't get things confused, programs like QEMM, 386MAX, and HIMEM.SYS are *memory managers*. They are not cache programs. A memory manager's job, in part, is to make sure programs get the right amount and kind of *memory*. A caching program's job is to make it easier for programs to have the right *command* at hand. The caching program uses memory — supplied by the memory managers — to do its job. So, if you've got QEMM et al installed, don't worry about a conflict of interest — the two kinds of programs are simpatico.

Chapter 9
Norton Change Directory

● ●

In This Chapter
▶ Foolproofing changing directories
▶ Giving your directory system a face-lift

● ●

*T*here are two sides to Norton Change Directory (or NCD, for short). On the "A" side, NCD takes the anguish out of negotiating DOS's CD (change directory) command. On the "B" side, NCD empowers you with the capability to actually make changes *to* a directory — like renaming it or deleting it or what have you. If all this talk of directories has your head spinning, go back to DOS Boot Camp in Chapter 1 for a pick-me-up on the topic.

Foolproofing Changing Directories

The problem with DOS's CD (change directory) command is that it's too easy to mess up. To move around on the hard drive, you have to know where you are in relationship to where you're going and whether that's up or down the directory structure — yikes! And, as disks get bigger and bigger, directory structures get more and more complex.

Norton's Change Directory (NCD) makes it simple. Honest.

Beaming across the computer

Here's the scene. You need to go to the WP51\DOCS directory to work. Normally, you have to type **CD \WP51\DOCS** and press Enter to get there. With NCD, all you have to do is type **NCD DOC** and press Enter. In a flash, NCD finds a directory in its list that matches DOC and takes you there. It's magic.

With NCD, all you type is the name of the directory you want to go to — not the whole path, mind you, just the desired directory name. And did you notice that I didn't even have to type the whole directory name? DOC was enough for NCD to leap into action. No more backslashes and backtalk from the computer when you don't get everything letter perfect. I always thought the computer at least should say, "Hey, that was close — I know you'll get it the next time" rather than `invalid parameters` or whatever.

There's only one catch to using NCD — and it's a tiny one. Before you can use NCD, you have to let Norton build a list of all the directories on your system. To accomplish this formidable-sounding task, all you have to do is ask. You don't even have to say please or thank you.

1. At the system prompt, type **NCD /R** and press Enter.

   The /R means "rescan," or it could mean "reconnoiter," because that's what NCD is carrying out on your hard drive. After carrying out Step 1, you should see something like Figure 9-1 as Norton Change Directory quickly scans the drive and assembles a list of directories. This process only needs to be done *once* — unless you do something like add or delete directories. Anytime you modify your directory structure, you need to rescan.

2. Once the list is compiled, you're left in the NCD dialog box, as in Figure 9-2. Press Esc to leave the dialog box.

   We'll be uncovering the secret life of the NCD dialog box in the next section. For now, just exit.

Figure 9-1: Before Norton's improved Change Directory command can function, it must be coaxed into compiling a list of directories on your hard drive.

The current directory is highlighted
when you get into the NCD map

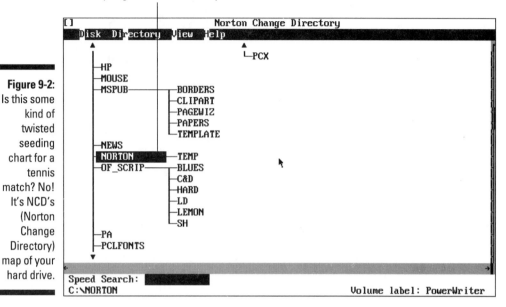

Figure 9-2:
Is this some
kind of
twisted
seeding
chart for a
tennis
match? No!
It's NCD's
(Norton
Change
Directory)
map of your
hard drive.

Now that NCD has its little list, you're all set! Give NCD a whirl. At your system
prompt, type **NCD** and *someplace on your computer* and press Enter.

✔ In Figure 9-2, typing **NCD LEMON** and pressing Enter would be the same as
typing **CD \OF_SCRIP\LEMON** and pressing Enter. A considerable shortcut.

✔ If there is more than one directory with the same or similar names, NCD
takes you to the first occurrence. So if you type **NCD LETTERS**, Norton
may take you to BOB\LETTERS instead of, say, WP51\LETTERS. Just type
NCD LETTERS again and this time you are taxied to the right place.

✔ To make the most of NCD, give directories unique names — it makes it
easier on NCD to take you to the right place.

When NCD saves the information on your directories, it's put in a file called
TREEINFO.NCD. So, if you happen to run into this file in your travels, don't
delete it. Of course, if you do delete it, you can make another by using the
NCD /R command.

Voyaging with a map

Even if you aren't at all sure about the name of the directory you need to go to, NCD can still help.

1. To get to the NCD dialog box in Figure 9-2, use one of the following:

   - From the Norton Utilities menu, highlight Norton CD and press Enter
   - From a system prompt, type **NCD** and press Enter
   - From Windows, in the Norton DOS Utilities group, click the NCD icon

2. Move the highlight until the directory of your desires is in the spotlight.

3. Press Enter — or double-click with the mouse.

   You will now find yourself out of the NCD dialog box and in the directory you wanted.

✔ Looking at the directory map, you may spot the directory you want way down at the bottom of the screen. To avoid a long scroll, just type the first couple of letters of the directory's name, and the cursor jumps straight to it. In Figure 9-2, for example, if you type **P**, you'll find the directory PA highlighted. NCD calls this a *speed search*. The search starts from the current locale of the cursor and searches downward. When you're all set, press Enter.

✔ If you're highlighting a directory and you're not quite sure that it's the right one, press Alt+Directory ➪ File List, and a Directory Sort (see Chapter 3) window appears with a list of all the files in that directory. Do the filenames look familiar? Is this what you want? Good, then you're in the right directory. Now click the Close button to get back to the map and press Enter to get out of NCD. If it isn't what you want, click the Close button anyway, because you need to do more searching on the directory map.

✔ Do you want to look at another drive? NCD can accommodate if you press Alt+Disk ➪ Change Disk. You'll have to press Alt+Disk ➪ **R**escan Disk to rescan the new drive.

✔ Would you like to see more of the map on the screen? NCD can accommodate you there, too — but the more lines displayed, the smaller the printing. Figure 9-3 is using the 50-lines option, and you can see how much more of the tree is visible — assuming, of course, that you can read it. Alt+View is where you can adjust the focus to taste. Heck, your directory map may not even have 50 lines to display. Remember, though, you can always go back to the original, 25-line option.

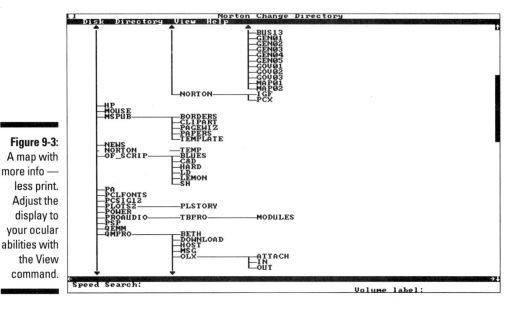

```
[ ]                      Norton Change Directory
  Disk  Directory  View  Help                                                  ↑
                                      BUS13
                                      GEN01
                                      GEN02
                                      GEN03
                                      GEN04
                                      GEN05
                                      GOU01
                                      GOU02
                                      GOU03
                                      MAP01
                                      MAP02
                          NORTON      IGF
                                      PCX
    HP
    MOUSE
    MSPUB         BORDERS
                  CLIPART
                  PAGEWIZ
                  PAPERS
                  TEMPLATE
    NEWS          TEMP
    NORTON        BLUES
    OF_SCRIP      C&D
                  HARD
                  LD
                  LEMON
                  SH
    PA
    PCLFONTS
    PCSIG12
    PLOTS2        PLSTORY
    POWER
    PROAUDIO      TBPRO         MODULES
    PSP
    QEMM
    QMPRO         BETH
                  DOWNLOAD
                  HOST
                  MSG
                  OLX           ATTACH
                                IN
                                OUT
Speed Search:                               Volume label:
```

Figure 9-3:
A map with more info — less print. Adjust the display to your ocular abilities with the View command.

Overhauling Your Directory System

NCD gives you the power — shazzam! — to delete, rename, move, and make new directories even if you don't know a lick of DOS.

However, be warned that whenever you delete, rename, or move a directory, you have the potential to screw something up. Your system is organized around certain givens. It relies on the fact that, for example, Windows is residing in a directory called WINDOWS. If you get the brainstorm to rename the WINDOWS directory WIN, you'll be unpleasantly surprised to discover that Windows no longer functions like it used to, if it does at all. So proceed cautiously and *vaya con Dios.*

The good news is that making a new directory won't hurt anything.

Making, renaming, and deleting directories

If you're ready to make the step into the big time by taking control of your directories, here's how:

1. Type **NCD** and press Enter to get to the NCD map.

   If you prefer, you can use one of the other methods outlined in the beginning of the preceding section. Anyway, you should end up looking at something like Figure 9-2.

2. Highlight the directory to be renamed or deleted, or where you want to create a new directory.

   Put the cursor at the root (\) of the map if you want to make a new, top-level directory.

3. Press Alt+Directory to drop down the menu shown in Figure 9-4.

Use these options to change your directories

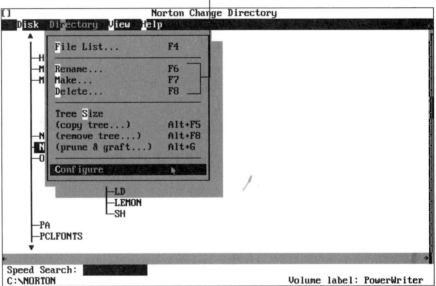

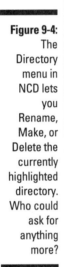

Figure 9-4:
The
Directory
menu in
NCD lets
you
Rename,
Make, or
Delete the
currently
highlighted
directory.
Who could
ask for
anything
more?

4. Select the action of your choice — **R**ename, **M**ake, or **D**elete.

   ✔ If you're renaming or making a directory, NCD asks for a new name. Respond and then click OK (or press Enter).

   ✔ If you're deleting a directory, NCD will either carry out the order or show you that there are files in that directory *that will also be deleted.* You have the option to either continue and delete the directory *and the files* in it or cancel the operation.

Pruning and grafting

Although pruning and grafting sounds vaguely like something to do with paying off politicians, it's actually the process of picking up a directory (and its contents) from one place in the directory structure and attaching it (and its contents) to another location. This is an amazing and powerful command, so NCD has gone out of its way to make sure only those who know what they're doing have access to it.

Although prune and graft isn't something you'll do every day, it's a real timesaver when it's needed.

So, if you really must prune and graft, the first step is to go into the configuration program and grant yourself the right to perform such a procedure. You may have noticed that the menu in Figure 9-4 shows the Prune and Graft commands turned off — which we will now toggle back on.

1. Type **NCD** and press Enter to get to the directory map.

2. Press Alt+**D**irectory ⇨ **C**onfigure.

3. When the NCD Configuration dialog box appears, as in Figure 9-5, select Enable Prune & Graft and click OK.

4. Highlight the directory to be moved, as I did with LEMON in Figure 9-6, and then press Alt+**P**rune.

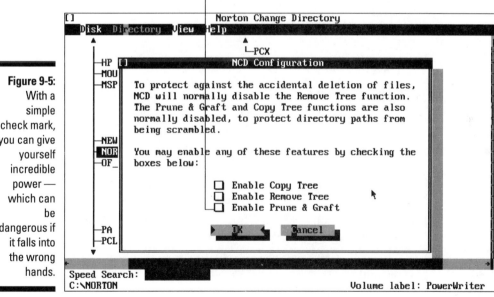

Figure 9-5: With a simple check mark, you can give yourself incredible power — which can be dangerous if it falls into the wrong hands.

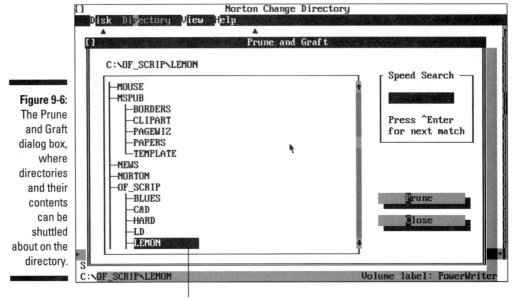

Figure 9-6:
The Prune
and Graft
dialog box,
where
directories
and their
contents
can be
shuttled
about on the
directory.

Before: LEMON is down here

5. Using the cursor keys, move the directory to its new home.

6. Press Alt+**G**raft.

   The directory becomes installed in its new locale — as in Figure 9-7 — and you're placed in a position to select another directory for movement.

7. When you're all finished, press Alt+**C**lose to bid a fond farewell to Prune and Graft.

✔ If you want to make sure that no one else using the computer can Prune and Graft, press Alt+Di**r**ectory and disable Prune and Graft (Steps 2 and 3).

✔ If you delete something in error, jump to Chapter 14 to learn about UnErase before you make another move.

✔ Prune and Graft cannot be reliably used from Windows — it has to do with caching programs and stuff like that. You'll get a warning from Norton if you try.

After: LEMON is moved up under the CLIPART Directory

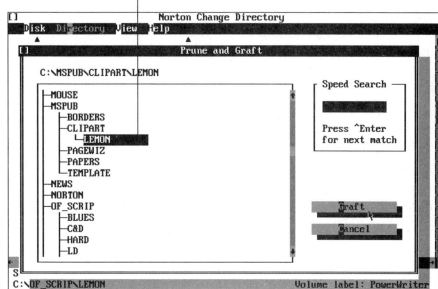

Figure 9-7:
Once the
directory is
in its new
position,
press
Alt+**G**raft.

Are you okay?

You see it in every dialog box, and every configuration option — it's the so-called word "OK." What the heck kind of a word is OK anyway? It's not even a word, it's two bloomin' letters!

Well, one theory places the origin of OK with the bastardization of the French word *au courant* (pronounced, sort of, as "oh-kooran") — which means "up-to-date."

However, according to my Webster's Unabridged dictionary, Democrats were the ones who coined the phrase OK when they created the Democratic O.K. Club back in the spring of 1840. O.K., it turns

out, is the abbreviation for a little town called Old Kinderhook—the birthplace of Martin Van Buren, whom the Club supported for a second term as president. Apparently, citizens of the United States didn't find Mr. Van Buren that OK, because he lost. Later on, he ran again, no longer as a Democrat, but as a member of a group called the Free-Soil Party. Fortunately, the Free-Soil Party didn't catch on that much — otherwise, we'd have "the gunfight at the FSP corral" and astronauts would be saying, "everything's A-FSP." Worst of all — by far — we'd all be clicking FSP to confirm our choices.

Chapter 10

Norton Control Center

· ·

In This Chapter

▶ Pumping up the cursor

▶ Looking at the world through a rose-colored monitor

▶ Sensitivity training for mice

▶ Setting the date and time

▶ Letting Norton Control Center control your system

· ·

*T*he Norton Control Center — the name just radiates power and strength, doesn't it? Sorry to disappoint you, but the Norton Control Center — NCC for short — lets you tweak and fiddle with a number of items that you probably never gave much thought to. After all, who worries about the size and speed of the cursor and whether the system prompt could be more colorful. Even though the goodies NCC gives you control over are — for the most part — not big ticket items, they can make a big difference in overall comfort. I'm reminded of the "Princess and the Pea" story.

If you've ever carefully adjusted a stereo system, you have no doubt experienced the frustration of having some less-than-sensitive person come along and change everything. You'll be happy to know that with NCC, your adjustments can be saved and loaded. That way, no matter what the philistines in your office may do to your settings, you can instantly come back to your 40 lines of display with a small yellow cursor.

Sounds great, but here's the catch — sometimes when other programs are started, they take control of the screen and toss the Norton settings out the Windows (so to speak). Fortunately, many programs are well-mannered enough to restore things to the Norton settings once you exit them.

Who put the NCC in NCC-1701?

Does the starship Enterprise really have Norton Control Center tattooed on its side? Well, no. As you might have assumed, the NCC on the Enterprise doesn't stand for Norton Control Center. NCC is supposed to stand for Naval Construction Contract (at least according to the official Star Trek blueprints). In other words, every ship in Starfleet is roaming the galaxy with a purchase order number painted on the outside. Tacky. Very tacky.

Controlling the Norton Control Center

We're going to browse through the options in the Norton Control Center. You can select the items you want to change, and stroll on by those you don't care about. When we're all finished looking, we'll save all our choices at once.

If, however, you're a speed shopper and you know what you want, then skip to that section, make your adjustment, and go straight for the checkout stand (Saving Settings) and save.

To get to the Norton Control Center dialog box in Figure 10-1, use one of the following:

✔ From the Norton Utilities menu, highlight Control Center and press Enter, or

✔ From a system prompt, type **NCC** and press Enter

The settings that you create with NCC probably will disappear when you start another program. Each application seizes control over the cursor and those other items. However, once you're back at the system prompt, the NCC settings will prevail.

Sizing up the cursor

If you're tired of big bullies kicking sand in the face of your pathetic underline cursor, now's the time to — pump him up!

1. Get into the NCC program as described at the beginning of the section (type **NCC** and press Enter).

2. With the highlight on Cursor Size, press Enter (or Tab) to move the cursor to the right.

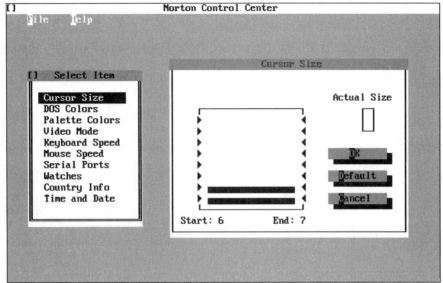

Figure 10-1:
The Norton
Control
Center, a
plethora of
possibilities
for perking
up your
picture.

3. Use the up-arrow key to increase the size of the cursor.

   You can see it growing in the sample box that's labeled Actual Size.

   • If you go up too many times, the box shrinks back down to the small size. No problem, just go back up again, but this time go a little slower.

4. When satisfied, press Alt+**OK** — or click on it with the mouse.

   You'll know you're out of the Cursor Size box when the highlight is back in the Select Item box, as shown in Figure 10-1.

Changing DOS Colors

One of the weird things about having a color monitor is that when you first turn on the computer, everything is in black and white. It isn't until you get into a program that you get to see the color.

If a black-and-white system prompt irritates you, you'll be interested in using the DOS Colors feature. You can make your system prompt — and everything else you do in DOS — just about any color you can think of. Even burnt sienna. Changing the DOS Colors doesn't make your computer perform faster or last longer — it'll just make it a little easier to live with. In fact, it makes the computer surprisingly more friendly.

1. Get into the NCC program as described at the beginning of the section (type **NCC** and press Enter).

2. Highlight DOS Colors, and the DOS Colors control panel appears (see Figure 10-2).

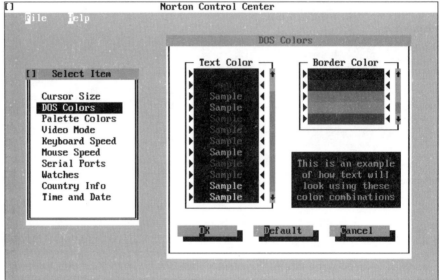

Figure 10-2: This is definitely somewhere over the rainbow — NCC lets you see all those thousands of colors you paid for when you bought that expensive graphics card.

3. Press Enter (or Tab) to move over to the DOS Colors control panel.

4. Use the up- and down-arrow keys to view all the colors and backgrounds available in the Text Color strip.

   The sample text box reflects what's currently highlighted.

5. If you want a border around the screen — press Tab to move to the Border Color box.

   If you're not sure about a border, see how it looks in the sample box. If you want no border, choose black.

6. When satisfied, press Alt+**OK** — or click OK with the mouse.

   ✓ If you alter the colors to the extent that you think you're flashing back to the Sixties, press Alt+**D**efault to put it back the way it was.

Creating a color palette

If you found the DOS Color options wanting in subtlety and variation, you can view more choices in the Color Palette. The Color Palette lets you trade out the standard colors found in the DOS Colors section for ones a little more extreme. For example, the Color Palette is where Barney Purple can be found.

1. Get into the NCC program as described at the beginning of the section (type **NCC** and press Enter).

2. Highlight Palette Colors to see the Palette Colors control panel.

3. Press Enter (or Tab) to move into the control panel.

4. Highlight the color you want to modify.

5. Press Alt+Change to see a panel with several variations on the color you selected.

6. Highlight the new color choice.

7. Press Alt+**OK**.

   The new color now appears in the Palette Colors control panel. Also, that color now appears in the DOS Colors options.

✔ If you want to change one color back to the way it was, follow Steps 1 through 5. Then, while in the smaller color control box, press Alt+**D**efault to restore.

✔ If you've changed several colors and want to put them all back, follow Steps 1 through 3 and then press Alt+**D**efault to restore.

Video à la mode

The standard number of lines displayed on a screen is 24. If you want more — and if your graphics card can support it — you can have more. You want 40 lines of display? Take 50, it's on me.

1. Get into the NCC program as described at the beginning of the section (type **NCC** and press Enter).

2. Highlight Palette Colors to see the Palette Colors control panel.

3. Press Enter (or Tab) to move into the control panel.

4. Using the spacebar or mouse, select the number of lines you want to display and whether you want color or black and white.

   Figure 10-3 shows what you get when you select the 50-line display.

5. When you're satisfied, press Enter or click OK.

Figure 10-3:
In the ring for tonight's bout is a normal screen on the left weighing in at 24 lines of display. The contender, on the right, weighs in at a big 50 lines of display!

> ✔ If you want to change the colors of the Norton program itself, this isn't the place. Press Esc to get out of this wing of the Norton world and review Chapter 2, which covers configuring Norton.

Speeding keyboards

Unfortunately, there's no setting that instantly improves one's typing speed. And, since it isn't likely our typing speed will ever tax the computer, we can assume that the Keyboard Speed setting in the Norton Control Center doesn't have much to do with the speed of human typing.

When Norton refers to keyboard speed, it's talking about two things. The first has to do with what's known as the *typematic rate*. Typematic is the conflation of *type* and *automatic*. You've seen the typematic rate in action plenty of times. When you hold down on a key on the keyboard for too long, you end up with a thousand of that letter. That was typematic at work. Although you never want 10,000 letter Es, you may want the cursor or the Backspace to repeat automatically when you hold them down — which is controlled by the same typematic setting.

The other half of the speed equation is the *typematic delay* factor. When you press and hold down the letter E, for example, there's a nanosecond of a pause before the computer starts running wild making Es. If you're heavy-handed — in other words, you're always getting more letters than you want — you can increase the delay time to compensate for that.

If you have no complaints about your keyboard speed, why not take a look at the adjustments anyway — it's kind of fun to see how it works.

1. Get into the NCC program as described at the beginning of the section (type **NCC** and press Enter).

2. Highlight Keyboard Speed to see the Keyboard Speed control panel (see Figure 10-4).

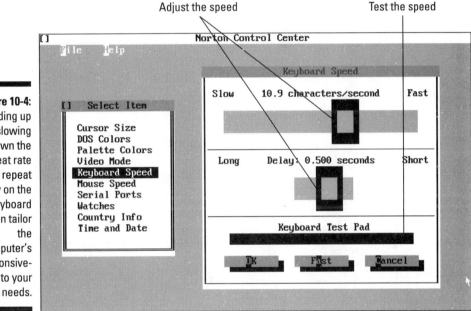

Figure 10-4:
Speeding up or slowing down the repeat rate and repeat delay on the keyboard can tailor the computer's responsiveness to your needs.

3. Press Enter (or Tab) to move into the control panel.

Once you're in the control panel, the up- and down-arrow keys move you between the adjustment boxes and the Keyboard Test Pad. The left- and right-arrow keys adjust the speed. Mousers can just click and slip-slide away. Also, the cursor is automatically placed in the testing area.

4. Adjust the speed and delay rate to taste.

5. Try out the new speed by pressing E — or any other letter — and holding down.

You'll see — in the testing area — how fast, or slow, the computer spits out the letters.

6. Repeat Steps 4 and 5 until you're satisfied and then press Alt+OK.

✔ For a thrill, first set everything to a slow speed and test via the testing pad. Then move everything to a fast speed and feel the difference. Another way to learn the difference between the typematic rate and the delay is to speed up the typematic rate and slow down the delay.

Sensitivity training for mice

If your mouse doesn't seem sensitive to your needs, you may have considered group therapy in the past. Much easier, however, is to use the Mouse Speed setting in NCC to instantly increase the mouse's sensitivity — a.k.a. the mouse's *speed*. Nothing's worse than a slow mouse.

1. Get into the NCC program as described at the beginning of the section (type **NCC** and press Enter).

2. Highlight Mouse Speed to see the Mouse Speed control panel (see Figure 10-5).

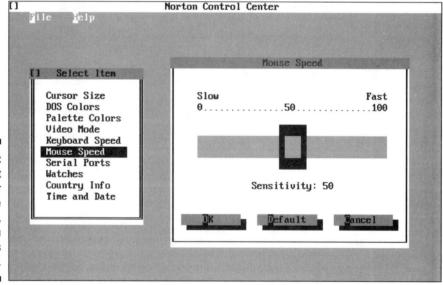

Figure 10-5: If you're not getting your mouse needs met, NCC lets you increase its sensitivity.

3. Press Enter (or Tab) to move into the control panel.

4. Use the left- and right-arrow keys to slide the control to a faster or slower speed.

   • As you change the sensitivity, try moving the mouse around. You'll see the difference.

   • If you change the Sensitivity to zero, the mouse won't respond at all and you'll have to use the arrow keys to crank it back up.

5. When you're satisfied with the sensitivity level, click OK.

A toast with serial ports

For all intents and purposes, the serial port settings on your computer are handled by your communications software. You don't have to deal with them at this level. The only port you have to deal with is Fonseca or Jerez, so skip the Serial Ports option in the NCC.

Watches? We don't need no stinkin' watches!

Okay, this is also another command that a normal person doesn't need. My goodness, if you need to time something, look at your own watch — or buy a stopwatch.

However, there is one fringe use for this command that's mentioned in the — *shudder* — Norton manual that's kind of cool, so I thought I'd translate it into English and share it with you.

Be forewarned, however, that you have to create a batch file to use this feature. I'll guide you through it step-by-step, but if it's all too much for you, don't worry about it. Maybe this is something you'll want to save for later.

Ready? Here's the scenario — you want to keep track of how long you work on your computer while doing a particular project. Assuming you're determined not to buy a stopwatch or timer of some sort, here's the technical solution to tracking your efforts.

Before creating the batch file, we need to learn a little about the stopwatch command. First of all, it's best used from a command line. To start the stopwatch you type **NCC /START:1** and press Enter. To stop, you type **NCC /STOP:1** and press Enter. The NCC part of the command invokes the Norton Control Center, the /START or /STOP does what you might expect with the stopwatch. The :1 refers to the fact that there can be up to four stopwatches going at the same time. We're not getting fancy here. One stopwatch is enough.

Okay, let's make that stopwatch batch file:

1. Type **EDIT LOG.BAT** and press Enter.

   Confirm that you want to create the file when asked to do so by DOS's EDIT command.

   • If your EDIT command isn't working, create the file by using your own word processor, but pay careful attention to saving instructions in Step 3.

2. Type the following in the file:

NCC /start:1 /c:%1 >> %2

word %1

NCC /stop:1 >> %2

Important note: Where I've typed *word*, you need to substitute the command that starts *your* word processing program or spreadsheet name — whatever you'll be using while working on the project. For example, if you use WordPerfect, your second line is *wp %1*.

3. Save the file and exit.

If you're using the DOS EDIT command, press Alt+File ⇨ **S**ave, and then Alt+File ⇨ **E**xit. If you're using a word processing program, make sure that you save it as a text or ASCII file or, in WordPerfect, use the Text Out function.

If you've typed and saved the file, congratulations for hanging in there. Now all that's left is to see how to use the thing.

Imagine if you will — you're working on a project called Johnson. As you toil over every aspect of the project, you want to keep a file called JOHNSON.LOG that records how long was required to accomplish each task. In fact, you're about to write a letter that will be called JOHN_LET.DOC, and you need to track that. By using the LOG.BAT command you just created, here's what you type: **LOG JOHN_LET.DOC JOHNSON.LOG** and press Enter.

Typing LOG starts the stopwatch on the JOHN_LET.DOC file and records the starting time in the JOHNSON.LOG file.

When you've finished working on the JOHN_LET.DOC file, be sure to save the file and exit the word processing program you used to write the letter. The moment you exit, the stopwatch automatically stops and records the stopping time in the JOHNSON.LOG file.

After working on a report and other things, your JOHNSON.LOG eventually will look something like Figure 10-6. It's crude, but effective. If you want something elegant, then drop a few bucks on TimeSlips.

Country Info — the lowdown on Garth Brooks

This has to do with settings for time, date, currency, and so on for various nations around the world. My recommendation is not to futz with this. First of all, you're probably already set up properly. Second, to change it, you need to put a country statement in your CONFIG.SYS, and it gets worse from there. Let's move along.

Figure 10-6:
One way to keep track of time worked on projects is via the stopwatch command. Of course, like any stopwatch, it's only as accurate as the person at the plunger.

```
john_let.doc 3:51pm, Tuesday, October   8, 1994
             4:00pm, Tuesday, October   8, 1994
                    9 minutes, 18 seconds

  report.doc 4:21pm, Tuesday, October   8, 1994
             4:29pm, Tuesday, October   8, 1994
                    8 minutes, 35 seconds

 summary.doc 4:30pm, Tuesday, October   8, 1994
             4:50pm, Tuesday, October   8, 1994
                   19 minutes, 38 seconds
```

Setting the date and time

Let me clear the air for commitment-shy guys — this kind of "setting the date" has nothing to do with getting married, okay? This is strictly setting the date and time on your computer clock. Relax. Take a couple of deep breaths.

Are you one of those people whose computer clock is correct only half the time because you never learned how to change the time with the seasons? Or, possibly you have an older model computer in which changing the time was an incredible hassle. In either case, changing the date and time with NCC is very, very simple.

1. Get into the NCC program as described at the beginning of the chapter (type **NCC** and press Enter).

2. Highlight Time and Date to see the Time and Date control panel (see Figure 10-7).

3. Press Enter (or Tab) to move into the control panel.

   Change the date or time by typing the correct info, or by pressing the plus and minus keys to increase or decrease the current setting if typing is too much of a chore.

4. Once it's all set properly, press Alt+**OK**.

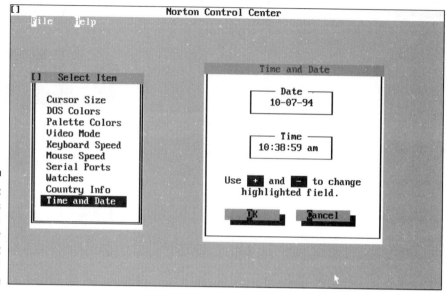

Figure 10-7:
Does
anyone
really know
what time it
is?

Saving Settings

Okay, you've changed your cursor size and colors, and everything is just so. Now, it's time to save the settings so that they can be loaded every time the computer is turned on.

Assuming you're in NCC (as in Figure 10-1), do this:

1. Press Alt+**File** ⇨ **S**ave Settings (the shortcut is to press the F2 function key, if you're into that sort of thing).

2. When you see the Save Settings dialog box, shown in Figure 10-8, type a name for your settings. *Hint:* Use your name so that you won't forget it.

   For the sake of example, I'll pretend I've saved mine under the name of Madonna. After all, who could forget Madonna?

3. Press Alt+**OK**.

4. Press Esc to exit NCC.

Loading NCC settings

Getting NCC loaded is simple. It's easier to use the command line method rather than going through a whole chain of commands in the NCC dialog box. Of course, using the dialog box is always delightful, but sometimes we don't have time for pleasant chit chat.

What you've changed has been checkmarked

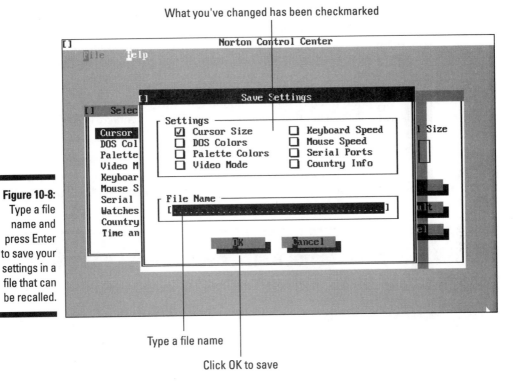

Figure 10-8:
Type a file
name and
press Enter
to save your
settings in a
file that can
be recalled.

Type a file name

Click OK to save

1. At the system prompt, type: **NCC filename/SET** and press Enter.

   In my example, where I saved the settings as MADONNA, I would type
   NCC MADONNA/SET and press Enter.

For this to work, you have to be in the directory where the MADONNA file is
saved. Otherwise, you must also specify where the MADONNA file is. For
example, if it's in the NU8 directory — where NCC is — you would type
NCC \NU8\MADONNA/SET and press Enter.

If you fall in love with your NCC settings, you may want to put the loading
command in your AUTOEXEC.BAT file (remember AUTOEXEC.BAT in DOS Boot
Camp in Chapter 1?).

1. Get to the root directory by typing **CD ** and press Enter.

2. Type **EDIT AUTOEXEC.BAT** and press Enter.

   This gets you into the AUTOEXEC.BAT file with the DOS EDIT command. If
   your DOS EDIT command doesn't work, then use your own word processor — but pay careful attention to the saving instructions.

3. At the bottom of the file, add *your* loading command for your NCC settings
   — like **NCC \NU8\MADONNA/SET**.

4. Save the file and exit.

   If you're using the DOS EDIT command, press Alt+File ⇨ **S**ave, and then Alt+File ⇨ **E**xit. If you're using a word processing program, make sure that you save it as a text or ASCII file, or, in WordPerfect, use the Text Out function.

Now, every time you turn on the computer, the NCC settings will be loaded for you automatically. Isn't that wonderful? It just doesn't get any better than this.

Actually, it does — as you'll see in later chapters.

If you accidentally delete or alter something else in the AUTOEXEC.BAT file, you can always bail out with no harm done by exiting and *not* saving. Then start again.

ANSI.SYS — it's not a sister who can't keep still!

For NCC's color stuff (DOS Colors and Palette Colors) to work, you have to have two things: A color monitor and — take a deep breath — ready? — ANSI.SYS must be in your CONFIG.SYS file.

I know what you're thinking. What's an ANSI.SYS and how do I tell whether it's in my CONFIG.SYS, especially if I don't know what a CONFIG.SYS is?

A CONFIG.SYS is a file that should be sitting in your root directory. CONFIG.SYS is short for *configure system,* and it's sort of the self-esteem part of the computer. Every time the computer is turned on, the CONFIG.SYS file tells the computer what's attached to it and what all it's capable of.

ANSI.SYS is another file, probably in your DOS directory, that is a video device *driver.* That means it chauffeurs your video capabilities. The driver gets employed in the CONFIG.SYS file — so that the computer knows there's somebody there to do the extra video work.

To install the ANSIS.SYS driver in the CONFIG.SYS file — which is a good thing to do whether you're using DOS Colors or not — do the following:

1. Get to the system prompt and go to the root directory — type **CD ** and press Enter.

2. Next, type **EDIT CONFIG.SYS** and press Enter.

   This starts the DOS EDIT program. If you see bad command or file name instead of the EDIT program, call up the file with your regular word processor, but pay careful attention to saving instructions at the end.

3. Look in the file for DEVICE=\DOS\ANSI.SYS.

   If you see this line — or at least something with the words DEVICE and ANSI.SYS in it, then you're all set. Exit the EDIT program without saving by pressing Alt+File ⇨ **E**xit.

4. If you don't see the line containing ANSI.SYS, you'll have to type it in yourself. Stick it in as the third line.

5. Save the file and exit.

   If you're using the DOS EDIT command, press Alt+File ⇨ **S**ave, and then Alt+File ⇨ **E**xit. If you're using a word processing program, make sure that you save it as a text or ASCII file, or, in WordPerfect, use the Text Out function.

You have to turn the computer off and then on again for this change to take effect.

Chapter 11

Safe Format

• •

In This Chapter

▶ Formatting a floppy disk — the basics

▶ Foiling formatting foul-ups

▶ Taking formatting shortcuts

• •

Safe Format? What's an *unsafe* format? More to the point, what's a *format*!?

Format is a verb. It's an action that must be performed — a deed that must be done — to all new floppy disks before they can be used. You don't need to have a clue as to what formatting is or what it does; all you really need to know is that you have to do it and Safe Format will do it for you.

Now, about the *safe* aspect. Normally, if you happen to format a disk that is already formatted, then FORMAT wipes out whatever material used to be on that disk. Isn't *that* special? With kindly Safe Format, you are warned that the disk contains data, and you even are offered the opportunity to call the whole thing off. Now that's safety.

Safe Format does not deny adrenaline junkies the thrill of formatting unsafely, though. There's an option to throw caution to the wind and ignore the safety factors. After all, sometimes you really do want to boldly go and wipe out what was on the disk before.

Formatting a Floppy Disk — The Basics

Let's get down to the business of formatting a floppy disk.

1. Insert the floppy to be formatted into the floppy drive.

2. Type **SFORMAT** and press Enter.

As usual, you have the option of starting the program the direct way, as just described, or via the Norton Utilities menu. In the menu, highlight Safe Format and press Enter. You want to end up with something like Figure 11-1.

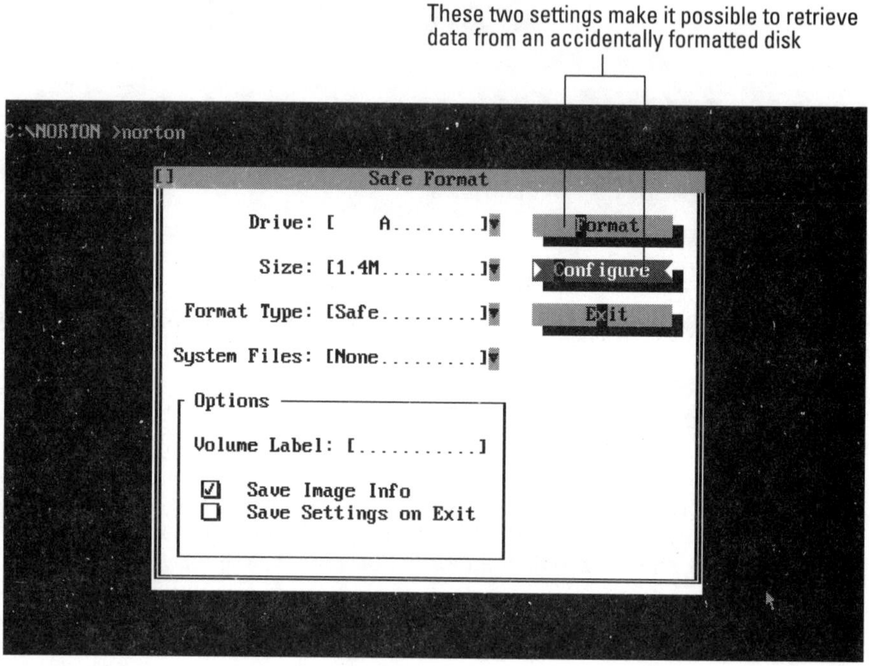

These two settings make it possible to retrieve data from an accidentally formatted disk

Figure 11-1:
Your basic plain-vanilla Safe Format dialog box. Verify that your options are set correctly and then click **Format** to start the process.

```
C:\NORTON >norton

[ ]                  Safe Format

         Drive: [   A........]▼      Format

          Size: [1.4M........]▼    ▶ Configure ◀

   Format Type: [Safe........]▼        Exit

  System Files: [None........]▼

  ┌ Options ──────────────────────┐
  │                                │
  │ Volume Label: [...........]    │
  │                                │
  │  ☑  Save Image Info            │
  │  ☐  Save Settings on Exit      │
  │                                │
  └────────────────────────────────┘
```

3. Make sure that the options are properly set.

   If the options aren't correct, use the drop-down arrow to reveal the alternatives.

   • The Drive will be either A or B — you have to figure that out yourself. If you guess wrong, you can always change it and try again. No harm done.

   • The Size of the disk is determined by whether it's high density or low density and whether it's a 3 ½" or 5 ¼" disk. (See "Help! I don't know what kind of floppy disks I have!" in Chapter 4 if you're unsure.)

   • The Format Type can be one of three choices: *Safe* — which enables you to unformat the disk later; *Quick* — the fastest method to reformat a disk; or *DOS* — the traditional "invading hordes" process that wipes out everything in its path. If you don't know which one to choose, go with Safe.

   • System Files should be left at *None* unless you're making a disk that is for booting the computer.

   • If you make changes to the options and you want them made permanent, be sure to check the Save Settings on Exit box.

4. Press Alt+Format, and away you'll go!

   Well, almost. First, Norton puts up a sign saying Analyzing disk information... while it looks at the floppy disk to make sure that everything's
   on the up and up.

   - If files are already on the disk, Norton asks, Are you sure you want to
     format it? and provides a listing of the innocent files that will be
     eradicated if you continue. If you approve, choose Yes. If not, choose No.

   After a few seconds you should get Figure 11-2. When finished, Norton let's
   you know that the drive has been successfully formatted.

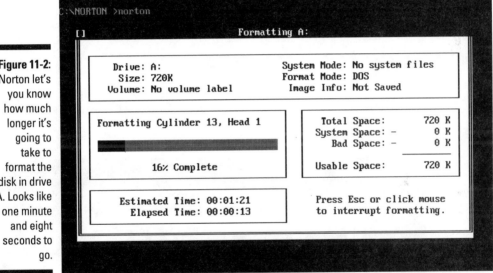

Figure 11-2:
Norton let's
you know
how much
longer it's
going to
take to
format the
disk in drive
A. Looks like
one minute
and eight
seconds to
go.

5. You can either stick another disk in the drive and start the formatting
   processes again, or press Esc to exit.

Foiling Formatting Foul-Ups

Sometimes Norton is unable to format a disk. When that happens, it pops up
with error messages like Unrecoverable Error! and The disk has bad
system values (not to be confused with *family values*) and other frightening
messages. There are many reasons this could happen, but here are a few you're
likely to run into:

✔ You've told Norton that the disk is a 1.4M size disk and it's really a 720K. Or vice versa.

✔ There's a write-protect tab on the disk. Those little notches on the side of your 5¼" disk are covered — or the little sliding things in the corners of 3½" disks are open.

✔ The disk actually has been physically damaged in some way. The next time you get a box of disks, try reading the information that comes with it — it warns you about the vulnerabilities of floppies.

 Although you've got a Safe Format icon in Windows, don't use it. If you do, Norton warns you that it's not safe to use Safe Format in Windows. My question is, *why* did they give us a bleedin' Safe Format icon if it wasn't safe to use it? Is this their idea of a fun time? Bah!

Formatting the Configuration

You may have noticed that there's a Configure option in the Safe Format dialog box. Mostly, I'd recommend leaving that alone, because the way it's set from the factory is how you want it to be (see Figure 11-3).

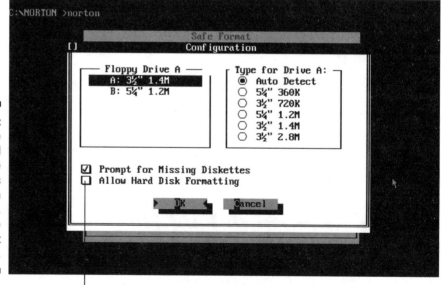

Figure 11-3:
Inside the hallowed halls of Safe Format's Configuration dialog box. It's best to look but not touch.

Don't select this option without fully understanding it!

The particularly frightening option inside the Configuration dialog box is the one that gives you the right to format your hard disk. Remember when I mentioned that formatting an already-formatted disk wipes out all data on the disk? Well, formatting your hard disk basically cleans the slate of your hard drive. Not a pretty thought. I'd even venture to guess that you would not be happy if this happened. Unless you really, really know what you're doing, don't check that box.

Taking Formatting Shortcuts

If clicking OK and using drop-down boxes to select the kind of format you want is too exhausting and tedious, try preselecting your favorite options via the command line. Table 11-1 illustrates some of the more useful command line switches.

If you've pressed Configuration ⇨ Alternate Names, covered in Chapter 2, to change the name of SFORMAT to FORMAT or SF, be sure that you use the command you've selected instead of SFORMAT. Table 11-1 tells you what's what. Also, if you're formatting drive B instead of A, substitute the proper letter. For example, if you've changed SFORMAT to FORMAT and you're using drive B, then instead of typing **SFORMAT A:**, you type **FORMAT B:**. Okay?

Table 11-1   Safe Format — Without All the Dialog

What to Type	What Happens
SFORMAT A: /A	Formats the disk using the current settings in the Safe Format configuration and doesn't stop to ask permission to proceed
SFORMAT A: /Q	Quick reformat
SFORMAT A: /D	Traditional, "unsafe" DOS format option
SFORMAT A: /S	Formats the disk so that it can boot the computer
SFORMAT A: /720	Formats a 3 ½" low-density disk

Remember, you can mix and match switches to fine-tune your instructions to Safe Format.

SFORMAT A: /Q /A   Quick format, without confirmation

SFORMAT A: /D /720 /A   DOS format, low-density 3 ½" disk, without confirmation

Who you callin' a general failure?

When attempting to copy or work with a floppy disk, you may receive an error message that says General failure reading Drive A. Although this is an alarming message, it doesn't mean what it says. The proper interpretation of this missive is that the disk in the drive hasn't been formatted yet. Abort what you're doing, format the disk, and then start again. Also, if you get a Not Ready Reading from the drive, that means you haven't closed the drive's latch. Do so now and try again.

If you use the /A — no confirmation — option, Safe Format goes straight to the formatting without a pause, even if there is data on the disk. It will not stop and warn you. It's quite conceivable that data you really wanted could be wiped out. Your best bet is not to use the /A option when formatting disks that may have data on them — but use your own judgment. Your mother and I trust you.

The 5th Wave   **By Rich Tennant**

"WHO'S GOT THE COMPUTER WITH THE SLOW RESPONSE TIME?"

Chapter 12

Speed Disk for DOS and Windows

● ●

In This Chapter

▶ Speeding up a disk in DOS and Windows

▶ Speedy Speed Disk shortcut

▶ Optimizing options

▶ Customizing Speed Disk in DOS and Windows

● ●

*W*hat does a teenager's bedroom and your hard disk have in common?

If you guessed that they're both messy, you're on the right track. The floor of a teenager's bedroom is traditionally a shrine to the theory of chaos. One sock here — its mate across the room. Wherever the teen could find a bit of floor space is where the clothes were dropped without any regard to order or neatness.

Similarly, whenever a file is saved onto the hard disk, it is also dropped down wherever there happens to be a bit of space. And, if the whole file can't fit in one spot, then it's broken up into several pieces and "continued" across the drive like a newspaper story. It's the duty of the File Allocation Table (or FAT — the hard drive's index) to keep track of where all the pieces are and how they fit together.

Whenever a file is loaded and saved, the hard disk is burdened with the task of taking the "scenic route" through the drive to gather all the pieces or file fragments. The longer you own the drive, the more fragmented everything becomes and the more time it takes to accomplish things that used to zip along. Plus, fragmented drives promote the possibility of cross-linked clusters — which is a situation almost as tragic as star-crossed lovers.

The purpose of Speed Disk is to clean up the bedroom floor. In other words, it puts the pieces of the files next to each other in an orderly fashion. This, in turn, reduces the time it takes to save and retrieve files and helps promote long-lived hard drives. This whole process is referred to as *defragging*, or *defragmenting*. There's another fun thing you can do to speed up the drive — *optimizing* — which is where stuff is moved to the front of the drive, within easy reach.

Basically, when the good people at Norton call the program Speed Disk, they're lying, because the disk isn't really going faster — there are no additional Rs in the RPMs. But getting what's on the disk happens faster — but who'd want a program called "Reduced Access Time"? Besides, then we'd have to call it RAT — which is not a good PR move.

Ooops, almost forgot the most important feature of Speed Disk — it's really fun to watch!

Speeding Up a Disk in DOS and Windows

Although you can't run DOS Speed Disk in Windows (and vice versa), both programs are practically identical when it comes to a no-frills launching. The similarity between the two is helpful because you'll probably end up using them both. The things that make the two programs different are in the options area — which you can skip if you're satisfied with the way the program works out of the box . . . which you probably will be.

1. To start Speed Disk, use one of the following methods:

   • From the Norton Utilities menu, highlight Speed Disk and press Enter, or

   • From a system prompt, type **SPEEDISK** and press Enter, or

   • From Windows, in the Norton Windows Utilities group, click the Speed Disk icon. You know, Norton did a great job on all the icons — but I can't help but think the Speed Disk icon looks like a race car with pancakes on top. Actually, though, the stack of pancakes is what a hard disk looks like when it's not in its protective shell.

If typing **SPEEDISK** doesn't work, you may have forgotten that you changed the name of the program via Norton's **Configuration** ⇨ **Alternate names** option (covered in Chapter 2). Try typing **SD** and pressing Enter instead.

2. When Speed Disk asks for a drive to optimize — as in Figure 12-1 (for DOS) and Figure 12-2 (for Windows) — highlight the victim drive and press Enter.

3. Both programs then quickly scan the drive and come back with a recommendation, as in Figure 12-3 (for DOS) and Figure 12-4 (for Windows).

It is conceivable that, instead of seeing the friendly Recommendation dialog box, you will receive an incredibly rude error message about invalid clusters or some such, along with a suggestion to use Norton Disk Doctor (NDD) and instructions about what to type. Actually, this suggestion is more like a demand, since Speed Disk will go on strike until you run NDD.

Write down the *suggestion* before exiting Speed Disk and then immediately follow up. More on Norton Disk Doctor in Chapter 26.

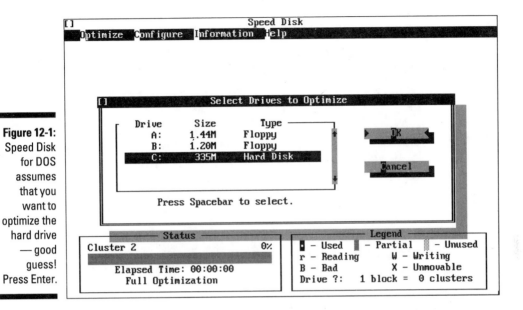

Figure 12-1:
Speed Disk
for DOS
assumes
that you
want to
optimize the
hard drive
— good
guess!
Press Enter.

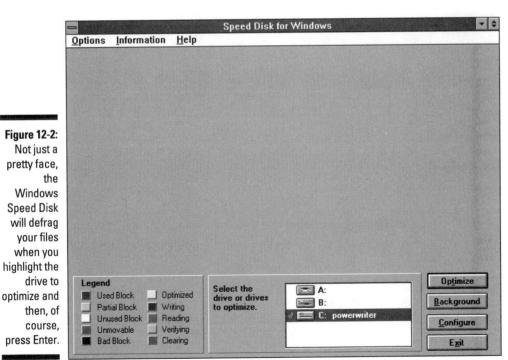

Figure 12-2:
Not just a
pretty face,
the
Windows
Speed Disk
will defrag
your files
when you
highlight the
drive to
optimize and
then, of
course,
press Enter.

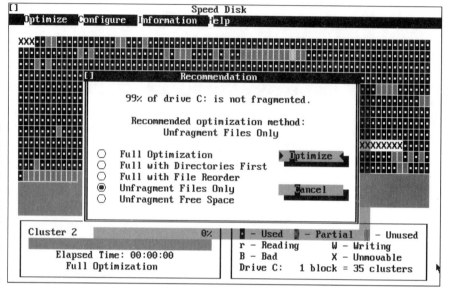

Figure 12-3:
To get a full explanation of the DOS Speed Disk options at this point, press F1 for help.

Figure 12-4:
Speed Disk for Windows is poised to optimize. To cancel the operation, click **C**onfigure.

4. For now, we're just going to follow Norton's advice and press Enter to start the defragging process.

   More about what all these choices mean in the next section.

5. Watch while Norton reads, writes, moves, and otherwise bulldozes your data around the hard drive.

   Speed Disk may take five or ten minutes to do the job the first time you run it. It could take several hours if you have a large hard disk (up to 2GB — that's *gigabytes*, which is short for "gazillion bytes"). That's because you've got such a messy room. After the first time, though, follow-up defraggings take only a minute or two — depending on the size of your drive, the speed of the computer, and the size of the moon.

One really great thing about Speed Disk for Windows is that it can run in the background. This means that you can take care of other business while Speed Disk works on your drive. In the DOS version, there's nothing you can do but wait — maybe return some phone calls?

There are certain files that Speed Disk will not defrag or move. These files are called Unmovable files. It's not that you can't move them — it's just that you shouldn't. For various reasons, moving or rearranging these files in any way can cause huge problems. Whenever Speed Disk announces that certain files won't be touched, know that it's a good thing.

6. When Speed Disk is finished, a window appears with the late-breaking news. Press Enter.

7. When you see Figure 12-5, press Alt+Exit Speed Disk to get out of the program.

✔ If you'd rather optimize another drive, then press Alt+Another Drive and repeat Steps 2-7.

✔ If you have a hard time saying goodbye, press Alt+Configure to stay in Speed Disk.

You can cancel optimization in mid-optimize if you want: Just press Esc (in either version). Although it's perfectly safe to cancel a Speed Disk operation, it's *NOT okay* to stop the process by turning off power or doing something equally grotesque. Even though Speed Disk is a no-brainer for *us* — it's really complicated for Norton, and since we're talking data manipulation here, try to have a little patience if you must interrupt.

Figure 12-5: Although this is the DOS Speed Disk screen, the options also appear in the Windows version after successful optimization has occurred.

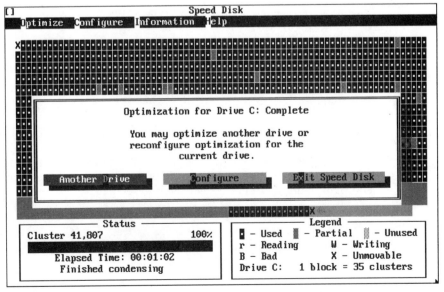

Go, Speed Racer!

Speed Racer, Speedy Gonzales, and Speedy Alka-Seltzer. What do these things have in common? That's right — all those words were in the preceding sentence!

To accelerate the use of Speed Disk, you can start the program from the command line and avoid prolonged interrogations with dialog boxes.

Speed Disk for DOS shortcut

To run Speed Disk on drive C with the Unfragment Files Only option, type **SPEEDISK C:** /U and press Enter.

To get a list of *all* Speed Disk command line options, type **SPEEDISK /?** and press Enter. Voilà! You get a nice reminder list. Or you *could* look in the manual.

Speed Disk for Windows shortcut

Even Speed Disk for Windows lets you start the program by using command-line options to override the default settings. For example, to start Speed Disk for Windows to defragment drive C, you type **SDW C:** /U. If you're used to clicking the little Speed Disk icon to launch the program, though, you may be wondering where the heck you're supposed to be typing the command line, right? There are a couple of ways to do it.

  ✔ From the system prompt, type **\WINDOWS\WIN \NU\SDW C:** /U and press Enter.

Okay, so the first suggestion was long and tedious. Let's try again.

  ✔ From Windows, press Alt+File ➪ **R**un and then type **SDW C:** /U and press Enter.

Of course, the slickest way to add a command-line option is to first copy the Speed Disk icon — highlight the icon and then press Alt+File ➪ Copy and make a clone in the Norton Utilities window. Then highlight the clone icon and press Alt+Enter to get into the Properties dialog box — and type the command line, as shown in Figure 12-6. Click OK when it's all set.

New command line

New name

Figure 12-6:
Technoids
can make a
new icon for
command-
line
variations.

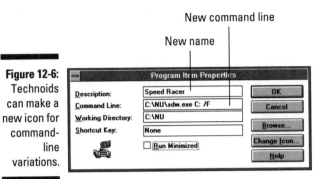

Program Item Properties	
Description: Speed Racer	OK
Command Line: C:\NU\sdw.exe C: /F	Cancel
Working Directory: C:\NU	Browse...
Shortcut Key: None	
☐ **Run Minimized**	Change Icon...
	Help

Optimizing Options

If you love getting right down to the real nitty gritty, you'll love the fact that Speed Disk allows tweaking and fiddling. Since Speed Disk likes to talk in jargon, however, we're forced to stoop to its level a bit to understand who's on first. Or was What on first and Who on second?

Making our own recommendations

In Step 4 of the basic process, illustrated in Figure 12-4, we're offered a lot of choices for optimization. You can make life easy for yourself by just going along with the optimization method suggested by Norton. For the sake of discussion, however, let's pretend like we care what all the options mean. Table 12-1 tells you what each option means.

Table 12-1	Optimization Methods
What Norton Calls It	*What It Is in English*
Full Optimization	Defragments files and shoves everything to the front of the drive.
Full with **D**irs First	Offers best chance of speed improvement. Defrags files and most-used directories, and files are, in theory, placed at front of the drive for faster access. Requires human intervention.
Full with File Reorder	Slowest and most complete. Same as Full with **D**irs First *plus* files not designated as most used by a human are sorted by their directories — again hoping for faster access.

(continued)

Table 12-1 (continued)

What Norton Calls It	*What It Is in English*
Unfragment Files Only	Fastest method. Defrags files, but doesn't move them to the front of the disk. Use this a couple of times a week, says Symantec. They should know.
Unfragment Free Space	Data is moved forward to use unoccupied hard disk space, but the files are not defragged.

Options that require human intervention to set — like directory and file order preferences — are handled in the Configure menu in DOS Speed Disk and by pressing **Options** ➪ **Preferences** in Speed Disk for Windows, as we'll see soon enough.

Enemies: A Love Story — Speed Disk and UnErase

UnErase (discussed in Chapter 14) is a program that lets you resurrect deleted or erased files. UnErase's job is made a lot easier if the deleted file can be found in one chunk rather than in fragmented bits — or bytes — all over the drive. As we just learned, Speed Disk puts files together in one neat chunk. So far, so good.

Another aspect of Speed Disk is to move files to fill empty spaces on the hard drive. So if a file is deleted, Speed Disk immediately writes over it — obliterating the deleted file and making it impossible to UnErase.

Talk about a love-hate relationship! Speed Disk and UnErase — codependent, self-destructive,

unable to compromise. Pretty soon they'll be making the tabloid talk-show circuit.

Is a bewilderment.

The only possible solutions are:

✔ Run Speed Disk only once a week — giving you a week to change your mind on deleted files before you overwrite them.

✔ Never run Speed Disk when you hope to retrieve a deleted file.

✔ Use Norton's SmartCan program (covered in Chapter 35), which allows you to UnErase files in spite of Speed Disk's best efforts.

Customizing Speed Disk for DOS

We have to cover DOS Speed Disk first because the stuff in Windows Speed Disk is so sexy I'm afraid you'll — you know — lose interest in the DOS version. The fact of the matter is that there are far fewer options in the DOS program — which also means it's easier to run, I guess.

Remember, you don't have to explore any of the inner workings of Speed Disk. The way it's set up out of the box is just fine — as you've already experienced.

Taking it on the road

In the Configuration menu, you have the option of actually moving Directories and Files on the hard disk. I'm recommending here, as I will again later in the Windows section coming up, that you leave this stuff alone until you're feeling very solid about directories, have a good grasp of what you're using the most, and so on. Unless you have a really old system anyway, moving directories and files around isn't going to make *that* much of an impact on the speed of the computer.

Other Options

In the Configuration menu you can press Other Options — Figure 12-7 — to specify how your leftover space is handled. The Read-After-Write option is most favored by the double-check twins. It tells Speed Disk to really make sure that the information it's handling is being cared for properly. It takes extra time to include double-checking. You may want to try it to see how much extra time it takes on your system.

Second, you can tell Speed Disk to scrub over the empty space on the hard drive to prevent anyone from getting in there and UnErasing files. If no one else has access to your computer, this is not an option you care about. On the other hand, if you're in the CIA, you'll want to select Clear Unused Space.

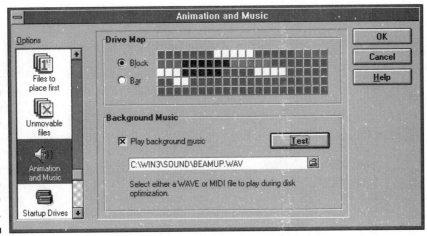

Figure 12-7: Other options in DOS Speed Disk let you determine the course of your data.

Finally, and this is a key option, you must decide whether Speed Disk should beep at you when it's all finished. The Beep is turned on by default. And, because you can't do anything with your computer other than wait while the optimization is happening, that beep tone will wake you up when the job is finished.

Saving

Once you've got all your options set, don't forget to save them via Alt+Configure ⇨ Save Options to Disk. It's quick, it's painless — it's done.

Customizing Speed Disk for Windows

A customized Speed Disk for Windows can become a veritable multimedia event with music and options to choose from. Of course, most of the options are technical and you don't really have to deal with them unless you're so inclined. After all, the thing already works — what else do you want? Dancing persons?

The various configuration options are available by pressing Alt+Options ⇨ Preferences and then highlighting an Option icon. Figure 12-8 shows the Animation and Music icon selected on the left, while the alternatives for that option are displayed on the right.

As you make your choices, use Alt+Save to record your selections. When you're finished with the section, click OK to exit. Don't forget: Whatsoever shalt thou select canst thou also deselect.

Figure 12-8:
Even though Speed Disk for Windows lets you add Animation and Music — don't hold your breath for "Beauty and the Beast," because you ain't even gettin' the Energizer Bunny here.

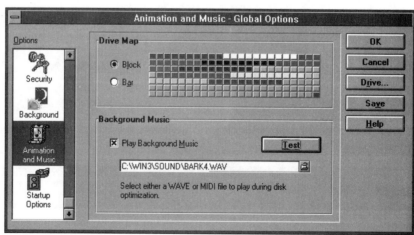

Animation and Music

Okay, because we're already looking at Animation and Music, let's briefly see what it can do.

First of all, Animation and Music lets you set what the *Drive Map* looks like. You remember the Drive Map, don't you — it was what took up three-quarters of the screen while Speed Disk was optimizing — with all the little squares? If the little squares irritated you, then click on Block if you want to see what the other choice looks like. It's quite a thrill.

 To change the colors on the Drive Map, you need to go to the opening Speed Disk screen and double-click on the colored boxes in the map legend on the left. A palette appears, allowing you to express your preference.

If you have a *sound card* in your computer, you can select your very own music to run Speed Disk by — as well as select your preferred Speed-Disk-is-finished sound. Speed Disk for Windows can accommodate WAV and MID files. If you don't have a sound card, none of this will make sense to you — don't worry about it. If you do have a sound card, you'll know what I'm talking about.

 To add your favorite sound, click on the little folder icon to gain access to the sound files. If you've got a sound card, you're an old hand at this.

Background and startup options

As mentioned earlier, Speed Disk can "run silent, run deep." Several ways to get it to strut its stuff in the background are:

- ✔ Choose **B**ackground when the Speed Disk first appears, as in Figure 12-2. If you do that, all Background Options and Startup Options — shown in Figures 12-9 and 12-10, respectively — as well as the other options already saved are used automatically.

- ✔ You can decide, after Speed Disk has begun optimizing, to minimize the program to a tiny, pathetic icon. Don't be deceived by small packages, however; Speed Disk is still hard at work and that icon isn't quite as pathetic as we first thought. You can actually watch your drive being worked on from the little icon.

- ✔ Choose Load with Windows in the Background Options to automatically kick Speed Disk into the background whenever Windows is launched.

- ✔ In the Start Up Options, also choose Load with Windows.

Figure 12-9:
Step right up
and choose
your
Background
Options
now! If
Speed Disk
is loaded
automa-
tically, it'll
use these
options.
Check out
Table 12-1
for further
help.

Starts optimizing if nothing happens
on the keyboard for one minute

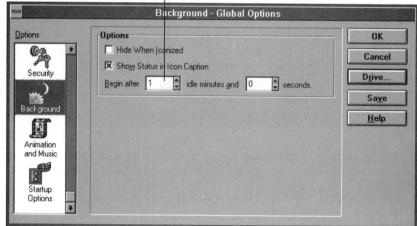

Figure 12-10:
Choose the
default drive
to optimize
and elect to
show
deference to
incoming
communi-
cations in
the exciting
Startup
Options
window.

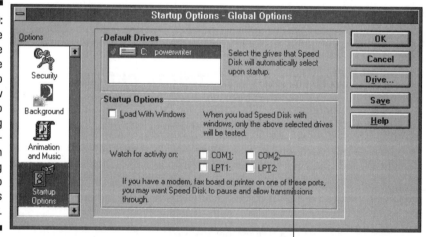

If you're expecting a fax — choose this option

Running Speed Disk in the background may be overkill in some situations, but it can be helpful anytime the optimization process takes longer than you have patience for — like with those big drives, or if you've gone and selected the most complex and time-consuming method of reorganizing the drive.

Don't be concerned about Speed Disk slowing your system down while running in the background. It's been engineered so that it runs only when the system is idle. It always makes it easier to recover from a crash when the system is not fragmented.

Optimization method

The Optimization methods are basically the same as in Speed Disk for DOS (see Figure 12-11). The only thing worth mentioning here is that whatever method you select will be used if the program is loaded with Windows. (It really is difficult to keep from making "loaded" jokes. Maybe Optimization did get loaded with Windows, but it just didn't inhale. Nah.)

Free bonus!

Figure 12-11:
You also can select which drive to Optimize while in the Optimization Method chamber. Be sure to Save when you're finished.

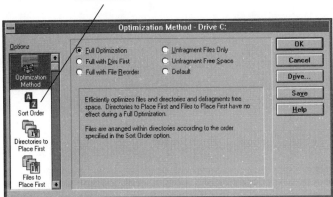

Security

You get both you're-in-good-hands security and *Sneakers* security in this option. Normally, neither of the Options in Figure 12-12 is selected.

If you're concerned about the health of your hard disk, check Verify Writes. If you're concerned about espionage on your computer, check Wipe Free Space. If you're concerned about your sanity, check out of work early and go see a movie.

- Verify Writes is a safety versus speed trade off. The safety is that everything is double-checked during the defragging to make sure that all Is are dotted and Ts are crossed — which, in turn, means that the operation takes longer to perform.
- Wipe Free Space makes sure that nothing in the unused space can be UnErased.

Figure 12-12:
The
Advanced
Options in
Windows
are
comparable
to the Other
Options in
DOS Speed
Disk. They
just give you
new words
to make
things — uh
— *clearer*!

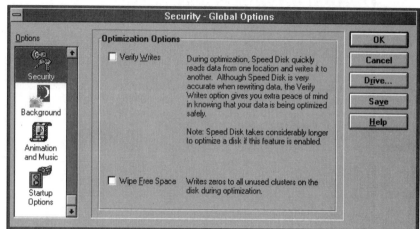

Sort Order

Speed Disk — not be outdone by those infomercials — throws in its own free bonus. Order now and get Sort Order. That's right, while the disk is being optimized, it can also be sorted à la Directory Sort (covered in Chapter 3). That way, when you exit Speed Disk and use DIR, the files will be in alphabetical order (or whatever order you want). If all you want is a sorted directory, Speed Disk is kind of overkill. Use Directory Sort instead. But, if you're here anyway or just want to quickly put a floppy drive in order . . .

Tote that directory — lift that file

Three other icons are Directories to Place First, Files to Place First, and Unmovable Files. This is where we have the power to designate which directory or file will be physically placed on the hard disk. This is also where there's some option for moving things that were meant to be left alone.

If you know what you're doing, moving directories and files in the order of use can speed up drive access. If you're still on shaky ground about what is, *exactly*, a directory, then leave these options alone for now.

Chapter 13

Sysinfo (System Information)

In This Chapter
▶ What you see is what you got
▶ Comparing your system to others
▶ Taking SI for a little ride

*I*t's ten o'clock — do you know where your extended memory is? If you're like most people, you don't. But Sysinfo does.

Basically, Sysinfo (also known by its nickname, SI) is like having a private detective assigned to your computer system. SI knows about all the secret nooks and crannies inside your box and is willing to print out a report on the topic at a moment's notice. So if you need to get the low down on your system, talk to SI. He knows where your memory is and a whole lot more.

SI is, among computer people, *the* standard for testing systems. After you run a few benchmarks on your computer, you can impress others in your office by saying, "My computer rates a 99.4 on SI." Be sure to have a doughnut in your hand so that after making your declaration you can quickly take a bite; your mouth should be too full to respond to any follow-up questions.

Anyway, we're just going to walk through a fraction of SI to get a peek at what's in there. And, if you're very good, we'll have a slide show later. Really.

Revving Up Sysinfo

Although SI is incredibly technical, kicking it into gear takes no special talent. It's just the usual drill.

To get to the Sysinfo System Summary, shown in Figure 13-1, use one of the following:

✔ From the Norton Utilities menu, highlight System Info and press Enter.

✔ From a system prompt, type **SYSINFO** and press Enter.

✔ From Windows, in the Norton DOS Utilities group, click the Sysinfo icon.

Figure 13-1:
SI's
summary of
your
system! To
impress
your friends,
click the
Print button,
and SI
obligingly
prints up a
report for
you.

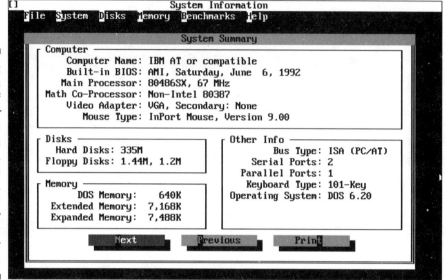

Sysinfo is another one of those programs whose name you can shorten with Norton's Configuration⇨Alternate Names option (see Chapter 2). So, if you type **SYSINFO** and press Enter and get nothing but grief from the computer, maybe you changed the name to SI. Give it a shot.

What You See Is What You Got

Figure 13-1 is but the tip of the iceberg of information available on your system. At least now if someone wants to know the size of your hard disk or how many serial ports you have, you can respond accurately.

Rating your system

Of course, you're above the notion of "keeping up with the Joneses," but a lot of really immature people like to know how their systems stack up against the other guy's. To get your Overall Performance Index:

1. Get into Sysinfo by using one of the methods described in the preceding section (like typing **SYSINFO** and pressing Enter).

2. Press **Benchmarks**⇨**O**verall Performance Index.

   SI flashes some messages on-screen, letting you know that it's testing one thing and then another. Eventually, you receive a Performance Index similar to the one shown in Figure 13-2.

This is *your* computer's performance

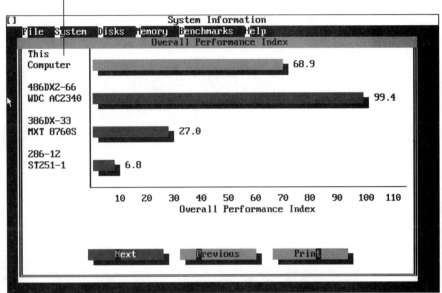

Figure 13-2:
How fast is
your
computer
compared to
a crankin'
486 or the
older 386 or
286 models?

✔ It's a good idea to run benchmarks before you change your system — like if you're changing hard drives, adding more memory, a memory manager, or cache software — to get a before and after picture.

✔ Knowing your computer's benchmarks when it's healthy facilitates a diagnosis when it starts acting up.

Sysinfo can print each and every one of the technical readout screens. Just press Alt+Print to activate the button at the bottom of every screen. It's also a very good idea, if you haven't done this before, to print your setup files as a backup. You don't even have to know what your setup files are — just know that if you don't have them, your computer won't work properly. In SI, pressing Alt+File shows you a list of the setup files — such as AUTOEXEC.BAT, CONFIG.SYS, WIN.INI, and so on. Call them up and print them out. That way, if you need help restoring them later, you can give your computer guru the printouts and it will make the job much, much simpler. Alternatively, INI Tracker (covered in Chapter 19) is very adept at restoring your system. ■

Getting technical

When installing new hardware in your system — like a CD-ROM or a tape back-up unit — you may have to decide which *interrupt* to use. Now, if you've always thought "interrupt" was another name for your kid, then you may be surprised to learn that a different definition of the word is associated with computers. ■

Basically, all the hardware in your machine has to be plugged into the system *someplace*, and that someplace is referred to as an interrupt, or an *IRQ* (for *I*nterrupt *Req*uest). There are a finite number of these little IRQs, and your new tape back-up unit will want one. Oh, and of course, no two devices can share an IRQ — because then they'd be interrupting each other.

So which one should you tell the tape back-up unit to take? Ask SI what's available:

1. Get into Sysinfo by using one of the methods described earlier (like typing **SYSINFO** and pressing Enter).

2. Press Alt+System⇨Hardware Interrupts.

   You get something like Figure 13-3.

In this system, the mouse uses IRQ 5

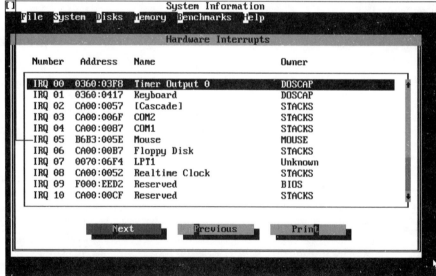

Figure 13-3: So many IRQs, so little time. A listing of hardware interrupts helps keep conflicts amongst your devices to a minimum.

Number	Address	Name	Owner
IRQ 00	0360:03F8	Timer Output 0	DOSCAP
IRQ 01	0360:0417	Keyboard	DOSCAP
IRQ 02	CA00:0057	[Cascade]	STACKS
IRQ 03	CA00:006F	COM2	STACKS
IRQ 04	CA00:0087	COM1	STACKS
IRQ 05	B6B3:005E	Mouse	MOUSE
IRQ 06	CA00:00B7	Floppy Disk	STACKS
IRQ 07	0070:06F4	LPT1	Unknown
IRQ 08	CA00:0052	Realtime Clock	STACKS
IRQ 09	F000:EED2	Reserved	BIOS
IRQ 10	CA00:00CF	Reserved	STACKS

System Information

File System Disks Memory Benchmarks Help

Hardware Interrupts

Next   Previous   Print

Revealing TSRs — quick and simple

TSR stands for "terminate and stay resident" — which pretty much explains nothing. A TSR is one of those pop-up type programs that isn't seen, but appears when you press a certain key combination.

Anyway, a question often asked during troubleshooting is, "Do you have any TSRs loaded?" (And I'll continue to resist the impulse to make a joke about "being loaded.") Here's a shortcut to a quick answer from SI. Just type **SYSINFO /TSR** and press Enter. Boom, you'll get your list of TSRs, as illustrated in Figure 13-4. You may not know what they are — but whoever asked you about them will.

Figure 13-4:
How much system memory is being gobbled up by your TSR? SI knows. SI knows *everything*. If only SI could tell me where I put my keys.

Here's where the mouse software lives

Address	Size	Owner	Hooked Interrupt Vectors
02B7	96	LOADHI	
02E5	1,360	EZTIMER	16 F7
034F	256	MOUSE	
0360	6,256	DOSCAP	08 09 10 17 21 30 60 61 62 ...
04E8	4,128	DOSKEY	2F
D1DC	2,640	COMMAND	22 24 2E
D28D	36,240	MSCDEX	
DB6E	17,888	SHARE	

Taking SI for a little ride

At the beginning of this chapter, I promised a slide show. Now I'll make good on that promise. You can get SI to make a slide show out of your system's technical readouts. Sounds inviting, no? It's a way to passively view all the screens, one at a time, to get a picture of what SI can really do. Maybe if you watch it often enough it'll have some sort of subliminal effect. I don't know. It couldn't hurt.

To get the slide show rolling, have someone dim the lights and then, at the system prompt, type **SYSINFO /AUTO:10** and press Enter.

This tells SI to show each screen, pause for ten seconds, and then move on to the next screen. If you want more than ten seconds, type *that* number instead of the *10* in the command in the previous paragraph. You can interrupt the slide show by pressing Esc if you've had enough. SI will understand.

Getting good marks

Did you know that one of the first benchmarks in the personal computer industry was a game? One of the hallmarks of a game called Flight Simulator was that it worked only on true-blue, 100% IBM-compatible computers. Companies were ruined and lives were left in shambles all because the little airplane wouldn't fly on their systems. I much prefer something like SI to sort things out for us.

Chapter 14

UnErase

● ●

In This Chapter

▶ UnErasing files by magic

▶ UnErasing directories

▶ Manual labor — UnErasing files by hand

▶ Planning for the future

● ●

*H*ave you ever seen a magician make someone disappear and then bring her back? Ever wonder how he did it? I may get into a lot of trouble for this, but I'm going to reveal the magician's secret: It's UnErase! Honest!

What magicians can do with volunteers from the audience, you can do with your files. Just because you've deleted a file doesn't necessarily mean it's gone forever. UnErase can find deleted files and bring them back to you — as if by magic.

One caveat for any program that promises to unerase files is that none of them can guarantee that any file can be recovered at any time. The rule of thumb is that the longer you wait before attempting an UnErase, the slimmer the chances for success. However, it doesn't hurt anything to try UnErase

There is one way to guarantee that everything you deleted in recent history is 100% recoverable — and that's to use the SmartCan program (see Chapter 35). It has its trade-offs, but if you find yourself constantly in a panic over accidental deletions, it's something to look into.

In this chapter, we'll assume that you're *not* using SmartCan and we'll walk through the process of UnErasing. We'll go from the very simple, nothing-to-it, automatic UnErase to the delicate surgery of the Manual UnErase for brave souls only.

If you're forced to turn your computer off and on before using UnErase, *do not* allow Speed Disk (discussed in Chapter 12) or any other disk optimizer to run on your computer. It'll make it completely impossible to recover the file.

If you realize that you've deleted a file in error, don't get disgusted and start another file with the same name. If you start another file — at all — it may immediately destroy your chance of UnErasing. If you start another file with the same name as the missing file, you've pretty much nailed shut the lid on the file's coffin.

If, when you realize you've deleted something important, your life starts flashing before your eyes, you break out in a sweat, and you begin hyperventilating, then the best thing to do is to walk away from the computer for a few minutes. Have a nice glass of cold milk, and take several deep breaths. Then, after you've calmed down a bit, come back and try UnErase.

UnErasing Files — The Basics

When the time comes — as it will eventually — that you accidentally delete a file, then lock and load UnErase and begin the recovery assault. In this example, we're looking for a file called TYPOS.DOC.

1. Get to the UnErase dialog box in Figure 14-1 using one of the following methods:

    • From the Norton Utilities menu, highlight UnErase and press Enter.

    • From a system prompt, type **UNERASE** and press Enter.

No matter how you get there, you should end up looking at a list of at least one erased file, as in Figure 14-1. Hopefully, among the files listed is the dearly departed, the one file you want to recover.

In our example, there are two files listed, including one called ?YPOS.DOC. Yippee! That's our missing file and — by some incredible luck — its chances for recovery are good.

If you don't find your all-important file among those in the list, it may be because you're not centering the search in the right directory. To see *all* the erased files on the hard disk, press Alt+A — or take the long way 'round and choose Alt+File⇨View All Directories. You may have to scroll up and down the list to locate your file (see Figure 14-2).

Unerase predicts whether it is likely
that a file can be recovered. These two
files are good candidates. Whew!

Here are your erased files — minus
the first letter of their names   Current directory

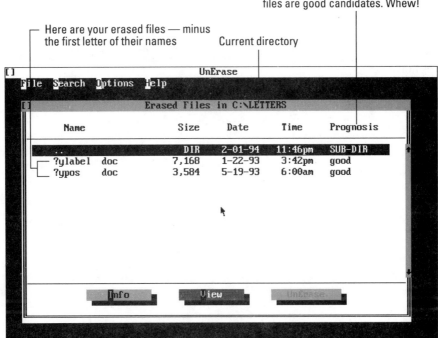

Figure 14-1:
UnErase is
the zombie
program —
it brings
dead files
back to life.

- If you still don't see your file — are you sure it's on this drive? Do you have a D, E, or F drive? Sometimes programs are kept on one drive and data files on another. It could happen. Press Alt+File⇨Change **D**rive and select the drive to be searched.

- The file's *still* missing from the list? I hope you're sitting down and have a pint of Häagen-Dazs at the ready. Your file is probably not recoverable. Yes, I said *probably*. If you're so desperate that you'll try *anything* to get that file back, go down to the Manual UnErase section and give that process a shot — or get someone else to do it for you and be sure to give *him* (or her) the Häagen-Dasz.

2. Highlight the file to be UnErased.

- Make sure that you highlight the filename, not the directory name. If you highlight the directory name, it'll seem as though UnErase isn't working.

You can see all erased files on
the drive by pressing Alt+A

Figure 14-2:
All the
deleted files
on your hard
disk — if
some of
them look
unfamiliar,
it's because
your
programs
create and
delete files
behind your
back.

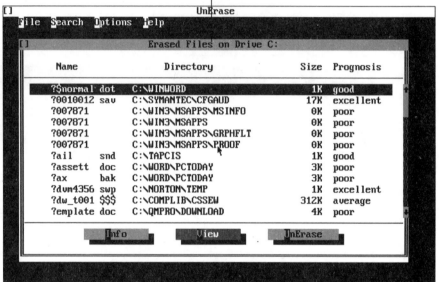

- If you want to recover more than one file, highlight each filename in turn and press the spacebar to tag them for recovery. If you've done something massively clever to wipe out a slew of files — for example, you deleted all your DOC files — you can use Alt+File⇨Select **G**roup, and when UnErase asks for the specs on the group to UnErase, type ***.DOC**.

- If you've got several files to choose from and you're not sure which file is *the* file, highlight one of the suspects and click the **V**iew button to see the file. When you try to view the file, one of two things will happen. The preferred development is that a view window opens up and the highlighted file is laid out for examination. Don't be concerned that the file looks funny: UnErase is presenting you with enough text to make a decision about recovering the file. If it isn't the right file, click Next to move to a view of the next file in the list. Choose Close when you've found the right file. The other thing that may happen after selecting View is that you're told UnErase is `Unable to display file data`. This isn't the end of the world, but it is the end of your chances to view that particular file. Try viewing the other files.

3. Press **U** — or use the mouse to select UnErase.

4. You get a dialog box like the one in Figure 14-3, where you are prompted to type the first letter of the missing file's name — type any letter you want.

- To recover our file, we type the letter **T**. However, just because TYPOS.DOC *used* to begin with T doesn't mean we *have* to type that letter. Any letter will do.

- If you're UnErasing a group, it could be tedious to supply missing letters for all the files, so you have the option of deselecting the `Prompt for Missing Letter` option. In this case, UnErase simply sticks an A at the front of each file.

5. In the best of all possible worlds, what happens next is Figure 14-4 — showing the file has been successfully recovered.

6. If you're finished recovering files, press Esc to exit.

✔ If the file cannot be recovered automatically by UnErase, Norton lets you know — and gives you some technical excuse for its failure. After reading the bad news, choose OK to return to the first screen and meditate on whether Manual UnErase is worth the effort.

All you have to do is type the first letter of the erased file's name!

Figure 14-3:
All the magic you need to know to make your file reappear is the first letter of the file's name. No beautiful assistant required.

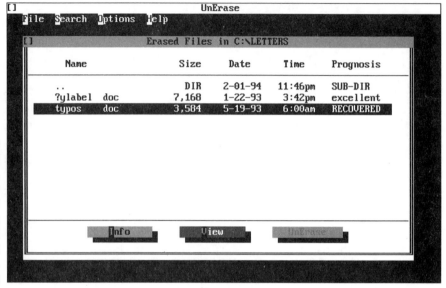

Figure 14-4:
TYPOS.DOC,
now fully
recovered
and sporting
its brand
new first
letter.

Taking an UnErase shortcut

If you know the name of the deleted file and you know what directory it's in, you can bypass the dialog boxes and other UnErase paraphernalia by using the command-line option:

1. Get to the system prompt.

2. Type **UNERASE**, a space, the name of the file to be recovered, and press Enter.

✔ In our previous example, we would have typed **UNERASE TYPOS.DOC** and pressed Enter, as in Figure 14-5.

✔ If the file cannot be recovered or you're in the wrong directory (or drive) you'll be told No erased files match... your filename. You may want to give Manual UnErase a shot.

Figure 14-5:
Being able to
immediately
UnErase a
file *is* a thing
of beauty —
and a joy
forever.

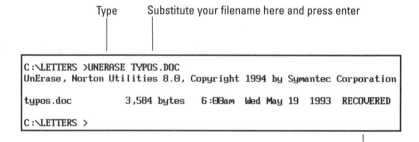

Unerasing Directories

You've erased a whole directory? Yikes. Well, you can even recover from an erased directory. Recovering a directory, however, doesn't automatically recover everything in it. You then still have to recover each file one at a time.

1. Get to the system prompt.

   • You need to be above the directory that was deleted. A good place to start is the root directory — type **CD ** and press Enter to get there.

2. Type **UNERASE** and press Enter.

   You get a screen like the one in Figure 14-6.

3. Highlight the directory to be recovered.

   I hope you don't have more than one directory to be reclaimed. One is plenty.

4. Press **U** or use the mouse to choose UnErase.

   With luck, the directory can be UnErased without incident. Then you can start recovering missing files, using the basic steps outlined in the preceding section.

A missing directory can be
brought back with UnErase

```
[]                               UnErase
  File   Search   Options   Help

   []                    Erased Files in C:\

        Name              Size     Date       Time     Prognosis

        TSCSI             DIR    12-20-93    10:46am    SUB-DIR
        TT                DIR    12-15-93    12:19am    SUB-DIR
        UTILS             DIR    12-15-93    12:20am    SUB-DIR
        UV                DIR    12-15-93    12:21am    SUB-DIR
        WAOL              DIR    12-15-93    12:21am    SUB-DIR
        WIN3              DIR    12-15-93    12:21am    SUB-DIR
        WINDOWS           DIR     1-30-94     5:20pm    SUB-DIR
        WINWORD           DIR    12-15-93    12:31am    SUB-DIR
        WORD              DIR    12-15-93    12:34am    SUB-DIR
        WSAWING6          DIR    12-15-93    12:38am    SUB-DIR
        X                 DIR    12-15-93    12:38am    SUB-DIR
        ?ETTERS           DIR     2-01-94    11:46pm    average

              Info              View              UnErase
```

Figure 14-6: UnErasing directories is much like UnErasing files.

If the directory cannot be UnErased, that doesn't necessarily mean the *files* cannot be UnErased automatically. At the screen shown in Figure 14-6, use Alt+Search⇨For Lost Names. UnErase tells you that it's scanning your disk and lists the lost names found, as in Figure 14-7. Proceed with the basic UnErase steps to recover your files.

These files used to be in
a directory that got nuked

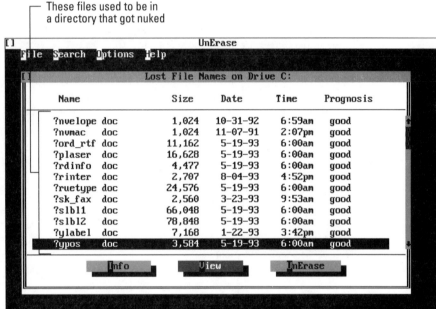

Figure 14-7:
Searching
for Lost
Names
sounds like
a job for
Robert
Stack — but
it's another
way to get
UnErase to
find deleted
files.

Name		Size	Date	Time	Prognosis
?nvelope	doc	1,024	10-31-92	6:59am	good
?numac	doc	1,024	11-07-91	2:07pm	good
?ord_rtf	doc	11,162	5-19-93	6:00am	good
?plaser	doc	16,628	5-19-93	6:00am	good
?rdinfo	doc	4,477	5-19-93	6:00am	good
?rinter	doc	2,707	8-04-93	4:52pm	good
?ruetype	doc	24,576	5-19-93	6:00am	good
?sk_fax	doc	2,560	3-23-93	9:53am	good
?slbl1	doc	66,048	5-19-93	6:00am	good
?slbl2	doc	78,848	5-19-93	6:00am	good
?ylabel	doc	7,168	1-22-93	3:42pm	good
?ypos	doc	3,584	5-19-93	6:00am	good

Going for a Manual UnErase

This gets very thick, very fast. You can get into trouble with Manual UnErase, so we're just going to skim through the highlights that are least likely to make things worse and most likely to pull the fat out of the fire, so to speak.

If you've ended up here in Manual UnErase, it pretty much means that your file will not be found totally intact. It means you may be able to recover some of it and cut your losses. That's the best we can hope for now.

You may decide that this is just too much hassle and you'll take your chances with a back-up copy of the file instead. That's fine. No one will think any less of you for bailing out.

The basic idea of Manual UnErase is that instead of letting the UnErase program figure out what pieces of data (called *clusters*) composed our file — *we* have to slog through the hard disk and gather up clusters on our own . . . with a little help from UnErase.

Even though this sounds massively complicated — and I won't lie to you and say that it isn't — sometimes UnErase can do most, if not all, of the messy stuff for us. So you may be very successful in finding your goods without too much anguish. Besides, it doesn't hurt anything to look. You can always quit without harm — as long as you haven't saved your efforts.

Starting a Manual UnErase is innocent enough — in fact, it starts the same as the automatic UnErase.

1. Type **UNERASE** and press Enter to start the UnErase program (you see something like Figure 14-1).

2. Highlight the file that you want to manually UnErase.

3. Press Alt+M (mousers can choose File⇨**M**anual UnErase).

   If you accidentally left the highlight on the directory name, Alt+M won't work. Make sure that it's the filename that's highlighted.

4. Type a first letter for the file to be UnErased, much like Figure 14-3, and you end up in Figure 14-8.

5. Choose **A**dd Cluster — your only option at this point — and you end up in Figure 14-9.

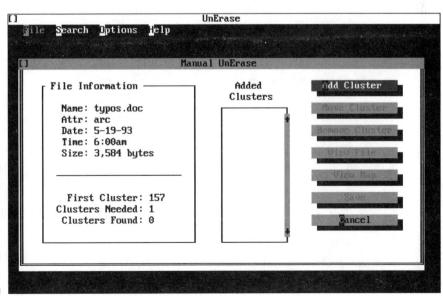

Figure 14-8:
This is
Manual
UnErase —
home of the
free, land of
the brave.

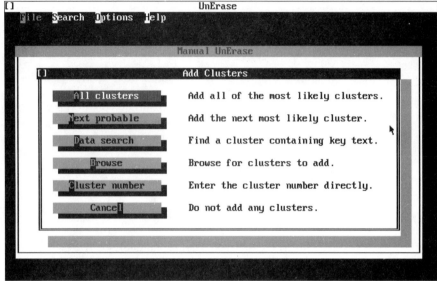

6. Cross your fingers and choose **All Clusters**.

   As the screen indicates, this is where UnErase takes its best shot at automatically finding your text. Each of the other options in Figure 14-9 provides other pathways to locating parts of your files. Each option is more arcane than the one preceding it.

   After carrying out your command, UnErase takes you back to the Manual UnErase screen, where you can evaluate the results of UnErase's efforts, as in Figure 14-10.

7. Use View **F**ile to see whether the data you want has been found.

8. Choose **S**ave to save the file you've put together.

   If all the file has not been put back together, go back to Add Cluster and use **B**rowse. You are shown a View window and all the erased data on the disk parades before you, one batch at a time. If you see some text that belongs to your file, then **A**dd it — whether or not it's in order and whether or not it also includes happy faces and screen garbage. If you see text that isn't from your file, then move along to the next cluster with Next. Eventually, you'll have all the clusters that are available from the drive.

   This is tedious, but it's the method you use to ensure that everything that can be found will be found, and it keeps at a minimum the likelihood of messing up something else.

9. Press Esc to exit UnErase.

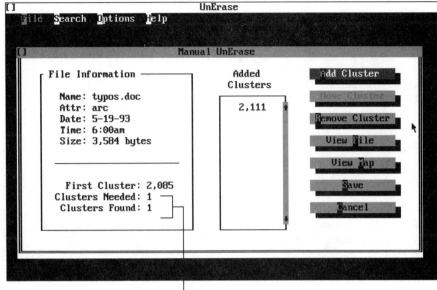

Figure 14-10:
UnErase has
added a
cluster —
and it looks
like it's all
we need!

This is your score box

Getting a Little Help from Friends

If you've gone through any of these steps to resurrect files, you may now be more receptive to using other parts of Norton Utilities that are designed to optimize chances for recovering files in the future. After all, you've already paid for all these tools — it's foolish not to use them to the max. Here's a few things you can do, in advance, to up your chances of successfully recovering files.

1. Use Speed Disk regularly, to keep files together and easier to find. See Chapter 12.

2. Use Image every time you turn on your computer. Read Chapter 16.

3. Use SmartCan to hold files that have been recently deleted. Chapter 35 discusses this feature.

4. This really has nothing to do with UnErase, but the best defense is a good offense, so back up often.

Why deleting a file doesn't really delete a file

How can we UnErase a file that's been deleted? Doesn't DOS delete the file when we tell it to? Well, not exactly.

The pathetic truth is that DOS is too darned lazy to actually delete a file when ordered to do so. DOS fakes you out by merely deleting the file from its index system (the infamous File Allocation Table) and removing the first letter of the file's name so that you can't *see* the file any more. You think the file is gone, but all the time it's still right there on the disk. Over the course of time, the file is erased as other files are saved over

it — kind of like recording over a VCR tape. But only after a file is recorded over does it truly become unrecoverable.

Sometimes the file is recorded over immediately, and sometimes it sits there for weeks. More likely, parts of the file are wiped out and other parts still survive. It's all mostly random.

Because of DOS's laziness, we can — sometimes — catch the file vacationing on the hard disk and summon it back to work.

Part III
An Ounce of Prevention...

In this part...

An ounce of prevention will keep you from pounding your head into the wall when disaster strikes. Team Norton has thoughtfully provided a suite of largely automatic systems to help keep things on the straight and narrow. All you have to do is provide an ounce of effort — and Norton will come through with the pound of cure.

Chapter 15

Rescue Disk

● ●

● ●

*B*ack up your system files and make a record of your system's settings, because some day the sky will fall and you'll be sorry . . . blah, blah, blah. If you've heard the warnings once, you've heard them a million times. My bet is that you're more than willing to do all those things — if you only knew what a system file *was*. And a system setting? If the truth be told, most people wouldn't know a system setting if it came up and gave them a byte.

Check this — Rescue Disk finds the system files and system settings and all that technical stuff on your hard disk and it copies it — plus some CPR-type programs — onto a floppy disk *for you*. All you have to do is shove a floppy disk in the computer and press Go. Rescue Disk even formats the floppy disk for you. This is my kind of program — a total no-brainer.

Once the Rescue Disk is made, you'll stash it away for a rainy day. Actually, you're saving it for more like 40 days and 40 nights of rain.

Since a rescue disk works only on the particular system that created it, a separate rescue disk for each computer you own — or each computer in your office — must be created. If you have more than one computer, take the time to clearly label the disks. You may want to resist the urge to label the rescue disk as "Steven's computer," because what if Steven leaves the company or he trades computers with someone else? Use a serial number or something that will not change.

Even though a Rescue Disk is child's play to make, its Restore function is very, very powerful — and can be used for good or evil. Chapter 21 outlines where Rescue Disk's Restore capabilities fit in the overall scheme of things. Since making a Rescue Disk is one of those "before the flood" type actions, we're bringing it up at this point.

Loading Up the Ark

The real first step in the process is to put a floppy disk in drive A. Since this disk may be used to start up — boot — your computer in an emergency, you should use a disk that works in your drive A. If you can, use a high-density floppy disk. We've got a lot of stuff to copy.

1. To get to the Rescue Disk dialog box shown in Figure 15-1, use one of the following methods:

   • From the Norton Utilities menu, highlight Rescue Disk and press Enter, or

   • From a system prompt, type **RESCUE** and press Enter

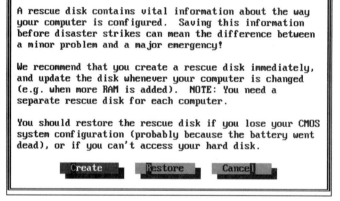

Figure 15-1: The welcome screen for rescue disk — nota bene.

2. Press Alt+Create to begin the process.

   Once you've chosen the Create option, you wind up with Figure 15-2.

3. Although Rescue Disk takes a guess at which drive and size of disk you'll be using to create the Rescue Disk — double-check to make sure that the Rescue Drive and Diskette Type are on the money.

   If you need to change them, either type the correct drive and diskette type, or press Alt+down-arrow to get a list of choices.

At this point, you can reduce or increase the items to be copied onto the Rescue Disk — if you're brave enough to branch out from the standard options. Although you can customize your Rescue Disk, Norton does not allow you to remove mission-critical items from its agenda, so you're fairly safe. The instructions for customizing your Rescue Disk are in the next section. We're just creating a normal All-American Rescue Disk now.

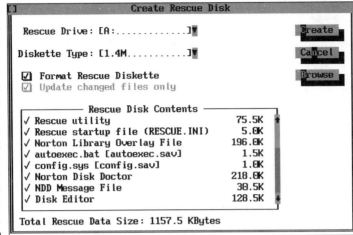

Figure 15-2:
Even though
the Create
Rescue Disk
dialog box
offers more
options than
Wall Street
— all you
really have
to do is
choose
Create.

4. All set? Press Alt+Create.

- If you're using a disk that has data on it for your Rescue Disk, Norton warns you that anything on the disk will be wiped by the formatting process. Choose Cancel if you need to use a different disk, or choose OK if you know what's on the disk and are happy to obliterate it.

5. When you're told to put a disk in drive A — you did put your disk in the drive, didn't you? — press Enter (or click OK), and Rescue Disk goes into action.

You can watch as the disk is formatted — party on! — and files are copied — yo, mama! — and all sorts of wild and crazy stuff goes on.

6. When everything's finished, you see Figure 15-3. After you read it, press Enter (or click the redoubtable OK).

Customizing the Rescue Disk

What goes onto the Rescue Disk is determined by Norton, the capacity of your floppy disk, and you.

Satisfying Norton's agenda

Norton *must* copy certain files to make a functional Rescue Disk. In the Rescue Disk Contents list, those important items are marked with an asterisk — you have to scroll the list down to see the asterisked goodies. When Norton sees what floppy disk you're using, it includes and excludes files accordingly.

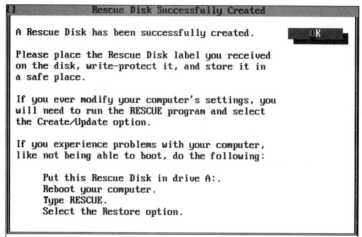

```
[]            Rescue Disk Successfully Created

A Rescue Disk has been successfully created.        OK

Please place the Rescue Disk label you received
on the disk, write-protect it, and store it in
a safe place.

If you ever modify your computer's settings, you
will need to run the RESCUE program and select
the Create/Update option.

If you experience problems with your computer,
like not being able to boot, do the following:

        Put this Rescue Disk in drive A:.
        Reboot your computer.
        Type RESCUE.
        Select the Restore option.
```

Using your best judgment

Optional files are indicated with a check mark and may be deselected with a click or by pressing the spacebar. The optional files are included on the Rescue Disk because in a time of need, you can use all the help you can get. As you add or delete files from the list, notice that the running tab at the bottom of the dialog box keeps track of how much you're planning to put on your floppy. Norton stubbornly won't let you accumulate more things than will fit on the disk.

Anything goes

You also can use the Alt+**B**rowse command to select files not initially listed by Norton. If you need a certain driver or something to start your computer, take advantage of the Browse feature to add your personal faves to the list (see Figure 15-4). If you don't know whether you have any special system files, you probably don't.

My personal advice for creating the perfect Rescue Disk is to remove one program — Disk Editor — and include another file in its place (if it's not already included). Here's how.

1. First, perform Steps 1-3 from the section "Loading the Ark."

2. Highlight Disk Editor and press the spacebar.

   This removes that program from the Rescue Disk list.

3. Press Alt+**B**rowse.

4. Type **\NU8\NLIB200.RTL** and press Enter.

Figure 15-4:
An
advanced
feature —
Browse —
gives you
point-and-
click access
to the hard
drive,
allowing you
the
opportunity
to put
unique
system
drivers on
your
personal
Rescue
Disk.

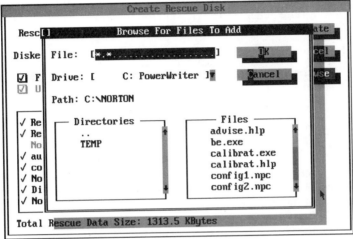

This adds a file called NLIB200.RTL (the *Norton Run Time Library*) to the Contents list. Other programs on the Rescue Disk need the Norton Run Time Library. It's a key file.

✔ If your Norton directory isn't called NU8, then substitute the appropriate directory name instead.

Updating the Rescue Disk

Every now and then, you should update your Rescue Disk. You should especially update it when you've mutated your system in some way — upgrading your DOS version, for example, should prompt some update action on the Rescue Disk. It doesn't hurt anything to update. So if in doubt, update.

1. Put the Rescue Disk in the drive.

2. At the system prompt, type **RESCUE/CREATE** and press Enter.

   If you just type **RESCUE** — without the **CREATE** — you have to look at that opening screen shown in Figure 15-2, and then press Create. This is a little shortcut.

3. Deselect `Format Rescue Diskette`.

This makes the `Update Changed Files Only` box come to life.

4. *If* you've customized the Rescue Disk in any way, add or subtract the appropriate items, as described in the section "Customizing the Rescue Disk." Otherwise, move to Step 5.

5. Press Alt+**Create**.

6. When the job is finished, you get that final screen shown in Figure 15-3. Just press Enter.

Returning from the Brink

Use the Rescue Disk Restore function with care. You should be considering using the Rescue Disk only if your computer won't boot. See Chapter 21 for troubleshooting tips.

1. Place the Rescue Disk in drive A and turn on your computer.

What you want to see are disk drive lights flashing — specifically on your floppy drive.

2. When you get a system prompt — `A:\>` — type **NDD** and press Enter.

This starts Norton Disk Doctor, which you should try to use before attempting a restore. See Chapter 26 for checkup info on Norton Disk Doctor (NDD). If NDD doesn't help, exit back to the system prompt.

3. Type **RESCUE/RESTORE** and press Enter, and you see the dialog box illustrated in Figure 15-5.

4. Select only those restore items you need.

Figure 15-5:
Nobody wants to use it — but if you're in trouble, there's nothing like Restore to put things back.

```
[]              Restore Rescue Information

Restore Rescue Information From:            ▐Restore▐
[A:\.................................]
                                            ▐Cancel▐
Select items to restore, then
press the Restore button                    ▐New Path▐

┌ Items To Restore ─────────────────┐
│ ☑ CMOS Information                 │
│ ☐ Boot Records                     │
│ ☐ Partition Tables                 │
└────────────────────────────────────┘
```

- Select CMOS Information if you've just changed your computer battery or if you're seeing an `Invalid setup` type error message.
- Select Boot Records if you get error messages like `Bad or missing command interpreter` or `Insert system disk and press Enter`.
- Select Partition Tables if your hard drive boots, but what you see on the screen is garbage — or you get a message about a `Bad File Allocation Table (FAT)`.

5. Press Alt+**R**estore.

   Norton asks you whether you're sure you want to Restore. Answer Yes and cross your fingers.

6. When the restore is finished, you get the chance to Reset or Cancel. Remove the Rescue Disk from the drive and choose Reset.

The information in the Rescue Disk should put you back on your feet. If not, go to Chapter 21 for additional suggestions.

See CMOS run. Run, CMOS, run.

In all likelihood, *CMOS* is a new vocabulary word for you. Although I don't like fussing with technical terms, CMOS is a technical word — actually, it's an acronym for Complementary Metal-Oxide Semiconductor, so it's several technical words — that you need to know because one day you'll have to go out and buy one.

Inside most computers is a battery that runs independently of the computer. Saved inside the battery is a list of your computer's *configuration* — the type of hard drive, the amount and kind of memory, floppy drives, and so on. That's your CMOS battery.

Every time your system is turned on, the computer goes to the battery — like a student to a guru — to find out about the nature of the universe. The CMOS responds with all the technical details about your system and everything turns on. Nirvana.

Now, here's something to chew on: What do all batteries have in common?

Give up?

Well, one thing is that all batteries eventually die and need to be replaced. Logically, then, all your important system settings will die, too. When that happens, you become the de facto keeper of the flame. It's up to you to pass on the system information to a new CMOS battery. You'll definitely lose your torchbearer license if you don't know what that system information is.

Now you see why Rescue Disk is doing you a huge favor by backing up all that CMOS information. All that great system information is stored in a file and can be restored when needed.

Mo' CMOS, Mo' CMOS, Mo' CMOS

When the CMOS battery is replaced, your computer tells you that the CMOS settings are invalid and demands new ones. You can use the Rescue Disk created in this chapter to Restore CMOS settings — or you can use another approach.

If you planned ahead, you may have a printed version of the CMOS settings, courtesy of Norton's own System Information program (see Chapter 13). If you didn't print out your system reports back in Chapter 13, then here's another chance. Really do it this time.

You need to print out two reports for your CMOS settings: CMOS Values (found under the System menu) and Partition Tables (found under the Disks menu).

After you pull up either the CMOS Values or Partition Tables screen, use the Print option to send the data to your printer.

✔ If you're using a laser printer, then after you print, you need to press — on your printer — the On Line button and then the Form Feed button to get the report to come out of the printer.

The bottom line is this — if you fail to print out a report, or fail to back up the CMOS information with Rescue Disk, then there will come a day when the battery runs out and you won't be able to use your computer. Period.

Without back-up information at the ready, you'll be forced to reconstruct your system settings by opening up your computer and foraging through your electronics. Maybe you'll get lucky and you won't have to take everything apart to figure out what you have.

Isn't it easier just to back things up?

Chapter 16

Image

*I*mages have had a bad name ever since the ancients decided to worship graven ones. Although I'm not suggesting that Norton's Image is worth worshiping, you may be praying while you're using it.

The Image program has but one job — keep up-to-the-minute stats on your computer system. Other Norton programs — like UnErase (see Chapter 14), UnFormat (covered in Chapter 27), and Norton Disk Doctor (refer to Chapter 26) — rely on the data in Image when called upon — by you — to pull a rabbit (or a file) out of the hat. Mere mortals such as you and I never get to actually use Image directly. Our job is over once we get Norton to stick the IMAGE command in the AUTOEXEC.BAT file.

Creating an Image

You don't have to hire a publicist or PR flack to get a good Image with Norton. Image is one of the "start-up" programs and can be installed easily — much like we did for Norton Cache.

Here's how:

1. At the system prompt, type **NORTON** and press Enter to get into the Norton Utilities menu.

2. Press Alt+**Configuration** ⇨ **Startup Programs**.

   You arrive at Figure 16-1, the amazing Startup Programs dialog box.

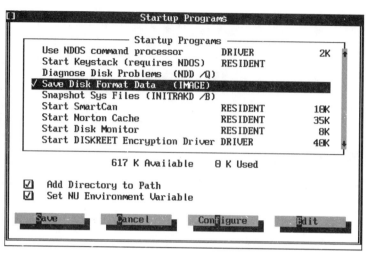

Figure 16-1:
The Startup
Programs
dialog box —
designed to
appear as
confusing as
possible —
check marks
those
programs
previously
activated.

3. As in Figure 16-1, highlight Save Disk Format Data.

4. Press Alt+Configure (or press the spacebar) to get to Figure 16-2.

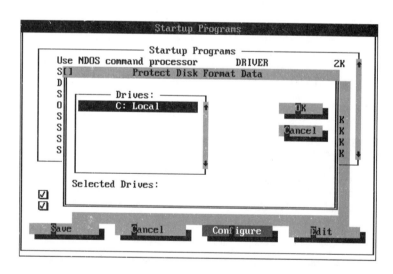

Figure 16-2:
If you have
more than
one drive
on your
system —
not counting
a CD-ROM
— Norton
lets you
create
images for
them all. In
this
example,
I've got just
one lonely
drive C.

5. Select the drives to be Imaged and press Alt+OK — or click OK if you're using a mouse.

6. When you're back in Figure 16-1, press Alt+**S**ave. Norton updates your AUTOEXEC.BAT file to include the Image program.

- When Norton has finished updating the file, a little note reminding you to reboot the computer appears — just press Enter to make the note disappear.

Finally, to see Image at work, reboot the computer. (The easiest way to reboot the computer is to press Ctrl+Alt+Del for a second or to press the reset button — if you have one — on the front of your computer.) Now, pay close attention — blink and you'll miss it. When the computer starts up again, it'll briefly say it's updating the Image file.

> ✔ To remove the Image command from the AUTOEXEC.BAT file, though I can't imagine why you'd want to — follow the same steps as installing the command. If you select a previously installed item, it uninstalls it. Like a light switch. On or off.

Tweaking Your Profile

There are two minor ways you can change the way the Image command works — neither is particularly dazzling, and both require some effort to effect the change, because although Norton has made it easy to insert and delete the Image command, it hasn't made it simple to make changes to the command. If you really need either of these options, they'll be worth the effort, I'm sure.

> ✔ If you noticed the Edit option in Figure 16-1, you may assume that Norton has provided a convenient way to edit your AUTOEXEC.BAT or CONFIG.SYS files. Guess again. All you can do with this lame **E**dit command is highlight, Delete, and Move lines in the AUTOEXEC.BAT File. If you want to perform either of these exciting tasks, then use Norton's **E**dit command — it doesn't do much, so it's simple to use. We're going to skip it.

A slimmer profile

Where hard disk space is particularly dear — like on a laptop, for example — you can install the secret /NOBACK switch. The NOBACK option tells Image not to create a back-up file. A back-up file, in regards to Image, is the previous day's IMAGE.DAT file.

In other words, every day when Image is run, it's out with the old and in with the new. Image creates a new IMAGE.DAT file containing all the information about your computer. Yesterday's IMAGE.DAT is renamed IMAGE.BAK, as a backup. (And then, the previous day's BAK file gets tossed out, in case you were wondering.) The NOBACK option tells Image not to keep the previous day's file.

On my system, using the NOBACK option frees up 100K of space! It'll free up even more space than that if you're also using SmartCan (covered in Chapter 35).

The bad news is that to change your Image command, you have to edit the AUTOEXEC.BAT file — there's no automatic option in Norton.

1. At the system prompt, type **EDIT \AUTOEXEC.BAT** and press Enter.

    • If your DOS Edit command isn't working, use your own word processor instead, but pay careful attention to the saving instructions at the end.

2. Once you're in the AUTOEXEC.BAT file, look for a line that contains the word IMAGE.

    If you want, use DOS Edit's Alt+Search ⇨ **Find** command to locate it for you.

3. Go to the end of the line with IMAGE in it and type **/NOBACK**.

    The line should now read: **\NU8** NU\IMAGE /NOBACK.

    • If your Norton program is in a directory other than NU, you should see the name of your own directory in the place of NU.

4. Save the file and exit.

    If you're using the DOS Edit command, press Alt+File ⇨ **S**ave, then press Alt+File ⇨ **E**xit. If you're using a word processing program, make sure to save the file as a text or ASCII file. In WordPerfect, use the Text Out, save as DOS File option.

Okay! From now on, no IMAGE.BAK files will be created when Image runs.

Keeping Image quiet

The second option you have for Image appeals to people who believe programs should be run but not heard. Again, normally when Image is executed, it produces a little message on the screen to let you know that the IMAGE.DAT file is being updated. If you don't want to see that message, you can turn it off.

To do this, just follow the same steps as the ones used to install the NOBACK option in the preceding section. In this case, though, Step 3 should read:

3. Go to the end of that line and add **/OUT**.

The line should now read: \ **NU8** NU\IMAGE /OUT.

- If your Norton program is in a directory other than NU, you should see the name of your own directory in the place of NU.

- If you want both the NOBACK and the OUT options, then you'll end up with something like: \ **NU8** NU\IMAGE /NOBACK /OUT.

TIP

Mirror, Mirror on the Wall

As mentioned earlier, Mirror is a DOS command that attempts to do what Image does. DOS may have stuck Mirror in your AUTOEXEC.BAT file for you and that's okay. The two don't conflict. Although we, of course, think Mirror can't hold a candle to Image, it doesn't hurt anything to put it in your AUTOEXEC.BAT file along with Image if you want . . . just to be extra, extra safe. All that's needed is a line in your AUTOEXEC.BAT file that says **MIRROR**. Or, if you have more than one hard drive — like a drive C and a drive D — you need **MIRROR C: D:**. That's it. If your version of DOS didn't include Mirror, aren't you glad you've got Image?

Chapter 17

Calibrate

· ·

In This Chapter

▶ Testing your integrity

▶ Interleave me alone

▶ Seeing test patterns

· ·

Calibrate! Calibrate! Dance to the music!

Calibrate dances, shouts, and feels the burn as it puts your hard drive through an intense aerobic workout. All you have to do is sit and watch as Calibrate displays impressive-looking screens and graphs and reports back to you about the condition of your hard drive.

What Calibrate does is twofold. First, it tests the drive for the proper *interleave* (I'll explain what that means in a moment). Second, Calibrate checks the hard drive for defects that could endanger your data. If it turns out that one of your files is unfortunate enough to be sitting on a flaw, Calibrate airlifts your goods to a safe site and posts a warning sign so that DOS won't put other files in the bad place.

Calibrate may be more than just a pleasant little preventive measure if you've been getting Error reading sector type messages from your computer. If you've been ignoring those messages because you didn't know what they meant, now's your chance to do something proactive about actually fixing the problem — instead of patiently waiting for the hard drive to fail.

You know how they always tell you to talk to a doctor before beginning any new exercise program? Well, this is your warning to back up your hard disk before running Calibrate the first time. Since Calibrate does some intense things to your hard drive, it is best to have a fallback position *just in case* your drive is that unlucky one-in-a-blue-moon drive that doesn't work well with Calibrate.

Okay, now that the obligatory warning is out of the way, let's begin a few stretches — never start a workout without warming up first!

Testing Your Integrity

Before Calibrate adjusts your hard disk, it first gives the disk a thorough checkup. Does your drive have what it takes to withstand thorough testing without making things worse? And what kind of job does Calibrate need to do on the drive? All these questions and more are answered in this initial pass.

1. To get to the opening Calibrate dialog box, shown in Figure 17-1, use one of the following methods:

   • From the Norton Utilities menu, highlight Calibrate and press Enter, or

   • From a system prompt, type **CALIBRAT** and press Enter

It's useless to attempt to run Calibrate from Windows — a multitasking environment makes Calibrate screw up big time. Personally, I find handling a monotasking environment enough of a challenge.

Figure 17-1:
The opening
Calibrate
screen says,
basically,
that you're
in the right
place —
which is
always nice
to know.

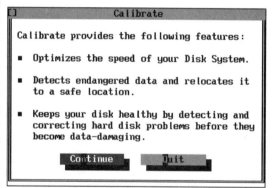

```
[ ]                    Calibrate

 Calibrate provides the following features:

  ■  Optimizes the speed of your Disk System.

  ■  Detects endangered data and relocates it
     to a safe location.

  ■  Keeps your disk healthy by detecting and
     correcting hard disk problems before they
     become data-damaging.

        Continue            Quit
```

2. After you see the screen shown in Figure 17-1, press Enter (or click Continue) to move along to another screen — Figure 17-2.

Figure 17-2:
Since I have
only one
hard drive,
my choice
here is
pretty
simple.

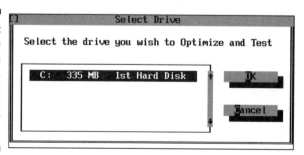

```
[ ]                   Select Drive

 Select the drive you wish to Optimize and Test

  ┌─────────────────────────────────┐
  │ C:   335 MB   1st Hard Disk      │        OK
  │                                  │
  │                                  │      Cancel
  │                                  │
  └─────────────────────────────────┘
```

3. Select the drive you want to test and press Enter or click OK.

4. Next you get a warning to back up your hard disk. Press Alt+Continue to move forward.

   It's always good advice to back up, but at this point all we want to do is the pretesting — which is safe.

5. You get another — yawn — screen, which tells you that before Calibrate does anything to your hard drive, it wants to run a few tests. That's what we want. Press Alt+Continue.

6. Sit and watch as Calibrate performs some system integrity tests, which only takes a couple of minutes.

   A system integrity test on a computer isn't like one of those sting operations they're always running on Congresspersons to test *their* integrity. This is a test to see whether the hard drive is running on all cylinders — so to speak.

7. Chances are — unless you have a very old computer — when the test is over, you'll get a message like the one in Figure 17-3. Press Enter to continue.

   If you're told about the joys of a new interleave, do not let the interleave start without backing up your system first and reading the next section.

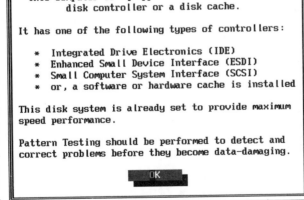

Figure 17-3: Congrats, you have no interleave problems — isn't that a relief!

Advanced Disk System

This computer is equipped with an advanced hard disk controller or a disk cache.

It has one of the following types of controllers:

* Integrated Drive Electronics (IDE)
* Enhanced Small Device Interface (ESDI)
* Small Computer System Interface (SCSI)
* or, a software or hardware cache is installed

This disk system is already set to provide maximum speed performance.

Pattern Testing should be performed to detect and correct problems before they become data-damaging.

OK

8. Next up, Figure 17-4 — at this point, we're going to take a break and press Alt+Cancel to prevent the process from moving forward.

Figure 17-4:
The Pattern
Testing
dialog box is
the gate-
way to
thoroughly
testing your
hard drive
— the
bigger the
pattern test,
the more
hours your
computer is
tied up.

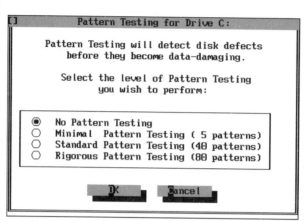

```
[]              Pattern Testing for Drive C:

           Pattern Testing will detect disk defects
                before they become data-damaging.

           Select the level of Pattern Testing
                    you wish to perform:

      ┌─────────────────────────────────────────────┐
      │  ◉   No Pattern Testing                      │
      │  ○   Minimal  Pattern Testing ( 5 patterns)  │
      │  ○   Standard Pattern Testing (40 patterns)  │
      │  ○   Rigorous Pattern Testing (80 patterns)  │
      └─────────────────────────────────────────────┘

               ▒ OK ▒           ▒ Cancel ▒
```

9. After you choose Cancel, Calibrate tries to woo you with a hard disk report — letting you know the results of its testing.

   • If you don't have any printed specs on your hard drive, you may want to Alt+**P**rint the report.

   • If you prefer, you can read the report on-line by scrolling through it. If your report has "best-seller" written all over it, then by all means print it out.

10. When you're finished, press Alt+**D**one. You are delivered back to Figure 17-2.

11. Press Esc or Alt+**C**ancel to leave.

This concludes the guaranteed no-harm-done portion of the Calibrate program.

Interleave Me Alone

Chances are, you won't need your interleave redone. So what the heck is an interleave? Let's just say that it's part of the method the computer uses when it's looking for information on the hard disk. If the interleave isn't set properly, the hard disk has to work harder and data retrieval is slower.

In the old days (five years ago), interleaves were set without much regard to performance — everyone was just thrilled that the hard drives worked reliably. However, one day someone woke up to the interleave connection, and the world hasn't been the same since. Most hard drives these days have perfectly wonderful interleave settings, and the whole topic has almost become a nonissue issue.

What makes a drive lose its charm?

Over time, all drives start to lose their magnetic personalities. That's because magnetic waves are not a permanent storage media. It's certainly permanent enough for our purposes, but entropy never sleeps and eventually the original magnetic pattern fades. Fortunately, with programs like Calibrate, it's possible to rekindle those old magnetic attractions — extending the life of your marriage. . . uh, I mean hard drive.

The bottom line is that if Calibrate offers to reset your interleave — go for it only *after* you've completely backed up your system. What Calibrate must do to reset your interleave can do bad things to your data.

To get your interleave retooled, follow Steps 1-6 in the "Testing Your Integrity" section — which are briefly listed here — and then complete Step 7.

1. Get into Calibrate.
2. Press Enter.
3. Select the drive you want to test and press Enter or click OK.
4. Press Alt+Continue.
5. Again press Alt+Continue.
6. Sit and watch as Calibrate performs testing.
7. When given the opportunity to adjust the Interleave, choose the Optimal setting and press Alt+Continue.

   You should now be facing Figure 17-4. The actual interleave-changing takes place during the Pattern Testing, as described in the next section.

Seeing Test Patterns

Pattern Testing is the main engine of Calibrate. This is where the drive is actually worked and where every bit of data at every point on the drive is exercised. How many reps Calibrate performs is up to you.

Follow Steps 1-6 in the section "Testing Your Integrity" — briefly listed here — to get to Figure 17-4. Then follow Steps 8-10.

1. Get into Calibrate.

2. Press Enter.

3. Select the drive you want to test and press Enter or click OK.

4. Press Alt+Continue.

5. Again press Alt+Continue.

6. Sit and watch as Calibrate performs testing.

7. Press Enter to continue.

8. Using the down-arrow key and spacebar (or by clicking with the mouse), choose the level of Pattern Testing you want to use.

   - No Pattern Testing just lets you know what state the drive is in. Nothing is changed.

   - Minimal Pattern Testing is the least thorough, but it's good enough to ferret out the worst offenders on the drive.

   - Standard Pattern Testing is what Norton recommends, generally, to really get the job done. This is the level to use if you're getting seek error messages.

   - Rigorous Pattern Testing is for people with no real life, because this kind of testing takes almost forever. The only time I could imagine going to this much effort is if you're buying a computer from someone you don't know and you want to make really, really sure the drive is okay. Also, if your drive has been performing erratically, this is one way to save a $65 service call.

No matter which method you choose, you can interrupt the process at any time by pressing Esc. Then come back later to pick up where you left off. This isn't an all-or-nothing-type thing.

9. After you make your choice, press Alt+**OK** to continue. You get Figure 17-5.

   Once the testing has begun, all you have to do is wait. Norton does the work.

   As you can see from Figure 17-5, Norton estimated that it would take about an hour and a half to run a minimal five-pattern test on my 350MB hard drive.

Since it's not a good idea to leave the same image on-screen for hours on end, Calibrate has a built-in screen saver. While the test is running, press the spacebar to replace the normal screen with the screen saver — which reports to you what percentage of the job is done.

Calibrate at work

Here's the estimated finish time for
a minimal pattern test on my system

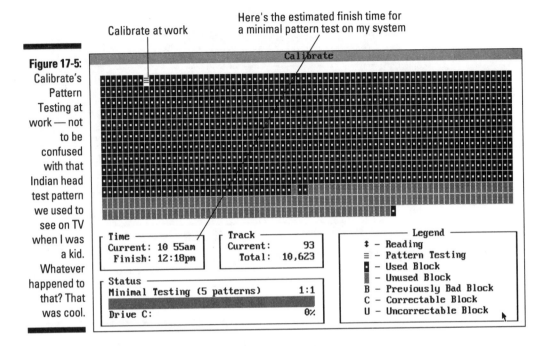

Figure 17-5:
Calibrate's
Pattern
Testing at
work — not
to be
confused
with that
Indian head
test pattern
we used to
see on TV
when I was
a kid.
Whatever
happened to
that? That
was cool.

10. When Calibrate finishes, you get a little notice indicating that everything's done, as in Figure 17-6. Press Enter (or click OK, if you prefer).

    Calibrate gives you another chance to see a report on what was done. Calibrate just *loves* issuing reports. Press Esc to exit.

After this workout, your hard disk will now be feeling wonderfully reinvigorated, the data will be feeling taut, and endorphins will be running rampant.

In case I confused any of you couch potatoes out there, an endorphin is a neurotransmitter that is released in the brain after exercising — don't panic, it makes you feel happy. And, no, endorphin is not the name of Samantha Stevens's mother — her name was Endora. Of course, Endora would have no right to complain that we got her name wrong — she never could get Durwood's . . . er, Darren's name right.

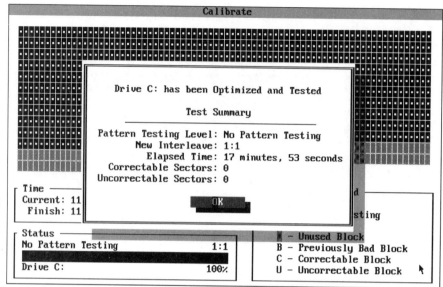

Figure 17-6:
Your
optimization
score card!

Identical cousins: Speed Disk versus Calibrate

Sometimes it's easy to confuse Speed Disk (covered in Chapter 12) and Calibrate. After all, they look alike and walk alike and at times they even talk alike — you could lose your mind — but Speed Disk and Calibrate are *not* two of a kind. Basically, Speed Disk is Patty — the crazy, frenetic one — and Calibrate is Cathy — the serious, intelligent one.

The basic philosophical difference between the two programs is that Speed Disk reorganizes *data* on the disk, and Calibrate checks out the *disk* itself.

Although both programs extend the life of your hard disk, Speed Disk takes only a few seconds to run, and a full-blown Calibrate session can take all day. You can use Speed Disk whenever you feel like it. Run Calibrate every three months.

Chapter 18

System Watch

- -

In This Chapter

▶ About SysWatch

▶ Making sense of the sensors

▶ Censoring the sensors

- -

System Watch (SysWatch) is a gas gauge for Windows. And, just like a gas gauge, System Watch alerts you if *resources* get too low.

The information provided by System Watch ranges from eye-popping to yawn-time, depending on how critical it is for you to know from nanosecond to nanosecond *exactly* what your computer is up to. As with any ecological system, however, depleted resources can bring things to a screeching halt. It's a good idea to take stock of the larder every now and again.

If you're constantly pushing the envelope of Windows' capacity, having a heads-up instrument panel like SysWatch is critical — and fun!

On the other hand, if you rarely have more than one application going at a time and you've never experienced a *system crash* — like when everything freezes up and you can't type anything or you get a message about a General Protection Fault — then you'll not need SysWatch on a daily basis.

However, whether you're a test pilot or a paper airplane pilot, if you've never lifted the hood off your Windows to see the engine run, now's a good time to take a peek.

About SysWatch

Doubtless the inspiration for SysWatch was Windows' own simple-minded *system resources* meter — which is okay enough if you've never had problems with Windows. Check in with Windows' version of System Watch from any Windows application by pressing Alt+**Help** ➪ **About**. You get something like Figure 18-1.

Figure 18-1:
To keep
from
crashing
and burning,
the rule of
thumb is to
keep your
system
resources
above 60%.
Click OK to
make the
display
disappear.

My name won't be on your software

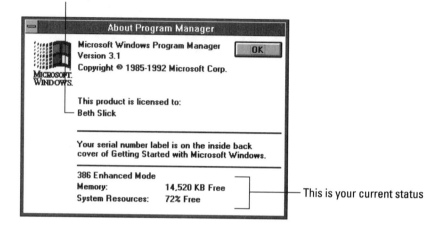

This is your current status

Now take a look at Norton's System Watch, which is shown in Figure 18-2.

Figure 18-2:
Nirvana or
Information
Overload? If
all you care
about is
Windows
Memory,
USER
Resources,
and the free
space on
your hard
drive,
SysWatch is
downwardly
mobile and
will agree to
display *only*
those stats.

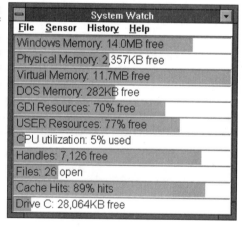

Here's how to get there:

1. Get in Windows.

2. From the Norton Utilities Windows group, click the System Watch icon.

That's really all there is to using System Watch in its most basic mode. Of course, the main thing about System Watch is being able to make sense out of what it's telling you.

Remember, there are 50 ways to leave your SysWatch — or any other Windows program. A few ways on everyone's top-ten lists are press Ctrl+F4, or press Alt+File ⇨ Exit, or double-click the Windows control menu box in the upper left part of the window.

Making Sense of the Sensors

System Watch gives you lots of wonderful information via what it calls *sensors* — as in Figure 18-2. The first hurdle to using SysWatch is understanding the significance of the displayed information.

✔ Windows Memory

The total memory, including Physical and Virtual Memory, available to Windows.

✔ Physical Memory

This number represents the available memory from installed memory chips and is part of the total Windows Memory.

✔ Virtual Memory

The other part of the Windows Memory figure. This is the amount of memory available from the Windows swap file.

✔ DOS Memory

The free memory left from your lower 640KB of memory.

✔ GDI Resources

This has to do with fonts and what's seen on-screen. A certain amount of resources has been allocated for displaying fonts — all that What You See Is What You Get business comes at a certain price. GDI, if you're concerned about such things, stands for Geraniums Drive Imprudently. No? Well, how about Graphic Device Interface?

✔ USER Resources

This is the grand total — sort of — of the preceding items. Basically, it's your "you are here now" status — much like the System Resources number you see when you access the **Help** ⇨ **About** screen.

✔ CPU Utilization

This shows how much of your computer hardware is at work. You'll see this number hop, skip, and jump when you do things like save, print, or call up another program.

✔ Handles

Just like in CB radio, where all good buddies have unique names so that they can be contacted — every file being used must have a system *handle* so that it can be found by Windows. The total number of available handles is limited, but usually that's not a problem. In Figure 18-2, you can see that there are 7,126 handles free.

✔ Files

This figure reflects more than just how many files *you* have opened in your application. Each application secretly opens a whole bunch of other files needed to run the program. Again, there's a finite number of files that can be open, and it's doubtful you'll hit the ceiling. But with SysWatch, you'll know for sure.

✔ Cache Hits

Your cache program at work! The higher the percentage, the better. If you're using a cache program other than SmartDrive, NCACHE 2, or Norton Speed Drive, this won't work for you. Sorry.

✔ Drive C

The amount of space left on your hard disk. When that figure gets much below 15,000K (or 15MB), it's nature's way of telling you that you need to buy a bigger hard disk or do some housecleaning to clear things out.

Generally speaking, the higher the memory and resources figures, the better. If your USER Resources — that combined figure — drops much below 60%, you *may be* more likely to crash.

On the other hand, don't start manufacturing symptoms just because you have a new measuring device. For example, if you call up your System Watch and realize that your Resources figure is 59% and you haven't even opened a single window, but you've never had any problems, don't start making yourself crazy worrying about it. If, however, you're at 59% and you're considering doing more with your system, then you may want to add more memory.

Watching SysWatch

Okay, so now you have some kind of idea of what System Watch is telling you, and you may have decided that it's a good thing — but you still have some reservations.

System Watch is a flexible little program that you can configure in a number of ways to fit your system. Available options range from *in your face* to *wallflower*. Of course, that's not what Norton calls them, but you'll see.

Getting graphical

In addition to the ever-changing numbers in the bar graph, each sensor can produce a graphical display that provides moment-to-moment information. I don't know who needs moment-to-moment usage stats, but they definitely are fun to watch, and bar charts are always impressive. Fortunately, making the bar charts is as easy as pie.

1. Of course, make sure that you're in System Watch by double-clicking the System Watch icon.

2. Press Alt+History.

   You see a list of all the sensors. At the bottom is `Close All`.

3. Click on the item you want to display.

   Figure 18-3 is a Windows Memory history chart. You can have more than one graphical display going at a time, of course.

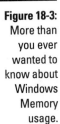

Figure 18-3: More than you ever wanted to know about Windows Memory usage.

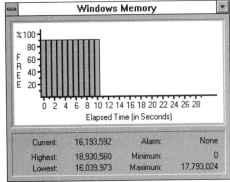

TIP

In the graphical window, the control menu contains a couple of items not normally seen in boring old control menus. To access the control menu, either press Alt+spacebar or just click on the control menu bar.

The item to look for in the control menu is called Always on Top. If you choose this option, it means that no matter what program you're using in Windows, this little graphical sensor will be sitting on top of the current program, whatever it may be. It's your window into the soul of the computer. Ain't that poetic?

The other cool thing about these little graphical windows is that when they're minimized, they continue to run and report what's going on. In Figure 18-4, for example, the Windows Memory and USER Resources are displayed on top of Excel.

Minimized sensors resting comfortably on Excel

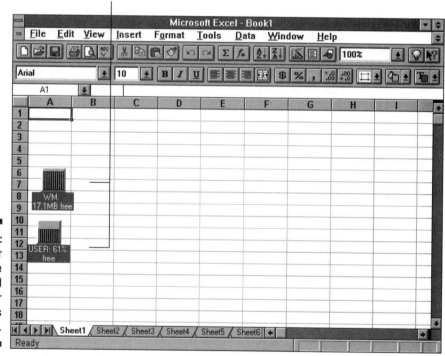

Figure 18-4:
Any sensor
can be
displayed
while other
programs
are working.

REMEMBER

If you don't choose Always on Top, the graphical window is buried the moment another application is used. You can unearth the sensor in the normal ways — including pressing Ctrl+Esc to bring up the Task List, which lists all the currently running programs, even the little graphical window.

Desensitizing SysWatch

If you're trying out commands as you read this book — I can dream, can't I? — you may notice that the first time SysWatch was opened, there were fewer sensors showing in your system than mine. That's because all the sensors are not normally turned on when you first use SysWatch.

I turned all mine on because I live on the edge. You can't hold me back.

Of course, if I can do it, you can do it. *You* can be just as wild and crazy by selecting your favorite sensors — and deselecting the ones that offend you.

To decide which sensors shall live and which shall die:

1. Make sure that you're in System Watch by double-clicking the System Watch icon.

2. Press Alt+**S**ensor.

   You see a list of all the sensors. Some are checked, some are not. At the bottom is Enable All, which turns them all on at once.

3. Click the items you want to include or hide.

That's it.

The SysWatch window performs a juggling act, trying to maintain the same basic window size as sensors are added and subtracted. What that means to you is that when you add or subtract from the System Watch window, the font suddenly changes or becomes smaller. If you don't like the size of the window, just grab that lower right corner with your mouse and adjust to taste. Also, as you'll see in a minute, you can decide exactly which font you want for your readouts.

Censoring the sensors

Naturally, you can futz away an entire afternoon exploring the gamut of options available to your sensors. It's so easy to pick out what color the sensors should be and how they are displayed and to set up alarms for those areas that you know have to be monitored that you could lose all track of time.

There are two sets of sensor alternatives. One is the General Options, which are choices that govern all the sensors. The second is Sensor Settings, which are applied one at a time to each sensor.

General Options

What's a General Option? It'll be a lot quicker to look at the General Options screen than to list a bunch of stuff, so take a look at Figure 18-5 to see what Norton Utilities considers General Options for System Watch.

Be the first on your block to get Figure 18-5 on your computer by pressing Alt+File ⇨ **O**ptions.

When you're finished with your changes and don't want to be in the configuration screens any more, just click OK or press Enter. If you want to move on to another configuration screen, just click the icon on the left — when you move to the next screen, the preceding one is saved for you.

When the General Options screen comes up, most likely the General Options icon on the left will be highlighted. If one of the other icons is highlighted instead, be sure to select the General Options icon. We'll be covering the un-general options in just a moment.

Apparently, there are three kinds of major options.

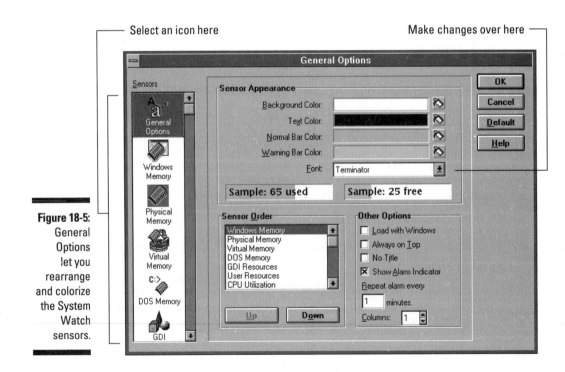

Figure 18-5: General Options let you rearrange and colorize the System Watch sensors.

✔ Sensor Appearance

The two samples show you what the sensors currently look like. You can select the various colors of your choice by clicking the little paint bucket icon — or, as always, tediously pressing Alt and the underlined letter — to see a palette of choices. Choose the one you want and click OK in the palette dialog box.

You also can change the fonts in which your sensors are displayed. In Figure 18-5, I've changed my font to the Terminator font. Just click on the down arrow on the font box — or press Alt+Font — and select your favorite font. The font selected applies to *all* sensors — that's why it's a general option.

✔ Sensor Order

This means that you can edit the pecking order for your sensors and determine in what sequence they are listed when the program is opened — as in Figure 18-2. Highlight the sensor to move and then choose Up or Down until you've got the placement just so.

✔ Other Options

For my money, there's nothing worse than being a miscellaneous option among miscellaneous options. I guess they really ran out of ideas for names. It's the usual drill here — click on an empty box to select an item — click on an X'd out box to turn a choice off.

If you want System Watch to automatically kick into gear whenever you get into Windows, use the `Load with Windows` option. Then you see something like Figure 18-2 when Windows is activated.

If you mess with your General Options too much, you can always have a clean slate — even after you've saved your changes — by pressing Alt+**Default**. Although Norton asks whether you're sure you want to go back to the factory settings and lose all your psychedelic choices — just say yes. Actually, you just say OK — but you get the general idea.

Sensor Settings

Knowing how sensitive sensors can be, Norton also provided ways to give each sensor the individual attention it needs. There are a variety of individual settings that can be set, including a command to sound an alarm when a sensor detects low resources. What constitutes low resources varies widely. Everyone is different. If your system is working fine, then don't worry about alarms. If your system has been weirding out on you, then maybe setting an alarm can help.

Once an alarm goes off, it's up to you to react appropriately. Norton doesn't take responsibility for seizing control of your system and delivering you to safety. It's perfectly willing to let you drive while your oil light is on.

To change individual sensor settings, press Alt+File ⇨ Options and select the sensor to be modified by clicking on the icon on the left — its screen pops up on the right, as in the example shown in Figure 18-6.

Turns sensor on/off

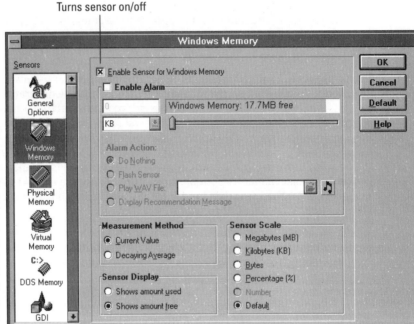

Figure 18-6: Each sensor has its own alarm system, which can be set to let you know that resources are getting low.

First, in the upper left corner is the all-important Enable Sensor option. If you don't want to use this sensor, have the decency to turn it off — uncheck the box with a click or by pressing Alt+Enable. This is the same as using the Alt+Sensor option from the System Watch screen — remember Figure 18-2?

Once you have turned on the sensor, there are four main types of sensor settings that can be adjusted — or ignored.

 ✔ Enable Alarm

   If you want to use Norton's early warning system, click Enable Alarm. Once the alarm is enabled, you may select at what point the alarm should go off — either by typing a number or by using the sliding scale. Your current settings are already on display. To make the experience complete, add sound — if you have a sound card — or use a visual cue. If you don't have sound, be sure to check your System Watch now and again for that flashing alert.

✔ Measurement Method

The two options are to display the moment-to-moment changes or to sort of even things out into a trend.

✔ Sensor Display

The half-empty, half-full option. Do you want to see what's used or what's left? Be careful, your choice brands you as an optimist or a pessimist.

✔ Sensor Scale

Do you like Megabytes, Kilobytes, Troglodytes, or just plain bytes? Experiment with your options — the numbers change in the sample to show you the ramifications of your choice. My personal recommendation is not to choose Troglodytes, though, because that's the fancy name for chimpanzees. Actually, it's Pan Troglodytes, but we don't want to show off.

To move on to the next sensor, just select the appropriate icon on the left. You are moved to that sensor's screen, and the modifications you just made are saved automatically — isn't that nice? Click OK when you're finished with all your icons. And, of course, choose Default if you want to go back to the way Norton intended it to be.

SysWatch Shortcuts

There are a couple of secret mouse-cuts in SysWatch that can be used when SysWatch is activated, as in Figure 18-2.

✔ Double-click on any of the sensor reports to make the command menu and title bar disappear.

✔ You can configure or view a graphical history of any sensor by pointing at it and clicking with the right mouse ear. A menu pops up, giving you familiar options.

Writing your System Watch memoirs

One of the best ways to troubleshoot is to compare the symptoms of the sick machine to that of the healthy machine. If your definition of a *healthy* computer is no more specific than *not broken*, then it makes it more of a challenge to figure out what's going on with the sick machine.

So, if you've got a healthy computer right now, why not take a snapshot for your memory book? That way, if your system starts to get weird on you, you — or whoever is working on the machine — can compare the sick settings with the healthy ones.

For instance, if today System Watch says you have 18MB of Virtual Memory free and the next time you look at System Watch you have no Virtual Memory, you'd know where to start digging. Or, at least whoever is going to work on your computer will know where to start digging.

Here's how to start your memory book:

1. Call up SysWatch by clicking on its icon in the Norton Utilities Windows group.

2. If all the sensors aren't turned on, then press Alt+**S**ensor ➪ Enable **A**ll to turn them on.

3. Press the Print Screen button on your keyboard.

   If you haven't used the Print Screen button, it's located somewhere in the upper right quadrant of your keyboard and is labeled Print Screen or some abbreviation of that, like PrtSc.

When you press Print Screen, it'll seem like nothing just happened. But it did. A picture of the current Windows screen was sent to your Clipboard.

4. Open the Main Group.

5. Double-click the Clipboard icon. It's easy to spot because it looks like — you guessed it — a clipboard.

   The Clipboard Viewer should display the picture you just took of your Windows screen, including System Watch — and including all your current healthy settings.

6. Press Alt+**F**ile ➪ Save **A**s.

   This is the first step to saving the picture — or *clip*, as they call it.

7. Type a filename to save it under and press Enter.

   One idea is to use the current date for the filename — 101494 for October 14, 1994, for example.

   Exit the Clipboard in one of the usual ways — press Ctrl+F4 or Alt+**F**ile ➪ **E**xit, and so on.

If you *really* want to go to the head of the class, you can get into Word for Windows — or WordPerfect or AmiPro or even Excel — and paste to the Clipboard (usually Ctrl+V) — and print out the screen. If you have a graphics printer, you should be able to do this without any problems.

Chapter 19
INI Tracker for DOS and Windows

· ·

In This Chapter

▶ Installing INI Tracker for DOS and Windows

▶ Automating current snapshots

▶ Restoring files

· ·

Do you get the feeling that someone's following you? Your friends tell you you're nuts — but you just can't shake the feeling you're being followed?

Well, your instincts are correct. Norton Utilities INI Tracker program *is* following your moves and taking daily (or more often, if you prefer) snapshots of the files important to your computer and to your very existence — like your WIN.INI and SYSTEM.INI files or even the AUTOEXEC.BAT and CONFIG.SYS files — as well as snapshots of the contents of selected directories.

Tracker keeps all the photographs in a Snapshot Log. When you view the log, it reveals a chronicle of how the files — or directories — have been modified over a period of time — a time period that you can set. This Snapshot Log provides you with what is called an audit trail, so you can go back and compare what was different with the file last week — as opposed to today, say, when things stopped working.

With the help of Tracker, you can restore a good system file and eliminate the one with the negative tendencies. However, determining which previous file is the good one requires some judgment on your part. Although Norton gives you a running commentary about what's different in today's CONFIG.SYS versus yesterday's, it's still up to you to decide — which is why Siskel and Ebert give this program a Three-Tech rating . . . a Four-Tech rating is about as techy as you can get.

Don't skip over the DOS version of Tracker. Although the Windows version is admittedly the superior program, the two versions work in tandem. One of the main things the DOS version may be called upon to do — in addition to restoring your common, garden-variety AUTOEXEC.BAT — is to restore a recalcitrant Windows INI file, without which Windows refuses to start up. That's right, DOS Tracker will restore a WIN.INI, SYSTEM.INI, or any other INI you've been tracking.

Establishing a Routine

To cover all the bases, it's best if *both* the Windows and DOS versions of Tracker are installed. That way, a snapshot is automatically generated every time the computer is turned on *and* every time you get into Windows. You also can schedule more frequent photo sessions if you're a life-in-the-ultra-fast-lane kind of person.

INI Tracker for Windows

 First things first — let's get into the program. Fire up Windows and go to the Norton Utilities Windows group and double-click the INI Tracker icon. You get something like Figure 19-1. Please note that the mouse arrow pointer turns into a little camera while it's busy taking a snapshot. Apparently, someone at Norton got some overtime pay on this design.

Since your screen doesn't have any snapshots yet, let's just move on to the task of setting things up.

 While in the INI Tracker screen, you can take a manual snapshot at any time by pressing Alt+File ⇨ New Snapshot — Ctrl+N for short.

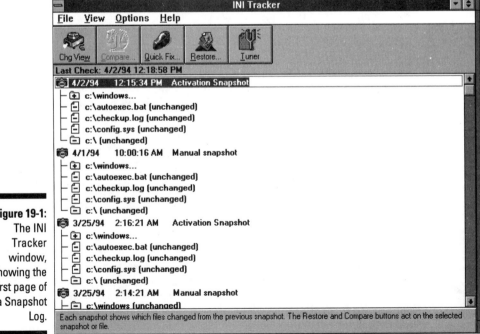

Figure 19-1:
The INI
Tracker
window,
showing the
first page of
a Snapshot
Log.

Configuring Snapshots

INI Tracker can handle a variety of monitoring duties — but you've got to ask. Here's how to set up the way INI Tracker will work.

1. From inside INI Tracker, press Alt+**O**ptions ⇨ **C**ustomize. You get Figure 19-2.

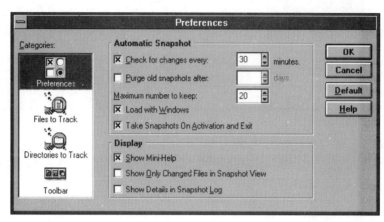

Figure 19-2: The scope of INI Tracker is apparent the moment you set foot inside the Preferences dialog box.

2. Make sure that Take Snapshots On Activation and Exit **is selected along with** Load with Windows.

   That takes care of regular picture-taking in Windows. In Fact, Windows takes a snapshot when it detects the words "install" and "setup" so that you'll always have a before photo to fall back on after a Windows installation.

   - You also can set here the maximum number of past Snapshots to keep and how many days to keep the snapshots. You don't want to keep them forever. Baby pictures you should keep forever. Not these.

   - If you want to track more than your basic system files, you can highlight the Files to Track icon and create your list of files to track. The more, the merrier. Figure 19-3 shows a basic setup of key files. As a minimum, make sure that your Tracker is set to track these files. Use the Alt+**A**dd command button to select from a file/directory list.

   - If you want to see what files have been added to or deleted from a certain directory, select Directories to Track and party on. If you're a software-aholic, you'll want to track your root (C:\) and Windows (C:\WINDOWS) directories, as in Figure 19-4.

   - If you don't like the position or shape of the toolbar, you can change that as well!

3. When you're finished, press Alt+**O**K, and you're outta there!

Figure 19-3: Press Ctrl+P to access the customization screens, where you can tell INI Tracker what files to track.

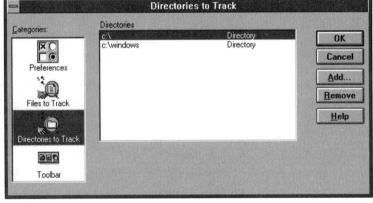

Figure 19-4: A simple little Directories to Track setup — click the Add command button to track additional directories as needed.

One universal problem with Windows is that if you need to delete a program, it takes a Ph.D. to undo all the adjustments made to the system files as well as to trace the files copied to various Windows directories. If you're tracking the directory containing Windows as well as your WIN.INI and SYSTEM.INI files, it's much easier to figure out what the newly installed program changed, in case you need to remove it later.

Reading the snapshot log

After a while, your screen will be full of filenames and changes — and it can be a little intimidating. However, you can follow the bouncing file folder. Tracker not only records your important files, it also provides a running list of which statements have changed, and how, since the last snapshot. Norton's diligence here can alert you to problems before they become worse. Here are a few clues about what you're seeing:

- ✔ When there's a plus sign (+) in the little camera or file folder icon, double-clicking it reveals more details about any changes between the current and previous snapshot.

- ✔ If the new version of the file differs from the old one, then Tracker shows a "before" and "after" of the line that's changed. A plus sign in front of the line indicates it's the current one — a minus sign indicates it's old news.

- ✔ If a new line has been *added* to the system file, then that line stands alone, with a plus sign. No comment.

- ✔ A minus sign in front of a line by itself indicates that the line was removed from the file.

- ✔ Our old friends from Algebra — the "greater than" and "less than" symbols (> and <) — indicate a line that was moved within the file.

If you prefer, INI Tracker can display more than just a few tantalizing hints about what changes occurred to the items being tracked. To always see exactly what's new, as in Figure 19-5, select Show Details in Snapshot Log in the Preferences dialog box (see Figure 19-2).

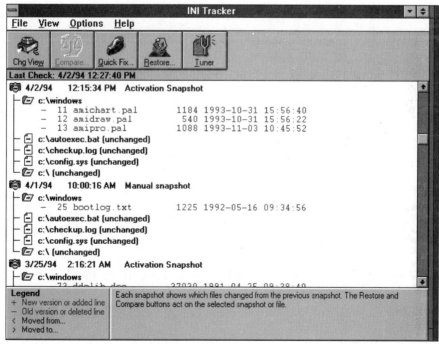

Figure 19-5:
INI Tracker lays it all out for you when you choose the Show Details option.

Commanding options

While using INI Tracker, it's good to note that you've got a number of choices in the toolbar and menu:

- ✔ **Chg View.** Clicking this icon organizes the Snapshot Log by file or by snapshot. Usually, you'll want to be in Snapshot view, which displays everything in chronological order — making it much easier to follow the audit trail. Take a look in the Alt+View menu to see your choices.

- ✔ **Compare.** Clicking this icon calls up the File Compare program, which is discussed in Chapter 7. This option makes it easier to see two files — or two directories — side-by-side and reinstate individual settings, rather than the whole file.

- ✔ **Quick Fix.** If you're in Snapshot view, use this option to restore one of the files, as long as it has just — a few minutes ago — changed. If you're not in Snapshot view, use Chg View to get there.

- ✔ **Restore.** Using this option replaces a current version of a file with an older — but better — file of your choice.

- ✔ **Tuner.** Use the Tuner to refine the Windows desktop. This is covered in detail in the next chapter.

- ✔ **File menu.** This menu contains items covered by tools, plus the New Snapshot command and the Print command, which lets you print the files currently on-screen.

- ✔ **View menu.** This also mostly duplicates the Chg View icon.

- ✔ **Options menu.** This is where we installed the automatic snapshot options. It is also where you can find the exciting Reset Snapshot Log command, which erases the Snapshot Log.

Once everything's set, when you're ready to leave, don't forget to turn out the lights. And remember, from now on, every time you enter or exit Windows, Tracker takes a set of photos.

Since Tracker works in the background, you don't have to allow it to take up space on your desktop — not even icon space. You can hide Tracker by pressing Alt+File ⇨ Hide.

If you choose to Reset the Snapshot Log — in the Options menu — you'll *wipe out* all the old snapshots.

INI Tracker for DOS

Setting up the Tracker in DOS requires a trip to the good old Startup Programs locale.

1. At the system prompt, type **NORTON** and press Enter to get into the Norton Utilities menu.

2. Press Alt+**C**onfiguration ⇨ **S**tartup Programs.

   You arrive at the Startup Programs dialog box.

3. **Highlight** `Snapshot Sys Files (INITRAKD /B)`.

4. Press the spacebar.

   A check mark appears in the left margin, signifying that Norton Utilities understands your selection.

5. Press Alt+**S**ave.

   Norton inserts a command in the AUTOEXEC.BAT file that makes the computer take a snapshot every time the computer is turned on.

6. You get a little note from Norton telling you that the snapshot action won't start until the next time the computer is turned on. Press Enter to make the message fade into memory.

You can only build a list of files and directories to be tracked in the Windows version of this program. The list of files and directories selected in Windows is used by the DOS version as well.

You can take a manual snapshot from DOS by typing **INITRAKD /B** and pressing Enter.

Restoring Files

The whole point of both programs is to have a preserve of recent system files that can be put back into action at a moment's notice. Well, actually, it's at no notice at all!

Restoring from Windows

1. Get into INI Tracker from Windows (double-click its icon).

   If you're not in Snapshot view, use the Chg View command icon to switch to it. It'll make it easier to find the most recent and next-to-most-recent files.

2. Highlight the snapshot you want to restore.

3. Click the **R**estore command icon in the toolbar.

4. Select any other files to restore from the Restore dialog box.

5. Once you're all set, select OK.

   A file preserved with the other files in the snapshot log takes over the place of the previous — bad — file.

If you're restoring because the INI files have problems, don't automatically restore the most recent snapshot — remember it's a photograph of the newest (and most screwed up) — files. Restore files that worked well from a few days back.

Restoring from DOS

If you cannot get into Windows, you have to restore files with the DOS INI Tracker.

1. Type **INITRAKD** and press Enter to get to the snapshot log screen.

   Make sure that Alt+View ⇨ Plus File Names has been selected. It makes the next step a lot easier.

2. Highlight the file to be restored.

3. Select the Restore button.

   You get something like Figure 19-6, where INI Tracker is confirming the choice to restore some files.

4. Confirm your selection with another OK.

   The selected file automatically takes its place as king of the heap. Watch out, Avedon!

5. You may now leave by pressing Esc, or Alt+File ⇨ **E**xit if you like to do things the long way.

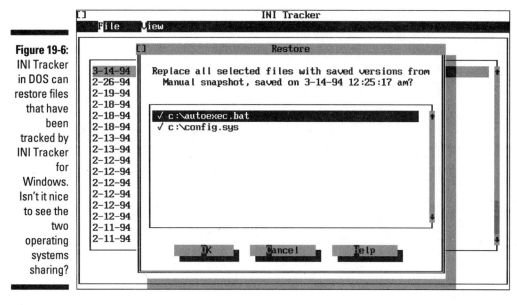

Figure 19-6:
INI Tracker
in DOS can
restore files
that have
been
tracked by
INI Tracker
for
Windows.
Isn't it nice
to see the
two
operating
systems
sharing?

MINI management

Tracker, File Compare (see Chapter 7), INI Advisor, INI Editor, and INI Tuner (all in Chapter 20) are all parts of a cohesive system to edit, fine-tune Windows, and protect INI files. Be sure to check them all out.

The 5th Wave   By Rich Tennant

Chapter 20
Hanging Windows

In This Chapter

▶ Introducing the Three Musketeers

▶ INI Advisor

▶ INI Tuner

▶ INI Editor

*I*sn't it kind of weird that Windows — the operating environment that's supposed to put the *Z* back into EZ computing — wants you to play Leonard Bernstein to WIN.INI, SYSTEM.INI, and a bunch of other high-strung INIs, all of which make AUTOEXEC.BAT and CONFIG.SYS look positively healthy. Am I the only one who thinks this is kind of backwards thinking?

Instead of just complaining about it, like me, Norton Utilities has taken the high road and provided a solution to the INI situation with three programs that at least pretend to be concerned about handling my SlowDither and 386grabber.

Since INI Advisor, INI Tuner, and INI Editor are all inextricably linked together, we're presenting them together as a group. When you use INI Tuner, for example, you'll find INI Advisor and INI Editor in its toolbar — likewise in INI Editor, where INI Tuner and INI Advisor stand by.

You can't have one without the other — and you really wouldn't want to, since they all complement each other. If you are editing your WIN.INI, for example, and have a question about something, you just pop up INI Advisor, and he'll patiently tell you what you need to know about the thing you're looking at. It's all for one, and one for all. Fortunately, the one they're all for is — you!

As you may — or may not — know, the WIN.INI and SYSTEM.INI files tell Windows all about your computer and its capacities, as well as a lot of information about your software. If you were to edit those files and take something out that was needed, you could disable Windows.

The reason people are drawn to editing their INI files, despite the dangers, is that they control the speed of your system. The more efficient the INI files, the more efficient the computer.

The purpose of INI Advisor, INI Tuner, and INI Editor is to help you traipse around inside your INI files and make intelligent changes to the system and the *desktop* — the Windows desktop is what you see on-screen when you're in Windows, but not in a program in Windows.

Although these programs are powerful and all that, they are also limited in scope — I mean, they're intensely focused . . . yeah, that's it. Anyway, since they are basically one-trick ponies, we can breeze through them pretty quickly. You'll be up and at 'em in no time.

Before you begin any exercise program, consult with a physician. Or at least use Tracker (covered in Chapter 19) to take a Polaroid of your INI files before you start messing with them. Tracker lives to restore files . . . as long as you put the files on record.

INI Advisor

If you have questions about Windows — terminology, error messages, statements in your INI files, what to do in various situations, and just about anything else — then the INI Advisor is here to help. If you're familiar with the Norton Advisor (see Chapter 21), then you can guess what INI Advisor is all about — it's just incredibly sophisticated and very cute. When it all comes down to it, the INI Advisor is one big teddy bear of a Help file. Generally, you'll use INI Advisor in conjunction with the other INI tools — unless you happen to be sitting in your office when someone pops by wondering what Int33h means. Then, you can just look it up with the INI Advisor.

To start up the INI Advisor

1. Get into Windows.

2. In the Norton Utilities - Windows Programs, double-click on the Dweeb icon.

   Initially, you get Figure 20-1.

As the INI Advisor points out, if you click your right mouse button, a shortcut menu immediately pops up right under your cursor — so you shouldn't have to reach all the way to the top of the screen where the menu bar is. This little come-as-you-are menu is called a PowerMenu and it offers faster-than-instant access to the menu bar options. Try it. It's fun.

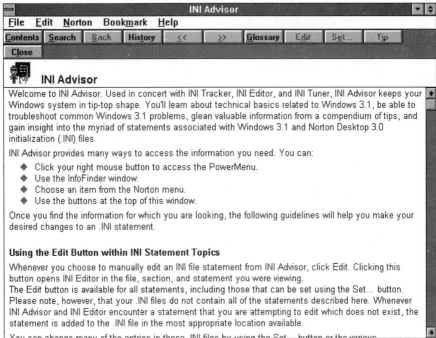

Figure 20-1:
INI
Advisor's
opening act
— which
explains
how to use
INI Advisor.

The other half of the INI Advisor is the InfoFinder — which you can call up by using the Contents command button. InfoFinder is your fast track to everything you want to know. Everything about Windows that you want to know, anyway, as in Figure 20-2.

Once you're in INI Advisor, it works like any other Windows Help system.

✔ Under the Alt+File menu, you can find the command to print out the current topic — the stuff you see on-screen at that moment. You can build your own reference book.

✔ Under the Alt+Norton menu, you can find specific help, including Trouble-shooting, Tips, and where to find Technical Support.

✔ Need to look up a specific term? Use the **G**lossary command button to bring the Norton Utilities Glossary to your beck and call.

✔ Finally, the **S**earch command button brings up the familiar dialog box that asks what you want to know.

For a good time, search GANG SCREENS. *Gang screens* are hidden lists of the names of those who wrote and tested the software. It's a way program-mers have of getting credit for all their work. Only insiders — like yourself — know where this information is stashed away and how to get to it. For example, to see the crazy folks who brought you Norton Utilities 8, open the Norton Disk Doctor for Windows icon. At the opening screen, press

Alt+Help⇨About. At the About screen, simultaniously press the letters NU8. If you don't do it all at the same time, nothing happens. If you do get it right, a photograph of these nutcases at Norton appears. Point to one with the mouse, and that person's name appears in the menu bar. It's fun! It sure beats work.

When you're finished with the INI Advisor, choose one of the close-this-window options you're familiar with now — you could hold a trivia contest in your office to see who can come up with the most ways to get out of a Window without turning off the computer. Let's see, there's Alt+F4, pressing the Close command button, Alt+File⇨Exit . . .

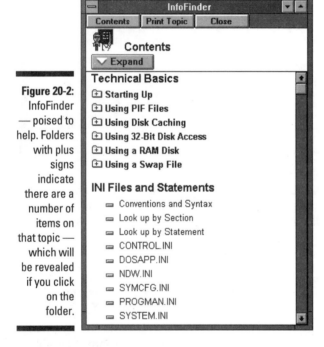

Figure 20-2: InfoFinder — poised to help. Folders with plus signs indicate there are a number of items on that topic — which will be revealed if you click on the folder.

INI Tuner

As dull and basic as INI Advisor is, INI Tuner is far cooler. The INI Tuner not only lets you easily change items found in the Control Panel, located in the Main Group window, but it also includes four *applets — little applications,* or programs — that let you adjust things you didn't know you could mess with and still have a good time.

C'mon along and see what I'm talking about.

1. Get into Windows.

2. In the Norton Utilities - Windows Programs, double-click the INI Tuner icon — the one that sort of looks like a cactus. Now I suppose I'll get a bunch of letters from psychologists explaining what it means to see a cactus in a tuning fork. But I can name that tune in three notes.

Initially, you get Figure 20-3 — be sure to say "hi" to our pals the Advisor and INI Editor.

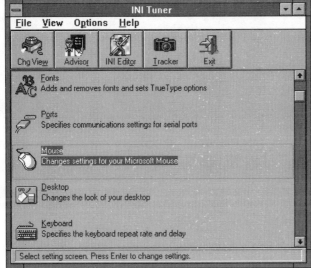

Figure 20-3:
The opening INI Tuner dialog box. Except for the fact that I've highlighted the Mouse section, this'll be what you get, too.

3. Highlight a feature you'd like to work with.

I've highlighted Mouse (see Figure 20-3).

4. Double-click or press Enter — and go forth and change things.

Another window pops up with all your options for that item. If you've messed with the Control Panel before, these will be familiar choices.

When I pressed Enter while the Mouse section was highlighted, I got Figure 20-4 for my efforts.

5. Press Alt+File⇨Restart Windows and choose Restart Windows.

Not all the changes you make using INI Tuner take effect immediately. You may have to exit Windows and restart in order to see the results of the modifications. To cancel, choose Continue.

Figure 20-4:
The Mouse
Manager
window is a
lot easier to
get to via INI
Tuner than
the Control
Panel — *if*
you can
remember
where the
Control
Panel is
buried.

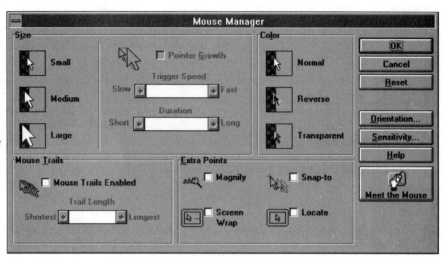

Using INI Tuner applets

This sounds far more complicated than it really is. To use these so-called applets, just scroll down to the bottom of the INI Tuner stuff. You bump into several items that you won't find in the Control Panel.

If you want to change Windows settings as often as you switch channels with a remote control, you can drag any of the applet icons to your favorite window. For example, you could highlight the Fonts icon and drag it to your Excel window — which you can select when the mood strikes you.

✔ **Help Colors.** You can easily change the colors of help to get rid of that ugly green color.

✔ **Advanced Desktop.** Okay, this is the fun one. Figure 20-5 is the Advanced Desktop dialog box, where you can easily adjust spacing between desktop icons and more.

✔ **Program manager options.** This one lets you restrict who is able to do what to the system. For example, is someone else always messing with your desktop layout and then saving the settings on exit? You can make that impossible.

✔ **Advanced Communications.** This is the yawner in the group. It lets you set the communication speed on the serial ports.

✔ **DOS Box and Others.** Sounds like a Saturday morning kids' show — you know, one of those things with aggressively gleeful hand puppets. Actually, it lets you do several things, including replacing the Program Manager for another program. Like, I suppose, you could even install Norton Desktop for Windows. Anyway, this section handles technical things for those parts of Windows that don't contain Windows applications.

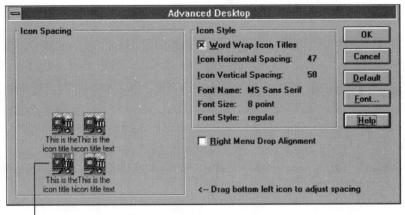

Figure 20-5:
Fit more on
the screen
by allowing
your icons
to get closer
in the
Advanced
Desktop
applet.

Grab and drag this icon to taste

Using the toolbar options

While in INI Tuner, you can avail yourself of the toolbar functions, like

✔ **Chg View.** This one flips between the nice graphical screen, as in Figure 20-3, and the text version of it. Click on the Chg View to see which you like.

✔ **Advisor.** This function summons the INI Advisor, which is discussed earlier in this chapter.

✔ **INI Editor.** Guess what? This calls up the INI Editor, which is discussed in the next section.

✔ **Tracker.** Use this function to fetch the Tracker, which is covered in Chapter 19.

Using the menu's bill of fare

There are four menu items, but we're not going to list Help and explain what that does because . . . let's just say that if you don't know what Help does, click on it and find out.

✔ File options allow you to instantly open — via the INI Editor — the WIN.INI, SYSTEM.INI, or any other INI file you want to look at. Also, the File menu can retrieve the Windows **S**etup screen or send you off to the exotic File Compare (see Chapter 7).

✔ View does basically the same thing as Chg View — translates the graphic screen to the written.

✔ Options lets you change the font for INI Tuner and relocate the toolbar if you don't like its present position.

Coining new words — Minting new phrases

One thing about the computer industry — it's added many new words to the language . . . though who's to say whether we're the richer or the poorer for having added words like "high-tech," "techno-weenie," and "hacker" to our vocabularies. The fact remains that words are being created — and new meanings being applied to others — at an alarming pace. Take this new word: *applets*. If we weren't listening closely, we might have thought it was epaulets — which are those hanging-down thingies on the shoulders of soldiers. The other thing about applets is — who *cares?* Okay, so an applet isn't a real program and it's something in a DLL with a CPL extension. But do we really need to know that to make it work? Why do they bother us with details that are really important only to the techno-weenie who makes the thing in the first place. To the rest of us, it doesn't matter one Twinkie what it's called — let's just point and click!

INI Editor

The final saga in the INI trilogy. Will Bilbo and Frodo make it? Will the Rings — wait a minute — wrong trilogy.

The INI Editor is a cleverly designed word processor that takes some of the tedium out of working with long INI files.

1. Get into Windows.

2. In the Norton Utilities - Windows Programs, double-click the INI Editor icon.

   Initially, you are asked to select an INI file to edit.

3. Highlight a file to edit and click OK.

   In Figure 20-6, a WIN.INI file has been loaded.

   Once a file has been pulled into the INI Editor, you may alter at will — with help of several command buttons on the right, plus, of course, the toolbar and the menus — which are discussed in the next sections.

4. When you're finished editing, click the Alt+**S**ave icon in the toolbar.

5. After you have finished editing, press Alt+**File**⇨**R**estart Windows and choose Restart **W**indows — to put the changes into effect.

Figure 20-6:
The INI
Editor
simplifies
working on
editing INI
files by
putting the
Section
titles in the
top window
and the
contents of
each
Section —
known as
the
Statements
— in the
bottom
window.

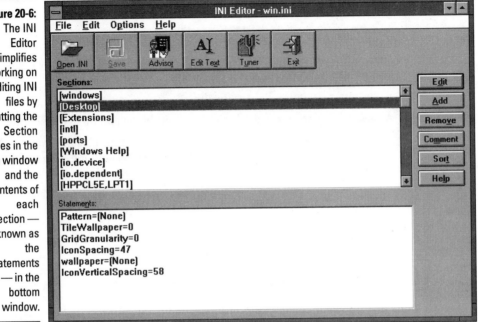

Editing with command buttons

You can fine-tune your INI file by

- ✓ **Edit.** Allows you to rewrite the currently highlighted item.

- ✓ **Add.** Add a statement or section head.

- ✓ **Remove.** Deletes the currently highlighted section or statement.

- ✓ **Comment/Activate.** Adds/removes a semicolon from the beginning of the line. Why would you want to add or remove a semicolon from the beginning of a line? Probably you wouldn't. But the purpose of a semicolon, in this context, is to turn an INI action statement into a written comment to be ignored. People who are troubleshooting conflicting goodies in the INI files comment things out as a way of isolating a problem. Don't select this option unless you know about editing INI files.

- ✓ **Sort.** Puts things in alphabetical order. *Caution:* When you use this, you may inadvertently separate comments from their corresponding program.

Bellying up to the toolbar

Several options are available right there while editing.

- **Open INI.** Pops up a dialog box that asks you to specify the lucky INI file that gets to be edited by you.
- **Save.** Saves changes made to the file.
- **Advisor.** Help system. See "INI Advisor," at the beginning of the chapter.
- **Edit Text.** Not the same as the Edit command button. This pulls up the INI file in a Notepad document, allowing traditional text editing — in the time-honored tradition.
- **Tuner.** Wakes up the INI Tuner, which is discussed in the preceding section.
- **Exit**. Hasta la vista, baby.

Grazing through the menu

There are, of course, additional features and more keystrokes tied up in the bona fide menu.

- File options allow you to instantly open — via the INI Editor — the WIN.INI, SYSTEM.INI, or any other INI file you want to look at. Also, the File menu can whisk you away to File Compare, Save As (to save the file under a different name), and, as usual, Restart Windows after your changes have been recorded.
- Edit gives you a basic editing setup with cut, paste, delete, and so forth.
- Options lets you change the font for INI Editor and relocate the toolbar to a vertical setup if you like.

The SkINI on INI

Just to make permanent note here, INI Advisor, INI Editor, and INI Tuner all work with File Compare (see Chapter 7) and Tracker (see Chapter 19) to provide a comprehensive INI management, tracking, and editing system. If you didn't know you had INIs before reading this book, it's probably overwhelming to receive five programs dedicated to taking care of them. Even if you never intend to edit or change your INI files, please be sure to at least check out Tracker in Chapter 19, which provides an easy way to restore INIs that get broken or corrupted. You don't have to understand anything about what you're doing to get complete protection. Sound like a plan?

Part IV
Rescue Me!

The 5th Wave   By Rich Tennant

"ALRIGHT, STEADY EVERYONE. MARGO, GO OVER TO TOM'S PC AND PRESS 'ESCAPE'...VERY CAREFULLY."

In this part...

1 f you're in the middle of a crisis and all you know is that the computer isn't working, you're in the right place. We'll do a little Troubleshooting 101 and then turn the whole problem over to Norton Utilities. After all, that's what they're here for.

Chapter 21

Disentangling from a Disaster

● ●

In This Chapter

▶ Starting from scratch

▶ Using the Rescue Disk

▶ Troubleshooting 101

● ●

*I*f you just purchased Norton Utilities and are in the middle of a major jam, do not install the Norton Utilities software until you've read this chapter — especially the section called "Starting from Scratch."

Welcome to the Nightmare

When things don't go right, it's definitely no fun.

If your computer doesn't start up like normal, if you can't find files you know you saved, if you erased files by mistake, and if you're getting messages from your computer that you don't understand or have never seen before — you're in a horror show that sends the pulse racing faster than any Hollywood movie ever could.

Okay, so you're in a disaster. What follows every disaster? Why, FEMA, of course. In this case, FEMA stands for Frightful Emergency Management Allocator. In other words, since most of this book is about using the various Norton Utilities to recover from a disaster, this chapter serves as a clearing-house of where you should go and what programs you should be using to recover.

We will not, however, be providing low-interest loans.

In addition to sending you hither and yon for help, we'll also give you some ways to work out problems on your own — since there's no way to cover every single possible contingency in this book. Once you know how to work out your own problems, you may even become the office guru. It could happen.

If you're convinced that troubleshooting is beyond your abilities, however, just remember that it won't hurt anything to try. You may discover that a degree from ITT Technical Institute isn't required to fix every computer problem. In fact, many predicaments can be corrected by applying a little common sense, as you'll see.

Starting from Scratch

Use this section *only* if

- ✔ The shrink wrap is barely off your Norton Utilities and you're hoping to use it to extricate yourself from a massive sinkhole that just opened up underneath you. Take two deep breaths and know that there is hope.

- ✔ You've been using Norton Utilities, but never made a Rescue Disk and now the computer won't start.

Norton Utilities comes with an Emergency disk. Find it and put it in your floppy drive. The Emergency disk contains several programs to help you recover from several really bad situations.

Once you get yourself out of the current scrape, go to Chapter 15 and make a Rescue Disk. A Rescue Disk stores information specific to your system and can restore your computer closer to normal than the Emergency disk.

If your computer won't boot up

If your computer won't boot up — in other words, you turn it on and you receive an error message like `This disk is not bootable` or `Bad or missing command interpreter` instead of a system prompt, place that Emergency disk in the drive and follow these steps:

If you left a disk in the floppy drive when you turned on the computer, it may cause the same `not bootable` error message. Double-check that you haven't left a disk in the floppy drive. If there is a disk in there, remove it and reboot the computer — everything may work again.

1. With the Emergency disk in the floppy drive, turn on your computer.

   If the computer was already on, then press the reset button — if you have one — or press Ctrl+Alt+Del simultaneously to reset the computer. If all else fails, turn the computer off — wait a minute — then turn it back on. The Emergency Disk is bootable and will start your computer.

2. When the Norton Utilities emergency screen appears, you have several choices.

- **Norton Disk Doctor.** Try this if you don't know what you did. (See Chapter 26)

- **Norton Diagnostics.** If you suspect a hardware problem, start here. (See Chapter 25)

- **Disk Editor.** Don't use this unless you *really* know what you're doing. (See Chapter 23)

3. Choose the program you want and follow the instructions in the appropriate chapter.

Also available on the Emergency disk, but not mentioned on the screen, are

✔ Disk Tools — See Chapter 22

You've wiped out your system files — you're getting that `not bootable` message. Or you're getting an `invalid setup` message.

✔ UnFormat — See Chapter 27

You just accidentally formatted your hard disk.

If you've accidentally deleted some files

If your computer works just fine but the problem is you've just wiped out something that you'd rather have back, then you need a quick shot of UnErase, discussed in Chapter 14. To use the Emergency disk to start UnErase:

1. Place the Emergency disk into the floppy drive.

2. Go to the directory on the hard disk that contains the erased files.

3. Type **A:UNERASE** and press Enter.

Go to Chapter 14 for further explanations about using UnErase.

Using the Rescue Disk

Did you create a Rescue Disk as instructed in Chapter 15? Bravo! You should be feeling a little less wonky in the face of a disaster. Hold on tightly to your Rescue Disk and read through Chapter 15 to come back from the brink.

Other programs on the Rescue Disk you may want to use are

- Norton Disk Doctor — See Chapter 26

  This is the one to use to examine and repair the hard disk.

- Disk Tools — See Chapter 22

  You've wiped out your system files — you're getting that `not bootable` message. Or you're getting an `invalid setup` message.

- Norton Diagnostics — See Chapter 25

  If you suspect a hardware problem, start here.

- UnFormat — See Chapter 27

  You just accidentally formatted your hard disk.

Troubleshooting 101

If the computer won't start up, it's pretty easy to interpret that as a computer problem. Most of the time, though, computer problems are a lot more subtle. Determining which Norton utility, if any, can help is a tricky business.

One way to approach a computer situation is to pretend you're playing the game "twenty questions," which, if you don't remember, works by one person asking an opponent a series of differentiating questions to determine what object the opponent is thinking of. Another name for this process is *deductive reasoning.*

Whenever you're troubleshooting, it may help if you assume the persona of your favorite deductive reasoner from TV — you've got lots to choose from, ranging from Perry Mason to Mr. Spock and, for the women, Maddie Hayes to Jessica Fletcher. Although, there's nothing to stop the women from pretending to be Perry Mason and the men from identifying with Jessica Fletcher — as long as it's in the privacy of your own home, I don't think anyone will mind.

Anyway, put yourself in whomever's shoes you want and let's walk through some questions that you need to ask yourself when you find yourself in some kind of serious trouble. You probably won't be able to answer every question — but *anything* you can do to help define the problem helps out.

Is everything plugged in and turned on?

It may seem obvious, but sometimes cleaning people, little children, or an accident of fate can unplug or turn off your devices. Unplug and replug all your connections — especially if you're having problems with things that are plugged into the computer — a printer, for example. Or if you've getting wierd colors on-screen, it could be as simple as a loose video cable.

Are there any error messages?

When something goes wrong, the computer may give you what is known as an *error message*. One error message everyone has seen at one time or another is `Bad command or file name`. You may have enough computer experience to know that means the computer does not understand whatever you've just told it to do. This could be because you simply made a typo, or because the program isn't on the hard disk or is on the hard disk, but the computer can't find it. The point is, when you see this message, you have some idea of what the problem may be. If the computer gave no reaction at all, you wouldn't have a clue what the problem was. So remember that, annoying as they may be, error messages are our friends.

So if something goes wrong — look for an error message and write it down.

You may not know what every error message means and how to respond, but that's okay. Because Norton knows. In DOS, there's the Norton Advisor, which can be accessed from the Norton Utilities menu by pressing Alt+**Help**⇨The Norton Advisor. Use the Search option to call up Figure 21-1. Type in the error message and press Alt+**S**tart Search, and Norton comes up with some helpful advice.

Figure 21-1: Can't exactly remember the error message? Do your best and Norton will do its best to guess the problem and provide a solution.

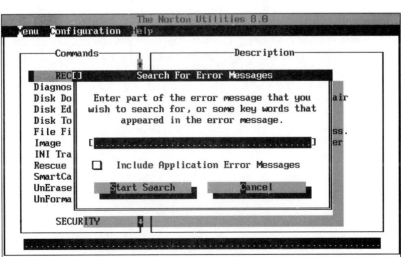

Windows has the INI Advisor, which has its own icon and is covered in Chapter 20 (see Figure 21-2).

Figure 21-2:
If you
Search for
error
messages, a
list of the
most
popular
Windows
problems
appears for
you to select
from.

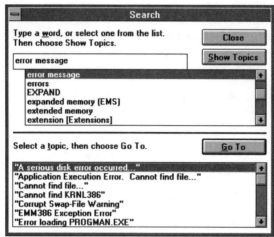

Both The Norton Advisor and the INI Advisor contain a wealth of riddle-solving knowledge that may help pinpoint your problem.

What, exactly, isn't working?

You don't have to know the techno-speak name for what isn't working in your computer. But it's far more helpful to think of the problem as "I can't copy to the floppy drive" rather than as "the computer is broken."

If you don't have a clue what the problem is, another approach is to ask yourself what *is* working. Can you turn the computer on? Does the monitor work? Do you get a system prompt? Can you get into your software? Can you print?

If, after thinking about it some, you determine that it may be a hardware problem, then Norton Diagnostics should help (see Chapter 25). A hard disk problem is best handled by the Norton Disk Doctor (refer to Chapter 26). Is Windows acting up? It's a job for Tracker (see Chapter 19).

Did it ever work?

It's one kind of problem when something that used to function has now decided to take an extended holiday. At least then you can compare what, if anything, has changed since those days when things used to work. You've got a bit more of a blank slate — clue-wise — if the thing never worked in the first place. In either case, running the Norton Diagnostics, which is covered in Chapter 25, may clarify the situation.

Has anything been changed on the computer recently?

More logic at work here. Lots of times adding on to the computer requires a bit of settling in before all the parts are working in harmony. Use the Norton Diagnostics to see if you have any conflicts. Again, read Chapter 25.

How serious is this problem?

Not every problem is a problem.

If your system crashes for no apparent reason but you can get back into your files and everything works, then just chalk it up to life's quirkiness. Maybe make a note of what happened, but don't make a big deal out of it. As Sigmund Freud once said, "Sometimes a cigar is just a cigar." Or in more modern terminology — cleaned up for gentle readers such as yourself — "Stuff happens."

Now, on the other hand, if the system crashes with a regularity that rivals Old Faithful, then you've got the sort of problem that Norton Utilities is dedicated to solving.

What were you doing before the bad thing happened?

The other half of the question is, Can you make the problem happen again? If you can re-create the problem, at least you can have a great starting point for solving the issue. For example, if your system crashes every time you try to spell check a document, then you can call up whoever made the spelling checker and lay your problem at their doorstep.

Chances are, though, that you won't be able to make the problem happen on demand. It is still very helpful to know as much as possible about the environment in which the error occurred. Questions to ask include: What program was I using? Was I in Windows? How many applications were open? How big were the files? Was I doing something different today than I did yesterday? Does the problem happen when I'm not in Windows?

Is there a utility that sounds like my problem?

If you're having a problem defining the problem, you may find that flipping through this book will uncover a Norton Utility that is suited to your situation.

Hardware troubleshooting: A case history

No matter what your computer problem, just ask yourself, "How would Mr. Spock — or whoever your role model is — handle it?"

Recently, when I cranked up a piece of Windows software that I had been using for several weeks, I was suddenly told the program wouldn't run and I got a "not enough memory" error message. That seemed kind of strange, because all the other Windows programs worked just fine. I double-checked the system resources in Windows and there was plenty of memory. As I suspected, memory was not really the problem.

I went through my mental Rolodex and came up with the fact that several days before I had installed a new graphics card. Could there be a connection somehow? I didn't know what the graphics card had to do with "not enough memory," but I did know that the program worked with the old graphics card. After the new graphics card was installed, the program had stopped working.

What I did next was change the video driver setting in Windows back to the setting for the old

graphics card. The program worked — and I'm getting an updated driver from the graphics card company.

Now, maybe you wouldn't have known what a video driver was or how to change it in Windows, but that doesn't matter. In fact, you didn't have to have a scintilla of technical knowledge to understand the most important clue — that the graphics card was the only variable in the situation. Even if you don't know what a graphics card is, in this situation, simple logic directs you to give the graphics card manufacturer a phone call. They would have told you how to do what needed to be done.

Sometimes the first place you call isn't the place with the ultimate solution, but they can point you to who does, because chances are they've seen the problem before and know what to do about it.

The whole point of troubleshooting — as with any good detective show — is to uncover the guilty party.

Chapter 22
Disk Tools

· ·

In This Chapter
▶ Giving a disk the boot
▶ Five-Step Recovery Program
▶ Unglitching a glitched disk
▶ Marking a cluster

· ·

Disk Tools is a program that contains a quartet of programs, which are
connected only by the fact that they've been tossed together under one
menu and given a semi-meaningful group name — Disk Tools.

It's Tool Time!

The first step in using any of the four disk tools is to get into the umbrella Disk
Tools program, shown in Figure 22-1. Getting into the tool box is standard stuff:

> ✔ From the Norton Utilities menu, highlight Disk Tools and press Enter, or
> ✔ From a system prompt, type **DISKTOOL** and press Enter

If you're planning to use one of these tools on a floppy disk, use Norton's
DupeDisk (covered in Chapter 4) or DOS's own DISKCOPY to clone the floppy
disk. That way, you can experiment with these programs on something other
than your one and only floppy. Remember, always have a fallback position.

Giving a disk the boot

The first program — coyly entitled Make a Disk Bootable — makes a disk
bootable. What that means is that the so-called *system files* are copied to a
particular location on the disk-to-be-made-bootable, which turns the ordinary
disk into a disk with the super power to start up the computer. System files are
kind of like the pilot light for the computer.

What it is   What it does

Figure 22-1:
On the left
side of the
window are
the four
programs;
on the right
is a
description
of the
highlighted
program.

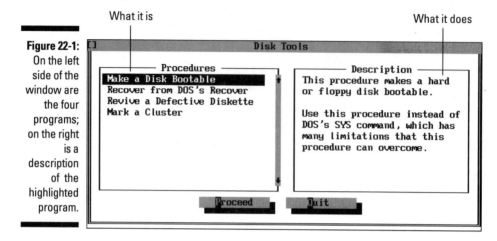

You should have a least a couple of bootable disks sitting around just in case something happens to the system files on your hard disk — unlikely, but it could happen — as discussed in Chapters 15 and 21.

Norton steps you through the process of creating a bootable disk:

1. Get into Disk Tools, as described earlier in the chapter (type **DISKTOOL** and press Enter if in doubt).

2. Highlight Make a Disk Bootable and press Enter.

   You see a dialog box like the one in Figure 22-2, asking which drive contains the disk to made bootable.

Figure 22-2:
Here's
where you
select which
disk gets the
capability to
pull the
computer up
by the
bootstraps.
Just don't
ask what a
bootstrap is.

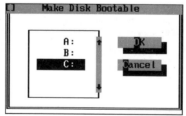

3. Highlight the drive and press Enter.

You'll probably highlight one of the floppy disk drives, like A or B. Drive C is your hard disk and, unless your computer isn't booting, you won't want to choose C.

- After you press Enter, you have nothing to do but sit and watch while Norton scans and copies and does all sorts of stuff. Finally some kind of dialog box pops up to say "all done" and you get to press Enter again.

4. To exit the Disk Tools dialog box, press Esc or Alt+**Quit**.

Five-Step Recovery Program

The second program in Disk Tools — `Recover from DOS s Recover` — is one utility you'll probably *never* use. DOS used to have a program called Recover — which was often mistaken as an undelete command back in the old days. What it really did was screw things up beyond belief.

If you have an older version of DOS and if you used Recover and if you now want to fix what Recover did, then you need `Recover from DOS s Recover`. But you probably don't, didn't, and don't. If you do

1. Get into Disk Tools, as described earlier (type **DISKTOOL** and press Enter, in case you forgot).

2. Highlight `Recover from DOS s Recover` and press Enter.

You get Figure 22-3, the first in a series of warning boxes telling you that the program will only work with Recover files and that Norton's about to wipe out everything. So don't play with this if you don't need it. Okay?

Figure 22-3:
Apparently you can't recover from Norton's Recover from DOS's Recover — so watch it!

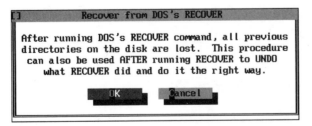

```
[ ]         Recover from DOS's RECOVER
 ┌──────────────────────────────────────────┐
 │ After running DOS's RECOVER command, all previous │
 │ directories on the disk are lost.  This procedure │
 │ can also be used AFTER running RECOVER to UNDO    │
 │    what RECOVER did and do it the right way.      │
 │                                                   │
 │          [   OK   ]      [ Cancel ]               │
 └──────────────────────────────────────────┘
```

3. Click OK or press Enter to continue if you really need to.

4. You see something similar to Figure 22-2, where you select the drive to be tooled and press Enter.

   You get another couple of warnings — press Enter when the words of caution show up.

   Finally, Norton does its thing and puts things back — to some degree. One of the things Norton does when it recovers from Recover is give recovered directories numbers instead of names; you still have to do a tremendous amount of cleanup.

5. To exit the Disk Tools dialog box, press Esc or Alt+**Quit**.

Unglitching a disk

If you get a `sector not found` error message on your floppy disk, then you need `Revive a Defective Diskette`. Who makes up these klutzy program names? (The person who came up with "Revive a Defective Diskette" was doubtless the same person who created "I can't believe it's not butter" and "Gee, your hair smells terrific."

Anyway, Revive basically does the same as what Calibrate does to the hard drive: it performs a nondestructive reformat of the floppy disk (see Chapter 17).

By the way, you can do this as a fun activity if you're bored some long afternoon. It won't hurt your floppy or the data on it.

1. Get into Disk Tools, as described earlier (type **DISKTOOL** and press Enter to get to first base).

2. Highlight `Revive a Defective Diskette` and press Enter.

   You get something along the lines of Figure 22-2.

3. Highlight the drive you want to Revive and press Alt+**OK**.

   You see Figure 22-4 as the disk is being reformatted.

4. To exit the Disk Tools dialog box, press Esc or Alt+**Quit**.

Marking a cluster

The last disk tool is called `Mark a Cluster`. It's another one to be careful about using. If you spill it on the carpet, you're in big trouble.

Figure 22-4:
The count slowly moves forward as a disk is reformatted... or should I say Revived?

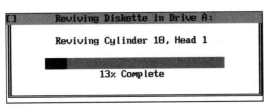

Here's the bad news: there are flaws and bad spots on your hard drive. The good news is that the manufacturer of the drive already knows about it and has notified the computer about those imperfections so that they won't be used for storing data.

The way the manufacturers cover the bad spots is not with Clearasil. What they do is mark the clusters as bad. You, too, can mark clusters as bad if you know the cluster number.

Now, you can do this by hand or let the Norton Disk Doctor handle bad clusters automatically (as described in Chapter 26). Please don't mark clusters as bad unless you know, for sure, what you're doing.

If Mark a Cluster finds data sitting precariously on a chunk of bad real estate, it cleverly moves the data to a safe place before branding the cluster as bad.

If you want to proceed, you must know the cluster number. This information can come from one of the other Norton diagnostic programs, or, in some cases, even from the manufacturer itself.

If you have the cluster numbers to be marked, then here we go:

1. Get into Disk Tools, as described earlier (type **DISKTOOL** and press Enter if in doubt).

2. Press Enter or Alt+**OK** at the Christmas greeting.

3. Finally, you get Figure 22-5 and the chance to actually do something. Type the cluster numbers to be marked and press Alt+**OK**.

   Eventually, you get a confirmation dialog box. Press Enter.

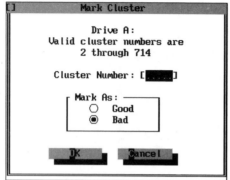

Figure 22-5:
One bad
cluster can
spoil the
whole
bunch!

4. After all the clusters are marked, exit the Disk Tools dialog box and then press Esc or Alt+**Quit**.

Tooling Around — The Shortcut

Because of the Disk Tools setup, you are forced to travel through several layers of dialog boxes before arriving at the actual command. Although we can't completely wipe out dialog boxes, we can at least speed things up a smidge. After all, those first few minutes are critical when a disk has gone down:

✔ **DISKTOOL /MAKEBOOT**

Creates a bootable disk.

✔ **DISKTOOL /REVIVE**

Why drives end up in wacky sizes

You may have noticed that when you purchase a 250MB hard drive, you end up with a 253MB — or some other odd number — hard drive. That's because the manufacturers make drives bigger than necessary because they expect to lose some of the space to bad spots. All manufacturers test their drives and mark out the bad spots before you get them because it is simply impractical to make truly perfect drives. So you get a little extra space instead.

Chapter 23

Disk Editor

● ●

In This Chapter

▶ How to stay out of trouble by not using Disk Editor

● ●

*T*his chapter is all about not using Disk Editor.

Actually, in all fairness, Disk Editor's Advanced Recovery Mode would put the Betty Ford Clinic to shame. Disk Editor can retrieve files from unsalvageable situations. However, it's not a program that you should try.

Read on.

If you're in the middle of a disaster and you need rescuing, try Norton Disk Doctor, Norton Diagnostics, Disk Tools, Rescue Disk, or the religion of your choice — but don't use Disk Editor.

First, don't confuse Disk Editor with the term *text editor*. They are not remotely the same. Disk Editor is not a word processing program like DOS's Edit command or any other normal editing program. Disk Editor lets you actually edit the hard drive — move clusters and so forth, like a super Manual UnErase times ten. It lets you gather bits and pieces of information and assists you in pulling together lost data — and more. In the process, though, you can implode your directory structure.

Unlike the other Norton Utilities — engineered so that most of the really hard decisions are made for you by the program — Disk Editor assumes you know gobs and gobs of stuff about your computer and endows you with the ability to override safety systems and get into things humans were not meant to tamper with. It's a program that's best left to professionals.

Use Disk Editor only when you have nothing left to lose!

If you don't believe me, let's take a quick look-see inside Disk Editor so that you'll know what I'm talking about.

To start Disk Editor, use one of the following:

- ✔ From the Norton Utilities menu, highlight Disk Editor and press Enter, or
- ✔ From a system prompt, type **DISKEDIT** and press Enter

The first message you get from Disk Editor (see Figure 23-1) lets you know that you can't do any harm — or good — until you change a setting in the **Tools** ➪ Configuration menu.

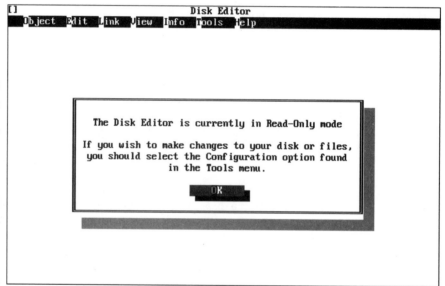

Figure 23-1:
Even Norton knows how dangerous Disk Edit is and disallows dilettantes from accidentally mucking up the works.

Of course, once you're actually in the program, you end up with something like Figure 23-2.

Finally, Disk Editor shows us what a file looks like to the computer (see in Figure 23-3).

There's more — lots more — but I think we get the idea here that Disk Editor isn't for us.

To exit, press Esc, or press Alt+F4, or double-click the close box. If you're asked, confirm that you want to leave by pressing Enter and clicking OK.

Satisfied?

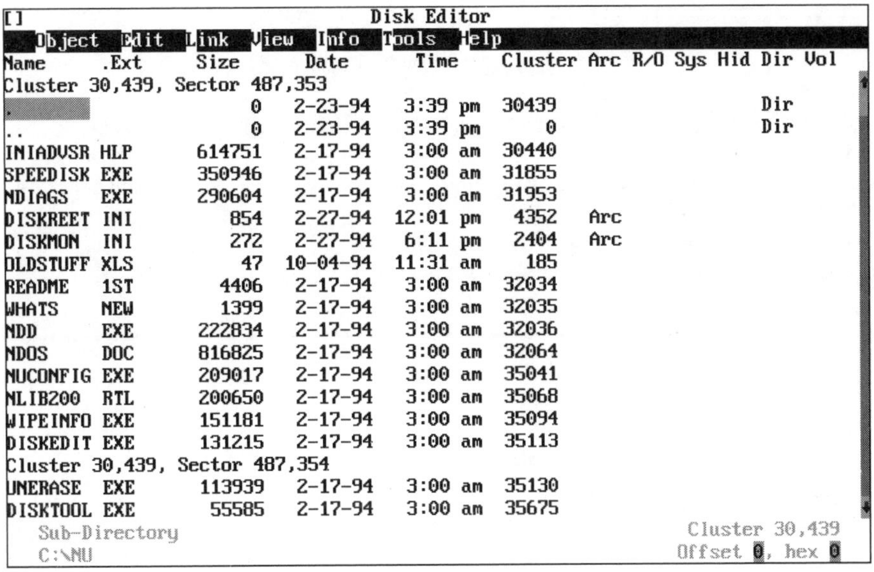

```
[]                          Disk Editor
    Object  Edit  Link  View  Info  Tools  Help
Name    .Ext     Size      Date      Time    Cluster Arc R/O Sys Hid Dir Vol
Cluster 30,439, Sector 487,353
.                        0    2-23-94   3:39 pm   30439                  Dir
..                       0    2-23-94   3:39 pm       0                  Dir
INIADVSR HLP        614751   2-17-94   3:00 am   30440
SPEEDISK EXE        350946   2-17-94   3:00 am   31855
NDIAGS   EXE        290604   2-17-94   3:00 am   31953
DISKREET INI           854   2-27-94  12:01 pm    4352   Arc
DISKMON  INI           272   2-27-94   6:11 pm    2404   Arc
OLDSTUFF XLS            47  10-04-94  11:31 am     185
README   1ST          4406   2-17-94   3:00 am   32034
WHATS    NEW          1399   2-17-94   3:00 am   32035
NDD      EXE        222834   2-17-94   3:00 am   32036
NDOS     DOC        816825   2-17-94   3:00 am   32064
NUCONFIG EXE        209017   2-17-94   3:00 am   35041
NLIB200  RTL        200650   2-17-94   3:00 am   35068
WIPEINFO EXE        151181   2-17-94   3:00 am   35094
DISKEDIT EXE        131215   2-17-94   3:00 am   35113
Cluster 30,439, Sector 487,354
UNERASE  EXE        113939   2-17-94   3:00 am   35130
DISKTOOL EXE         55585   2-17-94   3:00 am   35675
    Sub-Directory                              Cluster 30,439
    C:\NU                                      Offset 0, hex 0
```

Figure 23-2: Are we having fun yet?

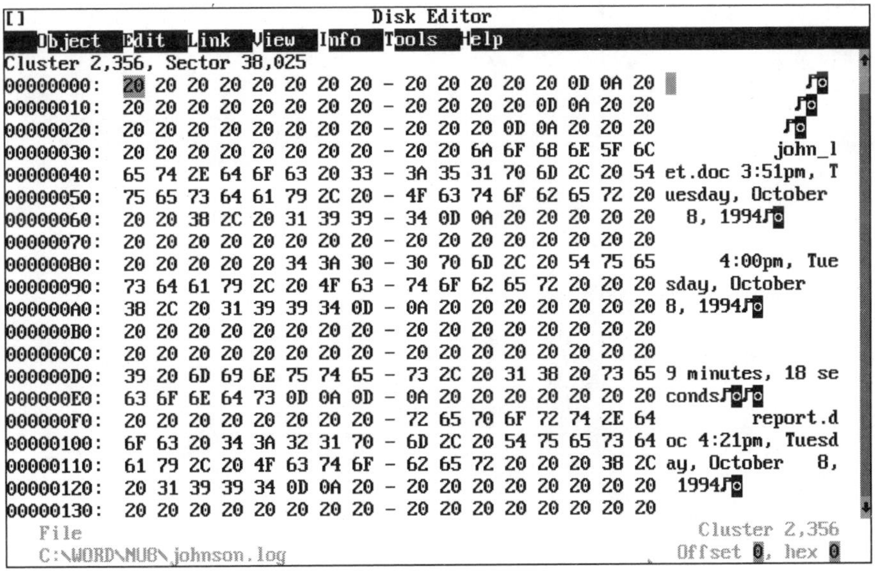

```
[]                          Disk Editor
    Object  Edit  Link  View  Info  Tools  Help
Cluster 2,356, Sector 38,025
00000000:  20 20 20 20 20 20 20 20 - 20 20 20 20 20 0D 0A 20
00000010:  20 20 20 20 20 20 20 20 - 20 20 20 20 0D 0A 20 20
00000020:  20 20 20 20 20 20 20 20 - 20 20 20 0D 0A 20 20 20
00000030:  20 20 20 20 20 20 20 20 - 20 20 6A 6F 68 6E 5F 6C        john_l
00000040:  65 74 2E 64 6F 63 20 33 - 3A 35 31 70 6D 2C 20 54   et.doc 3:51pm, T
00000050:  75 65 73 64 61 79 2C 20 - 4F 63 74 6F 62 65 72 20   uesday, October
00000060:  20 20 38 2C 20 31 39 39 - 34 0D 0A 20 20 20 20 20      8, 1994
00000070:  20 20 20 20 20 34 3A 30 - 30 70 6D 2C 20 54 75 65
00000080:  20 20 20 20 20 34 3A 30 - 30 70 6D 2C 20 54 75 65         4:00pm, Tue
00000090:  73 64 61 79 2C 20 4F 63 - 74 6F 62 65 72 20 20 20   sday, October
000000A0:  38 2C 20 31 39 39 34 0D - 0A 20 20 20 20 20 20 20   8, 1994
000000B0:  20 20 20 20 20 20 20 20 - 20 20 20 20 20 20 20 20
000000C0:  20 20 20 20 20 20 20 20 - 20 20 20 20 20 20 20 20
000000D0:  39 20 6D 69 6E 75 74 65 - 73 2C 20 31 38 20 73 65   9 minutes, 18 se
000000E0:  63 6F 6E 64 73 0D 0A 0D - 0A 20 20 20 20 20 20 20   conds
000000F0:  20 20 20 20 20 20 20 20 - 72 65 70 6F 72 74 2E 64          report.d
00000100:  6F 63 20 34 3A 32 31 70 - 6D 2C 20 54 75 65 73 64   oc 4:21pm, Tuesd
00000110:  61 79 2C 20 4F 63 74 6F - 62 65 72 20 20 20 38 2C   ay, October    8,
00000120:  20 31 39 39 34 0D 0A 20 - 20 20 20 20 20 20 20 20    1994
00000130:  20 20 20 20 20 20 20 20 - 20 20 20 20 20 20 20 20
    File                                       Cluster 2,356
    C:\WORD\NUB\ johnson.log                   Offset 0, hex 0
```

Figure 23-3: A simple file up close and personal — thanks to Disk Editor.

Greetings from the President

According to a book called *Information USA* by Matthew Lesko—which is now on-line, thanks to CompuServe—the President of the United States will send you a greeting card if you're celebrating either your 50th wedding anniversary or your 80th birthday. Just send a request at least a month before the date to: Presidential Correspondence, Old Executive Office Building, Room 94, Washington, DC 20500. You also can call 202-456-7639.

This has nothing to do with computers, Norton Utilities in general, or Disk Editor in particular. I just thought it was neat.

Chapter 24

File Fix

*T*he tell-tale signs are obvious — disinterest in schoolwork, lack of appetite, a bunch of strange new friends. This can mean only one thing — yes, your files have become corrupted! Don't take it personally: it can happen to the best of us. Power outages, system resets at the wrong moment, failing hard disks, and a lack of family values all lead to the corruption of our data files.

One of the unmistakable signs that your *data file* — that's computerspeak for the file that contains your work — has become corrupted is when the application software balks at your request to open the file. Maybe you're even getting error messages like `Don t recognize that file` or `Not a whatever file` or even `Invalid something or other`. In extreme cases, when you try to open the file, rather than you get a bunch of happy faces words or numbers on the screen!

If you have a glitch with a WordPerfect file, a spreadsheet file, or a database file, File Fix does its best to look inside, analyze what's wrong, and pull it back together.

The neighborhood watch

Sometimes a corrupted file is a hint from the computer that things are not going well. If the file wasn't corrupted during a power outage or something, it's a good idea to look for a larger disaster. In other words, look beyond fixing that one file and start scouting the neighborhood to discover the underlying causes for the corruption. Also, it wouldn't hurt to go to yellow alert and take some self-defense actions.

✔ Run Norton Disk Doctor (covered in Chapter 26) or, at least, Calibrate (discussed in Chapter 17) to make sure that the corruption wasn't caused by a hard drive problem.

✔ You also may want to get into Disk Monitor — covered in Chapter 29 — on the off-chance that the corruption was caused by a virus.

Of course, anytime bad things happen is a good time to back up the hard drive. You never know when a funny little problem will trigger the end of the world. Also, when backing up in a situation like this, use a fresh set of backup disks or a new tape: don't overwrite your most recent good backup with a set of suspect data.

Fundamental File Fixing

No matter what kind of file you want to fix, the process starts out the same:

1. Get to the File Fix dialog box, shown in Figure 24-1, by using one of the following methods:

    • From the Norton Utilities menu, highlight File Fix and press Enter, or

    • From a system prompt, type **FILEFIX** and press Enter, or

     • From Windows, in the Norton DOS Utilities DOS group, click the File Fix icon

Figure 24-1:
The opening File Fix dialog box asks you to choose the type of file you're hoping to restore.

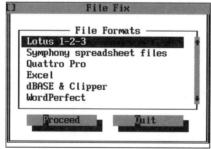

2. Highlight the program that originally created the broken file and press Enter.

   If your file does not belong to any of the programs listed in Figure 24-1, then File Fix won't work for you. If your data file belongs to a program that's compatible with one of those listed, then you're in the money. Otherwise, sorry.

3. Type the name of the file you want to repair, as in Figure 24-2, and press Enter or click OK.

   If when you start File Fix, you're not in the directory containing the corrupted file, you have to type the name of the directory as well as the name of the file.

Enter the name of the file to be fixed here   Then click OK

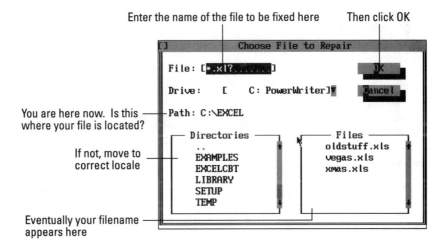

Figure 24-2: Before File Fix can go to work, it has to know what file you want to repair.

You are here now. Is this where your file is located?

If not, move to correct locale

Eventually your filename appears here

If you can't remember either the name of the directory or the file, use the Directories box to browse the hard drive until you run across the file. Remember, those two dots (..) mean go up one level on the hard disk. Keep scanning the Files box for the file you need to correct.

4. In the Repair dialog box, something like Figure 24-3, type a new filename that you want to assign to the repaired file and click the **B**egin button — or press Alt+**B**egin.

   The reason for this is that File Fix actually doesn't repair the original file. File Fix inspects the original file and then creates a new file — giving it the name you just typed — with its best repair job. The original file is not touched. That way, if the File Fix attempt doesn't work this time, you can try again.

- The Repair dialog box differs according to the type of file being repaired. However, the process is the same — whatever File Fix can recover from the defective file is placed inside the new file.

- Also, within the Repair dialog box is a Repair Mode section, which differs greatly depending on the type of file you're trying to repair. For now, go with the default setting, which is your best bet anyway. If the default doesn't work, then try one of the others, which are outlined in the following sections.

Figure 24-3:
A sample Repair dialog box. It looks different when dealing with WordPerfect or database files, but you still have to enter a filename and choose a repair mode.

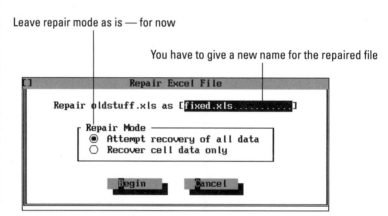

Leave repair mode as is — for now

You have to give a new name for the repaired file

5. File Fix may offer to print a report of what it's doing, as in Figure 24-4. Make sure that you press Alt+No Report — to avoid getting a long list of cluster and sector numbers — and then continue.

Figure 24-4:
The report File Fix prints out for you is detailed beyond sanity. It's far more pleasant to go the No Report route.

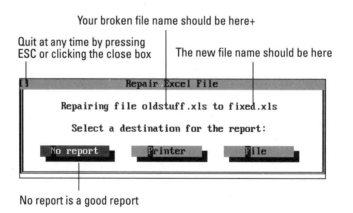

Your broken file name should be here+

Quit at any time by pressing ESC or clicking the close box

The new file name should be here

No report is a good report

6. If all goes well, you get a message saying File Fix is finished. Then click OK or press Enter.

7. Start your application and see whether the fixed file — that's the file with the *new* filename — comes up.

   If the new file is still unintelligible, follow Steps 1-3 and then jump to the appropriate section later in the chapter for more specific details on the type of file you're attempting to repair.

There are a jillion ways a file can go wrong, and File Fix cannot repair everything. Always back up your important work so that if a file gets defused, you've got a recent version to go back to.

Salvaging spreadsheet files

If you've followed the basic instructions and your spreadsheet file is still DOA, try using the `Recover cell data only` option in the Repair Mode box from Step 3. This method may at least recover the numbers and stuff in the cells. The new file may look like garbage, but you'll have *something*.

Warming up WordPerfect files

Assuming that you've still found no satisfaction in repairing your WordPerfect file by using the `Recover Document` Repair mode in Step 4, then it's time to try the `Review Start of Document` mode and take a trip down the rabbit hole. (Remember the repair modes differ between Word Perfect or database files.)

Once you choose this option, you have three more choices, all dealing with the stuff that you normally never see at the beginning of your file. This area at the beginning of the file — which Norton calls a *prefix* — contains all the stats and specs for your file. If the prefix of the file is corrupted, your file basically doesn't know who it is. It has amnesia. So we have to restore its memory.

✔ `Repair document offset`

   This is where you try to bring all the file's memory back. Unless you've got lots of links to other files and complicated formatting in your document, don't bother with this option.

✔ `Build simple file prefix`

   This is the default — and your simplest and safest option.

✔ `Import file prefix`

   File Fix can copy the prefix of another WordPerfect file and stick it on top of the current one. It's worth a try. You have to give File Fix the name of a WordPerfect file to use, but that shouldn't be too hard.

Once you've made your selection, click on Begin or press Alt+**B**egin.

After your file has been repaired, try calling up the file by using the new name. Assuming you get in, you may see a lot of * * B A D * * sprinkled throughout the file. File Fix is not commenting on the merits of the file. Rather, File Fix is just alerting you to areas that it knows are messed up.

Don't forget that you may have an automatically created BAK file sitting around on your disk someplace. A BAK file is the next-to-most recent version of your file. Even if BAK files aren't listed when you go to pull up a file, they are there nonetheless. If a file called REPORT became corrupted, try loading REPORT.BAK. You could get lucky.

Redoing database files

Database files have their own set of problems. If you've been inputting data into a database that someone else set up, don't try to fix the corrupted database. Let the person who set it up deal with it. You have to have some familiarity with the database's structure to perform Fix attempts beyond the basics.

However, if you want to try, it won't hurt anything because File Fix doesn't change the original corrupted file.

If the Fully automatic Repair mode from Step 4 didn't do the trick, you have to try one of the other selections.

✔ Review damaged records

   File Fix goes through the records in the database, occasionally asking for help from you when it hits something beyond its capability to fix.

✔ Review all records

   File Fix shows you each record in the database, giving you a chance to Accept, Reject, or fiddle with it to some degree.

File Fix also may ask you about the file header in your database. You can't have a database file without it. File Fix gives you the chance to Revise the damaged one. The easiest approach is to transplant — copy, actually — another database's header and then revise it. Try to pick another database that comes close to matching the structure of the one you're fixing.

Some database programs come equipped with self-repair options. Be sure to give them a try first because they probably have a better chance to repair the file than File Fix. No disrespect to File Fix, but the manufacturer of your database has a more intimate knowledge of how its own software works — and what can go wrong. Anyway, it's certainly worth a try.

Chapter 25

Norton Diagnostics

● ●

In This Chapter

▶ Making friends with Norton Diagnostics

▶ What's new in Norton Diagnostics

▶ Printing a report

▶ NDiag shortcuts

● ●

*W*henever you have a problem in life, it's nice to be able to talk with someone to get a fresh perspective — an objective point of view. If you're experiencing difficulties with your computer, the Norton Diagnostics (NDiags) can give an unbiased opinion about what's going on with your hardware. Basically, Norton Diagnostics runs tests on everything in your computer, from mouse to modem, and lets you know what's up.

As the name implies, Norton Diagnostics doesn't fix anything — it just methodically puts your computer's systems through their paces and reports the results back to you. In other words, NDiags lets you know whether anything is broken. This is particularly helpful when something just isn't going right and you don't know whether the problem is hardware, software, or wetware — that is, you.

When might NDiags come in handy? Well, mostly when something's not working correctly. Whenever things aren't going right, the first question to ask is, "Hardware, software, or pilot error?" NDiags can answer as to whether you're having a problem with the physical hook up — the hardware.

Consider an example. Suppose that you just bought a joystick and the thing doesn't work. Is it a bad joystick? Or did you install the software correctly? Run NDiags and find out whether it *sees* that a joystick is attached. If it does see the joystick, you know the problem is the software, and you can concentrate your troubleshooting efforts in that direction. Isn't that neat?

On the other hand, if you've just installed a new joystick — or a CD-ROM or sound card — and it's not working, you'll need to know about Norton's new IRQ testing. You don't have to know much about an IRQ, except that everything that hooks up to your computer needs its own unique one — and there are a finite number of them to hand out. Norton Diagnostics will help pinpoint situations where two devices are fighting over the same IRQ and provide options. If you're one of those about to take your shiny new multimedia kit back to the store because it won't work, check this out first.

You also can use NDiags another way. It can be set to run all its diagnostic tests in a continuous loop — for hours and hours — as a way of checking out a system. Although this sort of activity is mostly designed for professionals who need to test systems brought to them for repair, it's something you may want to use if your computer is new. You see, if your computer's a lemon, you'll know within the first 30 days of use. One way to accelerate that discovery is by running the continuous cycle of testing — known as *burning in* to computer professionals.

There are two things you need to understand about NDiags at this point — you don't have to know a serial port from a graphics card to run NDiags. As long as you can select Next, you'll be brilliant.

Granted, the information NDiags deals in is technical and esoteric — I mean, who cares about their UARTS and their CMOS, right? But the best time to take an introductory tour is now — when everything is working. Later, if things go bad — knock on wood — then at least you know what NDiags is and you'll feel more comfortable going back to it for help.

Although NDiags tests the hard drive, it does not test the stuff *on* the drive — the files themselves. That sort of testing is covered by Norton Disk Doctor (refer to Chapter 26).

If you're a hardware junkie, you'll be interested to know that Norton Utilities has added a couple more tests in this new version. In addition to the IRQ status test mentioned before, NDiags provides a video attribute test and a test for joysticks.

Getting an X-Ray

As mentioned just a moment ago, using Norton Diagnostics is a snap. Because NDiags looks kind of overwhelming, a roadmap to what we'll be in doing in this chapter goes like this:

- ✔ Get into NDiags.
- ✔ Start the test cycle or choose the test you want to run.
- ✔ If one of your systems fails the diagnostics, press F1 — for help — to find out what, if anything, to do about it.

That's about it in a nutshell.

Now we'll walk through it step-by-step:

1. To start the Norton Diagnostics, use one of the following methods:

    • From the Norton Utilities menu, highlight Norton Diagnostics and press Enter, or

    • From a system prompt, type **NDIAGS** and press Enter

2. Press Enter — or click **OK** to get past the first Description message.

    Every time you do something in NDiags, a message automatically appears, telling you about the selection you've made. If you don't want to see these informative screens, just press Alt+**D**isable Intro. Messages.

    NDiags takes a few seconds to determine your system contents, and then another jargon-filled description screen appears.

    In that first description screen, Norton Diagnostics asks that you unplug your modem and printer so that they don't foul up the testing. If you want, you can ignore that directive as long as you go into the options and disable those tests — as we'll do shortly.

3. Press Enter — or click **OK** — to get past the second Description message and on to Figure 25-1.

Either select a test

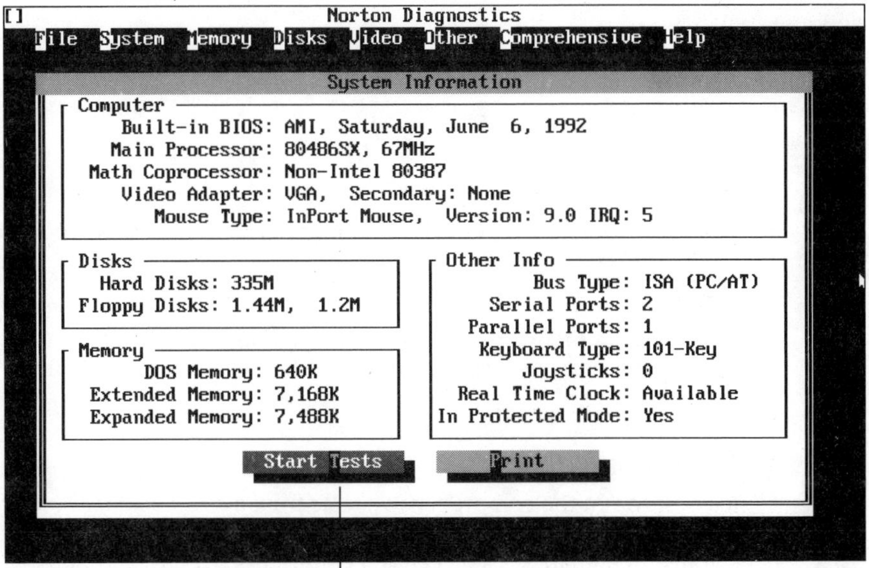

Figure 25-1:
No, we didn't screw up. It may *say* System Information, but this *is* Norton Diagnostics. NDiags and SI (see Chapter 13) just happen to share the same opening screen — isn't that a kick?

```
[]                          Norton Diagnostics
  File  System  Memory  Disks  Video  Other  Comprehensive  Help
┌──────────────────────── System Information ─────────────────────────┐
│  ┌ Computer ─────────────────────────────────────────────────────┐  │
│  │     Built-in BIOS: AMI, Saturday, June  6, 1992                │  │
│  │    Main Processor: 80486SX, 67MHz                              │  │
│  │  Math Coprocessor: Non-Intel 80387                            │  │
│  │     Video Adapter: VGA,   Secondary: None                     │  │
│  │        Mouse Type: InPort Mouse,  Version: 9.0 IRQ: 5         │  │
│  └───────────────────────────────────────────────────────────────┘  │
│  ┌ Disks ─────────────────┐   ┌ Other Info ──────────────────────┐  │
│  │  Hard Disks: 335M      │   │        Bus Type: ISA (PC/AT)     │  │
│  │ Floppy Disks: 1.44M,  1.2M │ │    Serial Ports: 2              │  │
│  └────────────────────────┘   │  Parallel Ports: 1               │  │
│  ┌ Memory ────────────────┐   │  Keyboard Type: 101-Key          │  │
│  │    DOS Memory: 640K     │   │      Joysticks: 0                │  │
│  │ Extended Memory: 7,168K │   │ Real Time Clock: Available       │  │
│  │ Expanded Memory: 7,488K │   │ In Protected Mode: Yes           │  │
│  └────────────────────────┘   └──────────────────────────────────┘  │
│            ┌ Start Tests ┐          ┌ Print ┐                        │
└──────────────────────────────────────────────────────────────────────┘
```

Or cycle through them all

At this point, you could select from any of the menus at the top of the screen and choose a test to perform — a roadmap of tests available follows this paragraph. You could even just press Alt+Start Tests and have Norton start automatically cycling through all the tests. But the best thing to do first is to exercise a modicum of willpower by visiting the configuration options in the next section.

To fully understand what all these computer system components are and what they do, you would need at least a whole other book about the personal computers. Naturally, there's a *PCs for Dummies*, which can introduce you to some of this stuff, if you care to investigate further.

File menu

The File menu is where the setup stuff is handled, like options, configuration — covered in "Configuring NDiags" in the next section — and the type of reports you want to receive.

System

Choose System to see System Information and to run a test on the main system board, the various ports where you plug in your printer or modem, the CMOS battery (see Chapter 15 for more on CMOS batteries), and IRQ Status.

Memory

You can order various memory tests to determine whether your memory chips are okay.

Disks

Test your hard disk and floppy disks.

Video

A number of tests are available here for your video card and your monitor.

Other

This tests your mouse and speaker (a fun thing to try, even if you haven't yet turned your computer into a multimedia center), as well as your keyboard and joystick.

Comprehensive

It's best to run the comprehensive tests from a *clean boot disk* (see Chapter 1 for information on what a clean boot disk is, if you've forgotten, or — ahem — skipped that chapter). You can run Calibrate (covered in Chapter 17), a memory test, and a bunch of UART tests.

UART the apple of my eye

Okay, we mentioned it twice — what's a UART? It stands for Universal Asynchronous Receive/ Transmitter. Duh. It's a technical thing, as you might have gathered, an electronic elf that takes data traveling in parallel formation and turns it into a single-file data stream. If this doesn't explain what a UART does, it should at least cure you from wanting to know. It's included so that if you're having problems with your modem, you have a place to start.

Configuring NDiags

Once you're in Figure 25-1, you can instruct NDiags about how your system is set up so that you don't get a bunch of unnecessary reminder screens. Just take a quick look at Figure 25-2 to see the Options screen, and you'll see what this is all about.

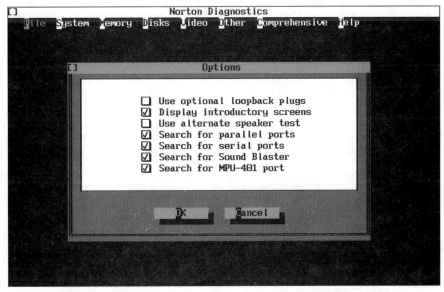

Figure 25-2: The Alt+File ⇨ **O**ptions screen lets you modify NDiags' efforts.

To get to the Options screen

1. Press Alt+**F**ile ⇨ **O**ptions.

2. Select or deselect the options to taste.

- Special note — if you don't want to disconnect your printer or external modem, deselect the Search for Parallel Ports and Search of Serial Ports options.
- Didn't buy the loopback plugs? Make sure the option is deselected. Don't know what a loopback plug *is*? See the story on those little guys at the end of this chapter.
- You can disable all those description screens by deselecting Display Introductory Screens.

3. Press Alt+**O**K when you're satisfied.

   You go back to Figure 25-1.

Now, go ahead and choose a test from the menu at the top, or if you're a little shy, press Alt+Start **T**ests to have Norton get the ball rolling.

REMEMBER

You can stop Norton from diagnosing by pressing Esc or selecting Cancel.

Finding the new stuff

TECHNICAL STUFF

If you're experienced with NDiags and just want to see the new stuff, look under Alt+**F**ile to find Interrupt Configuration and Burnin Report. Under Alt+**S**ystem, you'll discover the IRQ Status test (see Figure 25-3). Press Alt+**V**ideo to find the new Attribute Test. You can find the joystick testing by pressing Alt+**O**ther. Finally, the Advanced UART tests are in the **C**omprehensive menu. Oh, note that in the System Information, Other Info box is — instead of a Keyboard Command Set — a report on Joysticks.

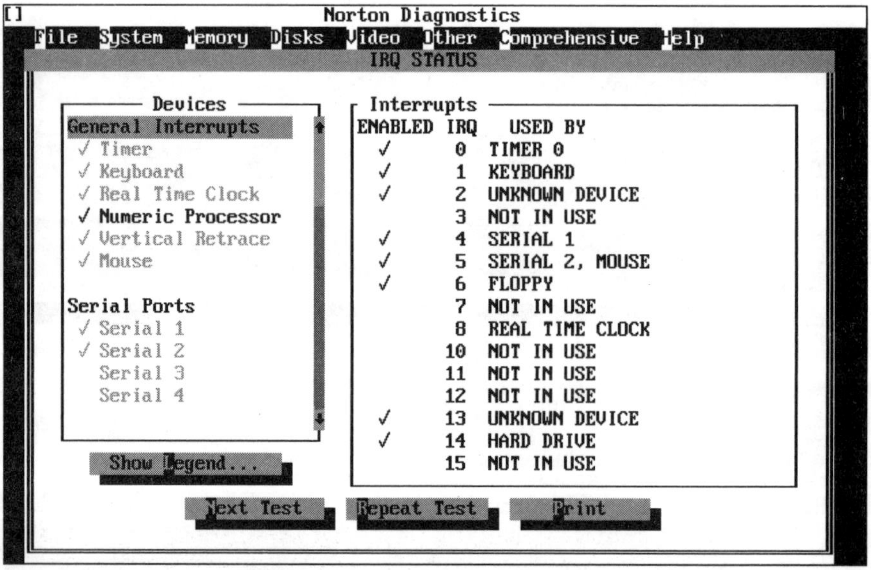

Figure 25-3: Where is it and whose got it? The New IRQ Status screen provides some illumination on this frustrating topic.

Zigging, Zagging, and N-Diagging

We're not going through every single little test and option here in NDiag-land — once you start testing, there are very few things to do besides move along to the next test. And remember F1 for Help is always a key press away — as in Figure 25-4.

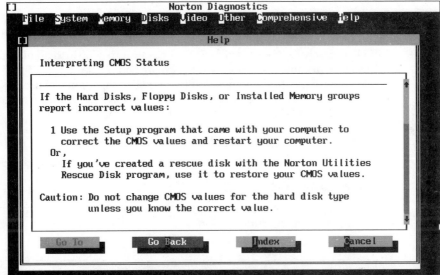

Figure 25-4: While in the Alt+**S**ystem ⇨ **CMOS** Status screen, pressing F1 delivers a typical help screen explaining what to do.

Another fun test is the Hard Disk test, shown in Figure 25-5, which measures the RPMs of the hard drive.

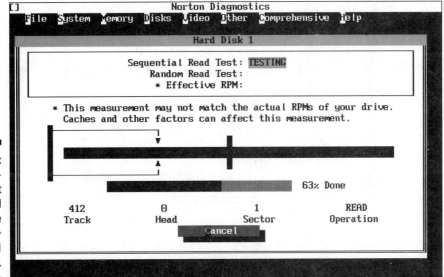

Figure 25-5: A cool-looking test of the hard drive in the Alt+**D**isks ⇨ Hard disk **1** test.

Printing a Report

One of my favorite things about this program is that in the opening screen it yells at you to disconnect your printer. Then after you've run a test, NDiags offers to print out a report of the test. Hello! Mr. Norton, sir! Am I missing something here? If we disconnected the printer, how are we supposed to print out a report?

I mean, really.

Well, one way around this is to print the report to a file instead of to the printer. Basically, printing the report to a file creates on the hard disk a file that contains the diagnostics' findings. After you quit NDiags, you can use your word processor, DOS's EDIT command, or even Norton's Line Print (explained in Chapter 34) to print it out.

Anytime you're in an NDiag screen where Print is an option, proceed as follows to print out a report:

1. Press Alt+**P**rint.

    You see a screen something like the one in Figure 25-6, where I'm planning to print an IRQ Status report.

Figure 25-6: Print the results of any, diagnostic for later review with the **P**rint command.

2. Press Alt+**File**

3. When asked, type a spiffy name for the report.

   Norton suggests a title — NDIAGS.RPT. If that's good enough, press Alt+**OK**. If you hate that, type in something else.

Taking NDiag Shortcuts

Of course, if you need instant gratification, you can order up a diagnostic straight from the command line, as follows:

- **NDIAGS /AUTO**

  Same as Start Tests in NDiags, except this only runs all the automatic tests — you know, no *keyboard press* tests or any of the others that require something from you.

- **NDIAGS /NOSEARCH**

  Tells NDiags not to determine the system contents at the beginning of the program.

Loopback plugs

Loopback plugs were mentioned earlier in this chapter, and now it's time to clarify what the heck a loopback plug is. Loopback plugs are plastic and metal caps that fit on the parallel port (where the printer is usually plugged in) and the serial port. When NDiags knows those plugs are in place, it sends a message out the port — which is echoed back by the loopback plug. Depending on the echo, NDiags can tell whether everything is functional with those ports. Since modems and printers don't talk back to Norton, they are useless for testing purposes. The loopback plugs can help answer questions like — Is it the computer or the printer that's the problem?

Crummy keyboards and de-energizer dust bunnies

Even if you live in Howard Hughes-certified clean rooms, debris will somehow, mysteriously, find its way inside your computer and into your keyboard. Debris, after all, never sleeps. It's a good idea to invest in a can of industrial strength air and blow out the accumulated flotsam and jetsam from your keyboard and computer every now and again. If you don't, just remember when a dust bunny finally turns on you that it can get pretty nasty.

The 5th Wave

By Rich Tennant

"YO-I THINK WE'VE GOT A NEW KIND OF VIRUS HERE!"

Chapter 26

Norton Disk Doctor for DOS and Windows

● ●

In This Chapter

▶ Using Norton Disk Doctor in DOS

▶ Using Norton Disk Doctor for Windows

▶ Installing Options in DOS or Windows

● ●

*N*orton Disk Doctor (NDD) is the program that makes your hard disk stick out its tongue and say, "Ahhh."

Norton Disk Doctor is so easy to run that you'll conduct a checkup a lot more often than once a year. In fact, a lot of people have things set up so that every time the computer is turned on, the disk gets a thorough exam. And the new Norton Disk Doctor for Windows seems to be the perfect program for hypochondriacs, because it can run in the background — continuously checking the health of the hard drive.

The way Norton Disk Doctor works, whether using the DOS or Windows version, follows these basic steps:

1. Run the Norton Disk Doctor program.

2. Watch for messages from NDD about the hard drive.

3. Say "yes" to whatever NDD suggests.

Just because you mostly work in Windows these days, don't toss aside the notion of using Norton Disk Doctor for DOS. It may be very helpful to include NDD as a start-up program and let it conduct a quick diagnostic whenever the computer is booted up.

Running a Checkup — In DOS

Getting a physical in DOS is almost a matter of simply pressing Enter a couple of times.

1. To get Norton Disk Doctor up and going (see Figure 26-1), use either of the following methods:

   • From the Norton Utilities menu, highlight Disk Doctor and press Enter, or

   • From a system prompt, type **NDD** and press Enter

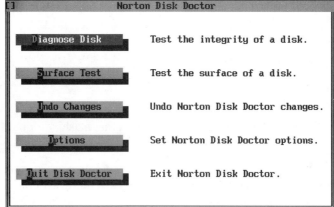

Figure 26-1:
The Norton
Disk Doctor
for DOS
opening
menu.

2. Choose Alt+Diagnose Disk by pressing Enter.

3. When asked to select a drive to diagnose, highlight the drive of your choice and press the spacebar — and then press Enter to kick the action into gear.

   You see a series of tests being performed, as in Figure 26-2.

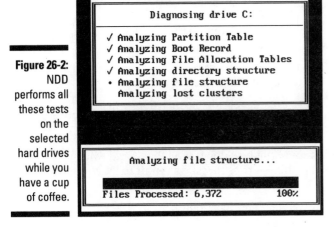

Figure 26-2:
NDD performs all these tests on the selected hard drives while you have a cup of coffee.

4. Eventually, NDD asks whether you want to perform a Surface Test — press Enter to start that test. It'll take a little while, so be patient.

5. When the test is finished, NDD has to give you a summary of what it did — Norton loves producing reports!

6. Back at the main menu, press Alt+**Q**uit to exit.

Getting a bad checkup

Fortunately, really, really bad checkups are very rare. NDD may occasionally find something to complain about, as in Figure 26-3, but for the most part, all you have to do is agree with whatever the doctor recommends.

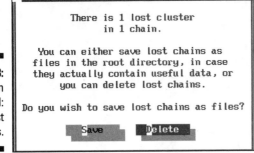

Figure 26-3:
As common as the cold: lost clusters.

1. When NDD notifies you of an error, go along with whatever is recommended. Just say yes.

2. If NDD offers to create an Undo disk during the recovery process, say yes to that option as well.

   You can use the Undo Disk to put things back if, for some very strange reason, you don't like what NDD did to fix the problem.

3. Specify that you want to create an Undo file on a floppy disk, so that nothing you might want to resuscitate from the hard drive will be wiped out accidentally.

   Dr. Norton lets you know what he's doing at all times, and when he finishes, he — but of course — tries to issue a report to let you know what all was done.

4. When it's finished, press Alt+**Q**uit Disk Doctor.

Using NDD for Windows

To rouse NDD for Windows

1. Click the Norton Disk Doctor icon in the Norton Utilities Windows group, and you get Figure 26-4.

2. Select the drive or drives to be tested.

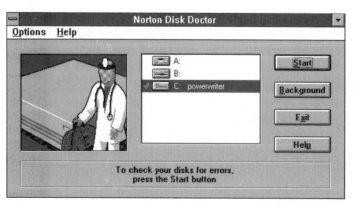

Figure 26-4: Here's something unique in the history of the universe — a doctor who does Windows!

3. Press Alt+Start.

Alternatively, you can choose Background to make the program work underground, but for the first time, let's watch it. And, if you've got a decent graphics card, a sound card, and a little bit of extra memory, what you're about to see is truly amazing. You get Figure 26-5, and as the various tests are conducted, the Norton doctor becomes "animated," examining the disk and so on, as the tests move forward.

Figure 26-5:
The testing of drive C continues apace as the little doctor provides amusement.

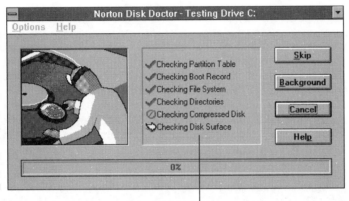

The surface test takes a while — you may want to skip it sometimes, or let it run in the background

Once the tests are over, assuming everything's okay, you see something like Figure 26-6.

Figure 26-6:
NDD gives you, literally, a clean bill of health.

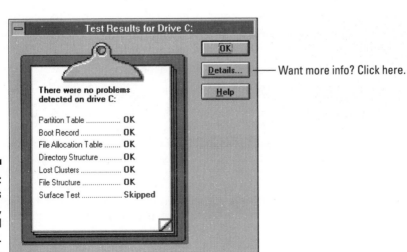

Want more info? Click here.

Getting a bad checkup

Remember, your motto is "Just say yes." If NDD finds a problem with a lost cluster or an allocation table entry, say yes to his offer to correct the problem, but always first let NDD create the Undo file on a floppy disk so that there's a fall-back position — just in case.

Installing Options — Both Programs

In opening screens of both NDD for DOS and NDD for Windows is an Options menu item. If you choose Options, you have a plethora of choices regarding which disk drive tests should be run or turned off, whether disk errors should be handled automatically when detected, and so forth.

My recommendation is to leave the settings alone. They are set for your safety. If you know enough to feel confident about changing them, then go for it. Otherwise, let the doctor do his business.

Installing NDD for DOS as a Startup program

Whether you spend most of the day in Windows or DOS, you can still set your Disk Doctor to run a quick diagnosis every time the computer is turned on. All it takes is a little Start Up magic.

1. Type **NORTON** and press Enter to get to the Norton Utilities menu.

2. Press Alt+**Configuration** ⇨ **Startup Programs.**

3. Highlight `Diagnose Disk Problems` and press the spacebar to choose Norton Disk Doctor.

4. When asked to select a drive to diagnose, highlight the drive or drives you want to diagnose and press the spacebar.

5. When you've finished selecting drives, press Alt+**OK.**

6. Press Alt+**S**ave.

Norton makes changes to the AUTOEXEC.BAT and notifies you that you must reboot the computer before the changes take effect on your system. All that means is that the next time you turn the computer on is when you'll see NDD run. If you need instant gratification, then — at the system prompt — press Ctrl+Alt+Del to reset the computer. That's like turning it off and on again. This time, you see your system flying through the NDD tests.

By the way, if you don't feel like sitting through the NDD diagnostic test, you can always interrupt the physical by pressing Esc. Sometimes you just don't have the minute and thirty seconds it takes to run.

Running in background

NDD for Windows has the capability to run in the background — sort of. When you stop typing or mousing, NDD seizes the nanosecond to go to work. If you use a screensaver, you can get a picture of how WDD works. When system resources are needed by you, NDD selflessly drops what it's doing and steps away until things free up again. If you need that kind of moment-to-moment examination of your hard drive, you may want NDD to load itself automatically whenever you get into Windows:

1. From the NDD opening screen, press Alt+**O**ptions.

2. Highlight the Startup Options icon.

3. Put a check mark next to Alt+**L**oad with Windows (see Figure 26-7).

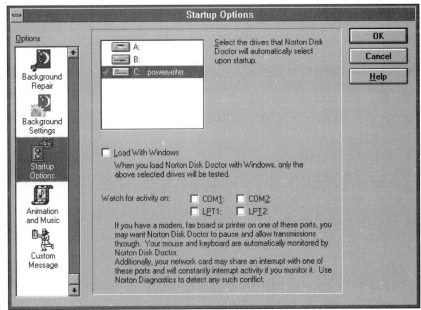

Figure 26-7:
The NDD
Startup
Options
screen.

4. Press Alt+**OK** to save your choice.

If you ever want to stop NDD from loading automatically, just follow the same steps again, making sure that you remove the check mark next to **Load with Windows**.

If you're already running Speed Disk (Chapter 12) in the background, then don't be shy about adding Norton Disk Doctor to the mix. Speed Disk and NDD actually share system resources.

Chapter 27

UnFormat

In This Chapter

▶ UnFormat a floppy or hard disk

*U*nFormat is one of those programs that you never want to use. It's not that it's a difficult program to use — quite the opposite — it's just that if you need to use it, you're in a bad place.

I hope you'll recall from Chapter 11 — the chapter about Safe Format — that every disk must be formatted before it can be used, including the hard disk. Unfortunately, if a formatted disk is formatted a second time, everything on the disk gets wiped out.

This very tidbit of information may be something you've just learned the hard way. In fact, your purchase of Norton Utilities may have been motivated by such an event.

Of course, once Norton is installed, Safe Format pretty much intercepts any formatting you do and prevents any accidental formatting of the hard disk — as well as inadvertent erasure of a floppy disk.

One other reason you might need UnFormat is a bit sinister. Sometimes computer viruses take over the computer and mischievously reformat the hard disk. Isn't that cute?

Anyway, even though what UnFormat does is extremely complicated, it's simple to use.

You can't undo an UnFormat. Make sure you've got the right disk this time and proceed carefully.

UnFormatting a Disk

Whether you're UnFormatting a floppy disk or a hard disk, the commands work the same. If you formatted your disk with Safe Format (covered in Chapter 11), or you faithfully use Image (covered in Chapter 16) or Mirror (a DOS program that does something similar to Image), your chances for a successful UnFormat are quite good.

If you haven't used Image or any of that other stuff, it doesn't mean UnFormat won't work — it just won't work as well. However, if you're using a version of DOS earlier than version 5, you can forget it.

So, to UnFormat

1. To get to the UnFormat dialog box (see Figure 27-1), use one of the following methods:

   • From the Norton Utilities menu, highlight UnFormat and press Enter, or

   • From a system prompt, type **UNFORMAT** and press Enter

Figure 27-1:
You're about to enter the world of UnFormat. What Norton has joined together let no person put asunder.

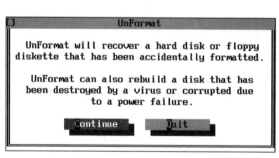

2. Highlight the drive to be formatted, as in Figure 27-2, and press Enter or click OK.

3. Press Alt+**Yes** to the question posed in Figure 27-3 regarding the use of Image or Mirror.

   What makes Safe Format so safe is that it creates an Image file that contains the genetic coding of what the disk was like before the formatting (see Chapter 16 for more about Image).

4. Press Alt+**Yes** to the Are you sure question in Figure 27-4.

Figure 27-2:
Don't worry
if you don't
have *A:*, *B:*,
and *C:*
drives like in
this picture.
You may
have more
— or fewer
— drives
than I do.

Be sure to pick the right drive!

Hard disk   Floppy

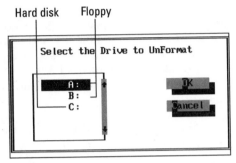

Figure 27-3:
My kind of
dialog box.
They ask the
question
and tell you
what to say.
Perfect.

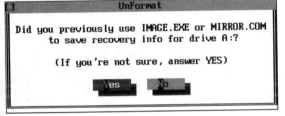

Figure 27-4:
Is UnFormat
poised to do
its thing on
the *right*
drive? If you
meant drive
C, then say
No and start
again.

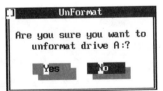

A bunch of computer stuff happens until — if you're lucky — you see Figure 27-5 where UnFormat asks whether you want to restore the disk to the status of the last Image update.

If an Image or Mirror file is not found, UnFormat still tries to do its job. However, all the directories get names like DIR0, DIR1, and so forth. You have to rename them with Norton Change Directory (see Chapter 9). Oh, then you also have to UnErase all the files in the root directory. Sounds like a drag, doesn't it? But it's better than no files at all, right?

5. Press Alt+**OK**.

You don't *have* to say OK; you could press Alt+**Cancel** if you want. But if you want the UnFormat to proceed, you must say OK.

Next, you get another warning, as in Figure 27-6.

6. Press Alt+**Y**es to Figure 27-6.

Once you say Yes, you get another question, as in Figure 27-7.

Figure 27-5:
Yippee!
Image info
was found!
The disk
can be
UnFormatted!
Quick — say
OK before
UnFormat
changes its
mind!

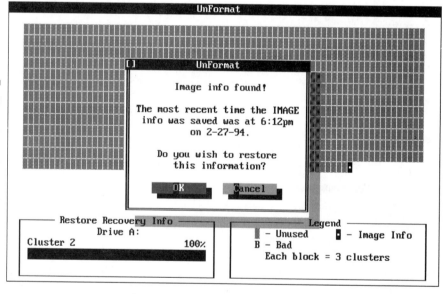

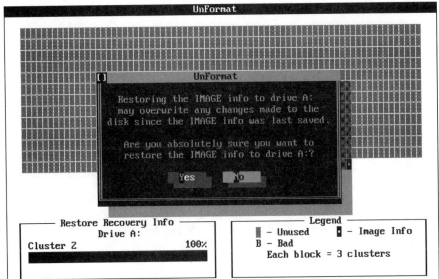

Figure 27-6:
All ashore who's going ashore! Last chance to jump ship! Remember, UnFormat can't be undone.

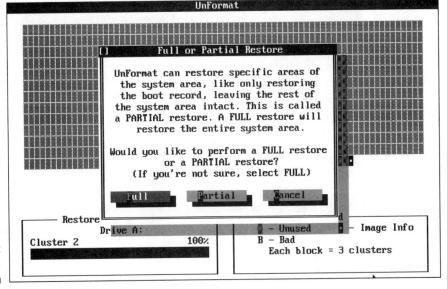

Figure 27-7:
Like Columbo, UnFormat keeps coming back with just one last question.

7. Press Alt+Full — just like Norton suggests.

As this question implies, you don't have to restore the whole disk if you only want a certain section or file. However, we'll assume that you want it all. Besides, if you know enough to want a Partial Restore, you don't need help from me on how to do it.

After you choose Full, Norton goes to work. Eventually, depending on the size of the drive and how much work there is to do, you see something like Figure 27-8.

Whether you UnFormat a floppy or a hard disk, be sure to use Norton Disk Doctor (discussed in Chapter 26) after the operation to check the disk out.

Since the Image file is the blueprint for UnFormat's restoration operations, an out-of-date Image file results in an incomplete or out-of-date UnFormat. Please keep your rescue disk up to date; it'll make UnFormat's job a lot easier.

Figure 27-8:
This is the message you want to see after UnFormatting a disk. Of course, if you've UnFormatted the hard disk, it would say *Drive C:* has been successfully restored.

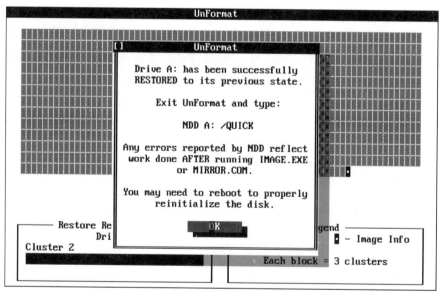

Why UnFormat was invented — A fable

Gather round, children, and I'll tell you a tale of yore. Long, long ago in the version of our DOS 2.1 — we are currently in the version of our DOS 6.2, so you can see that this was, indeed, a long, long time ago — the first hard disks appeared on our computer systems. Most of those first hard disks were only about 10MB in capacity, but it seemed like we'd never need more space than that!

Then it started happening. The horror. You see, to format a floppy disk, you had to type — as you do today if you're not using Norton Utilities — **FORMAT A:** and press Enter. In Version 2.11 of DOS, if you just typed **FORMAT** and pressed Enter — forgetting the all-important **A:** — the computer would immediately start reformatting the hard disk. No warnings, no hints of disasters. It just started chugging along — and we started screaming. And that's when UnFormat was invented.

Part V
The Norton Grab Bag...

The 5th Wave   **By Rich Tennant**

New Age PC Repair

"QUIET EVERYONE — LET THE CRYSTAL DO ITS WORK."

In this part...

You know what you usually find in so-called grab bags — merchandise so awful they had to hide it in a "mystery" bag and label it with giveaway prices. Although the Norton Grab Bag isn't quite as bad as that, the Grab Bag does consist of programs that mostly seem to be answers in search of questions — or fixes for problems that either no longer exist or are handled better by another Norton Utility.

Remember, there's always at least one really wonderful thing in every grab bag — and sometimes the most innocuous-looking program can be the answer to all our dreams!

Chapter 28
Batch Enhancer

● ●

In This Chapter

▶ Not all BATs live in caves

▶ Batch enhancers — where *does* Batchman get all those wonderful toys?

▶ Building a better batch file

● ●

*Y*es, it's true, Norton Utilities includes batch-enhancing commands. "Oh, boy, batch file enhancing!" you say, with all the conviction of someone who just received underwear for Christmas. "Just what I always wanted."

Here's the good news — if you don't know what a batch file is and are even less concerned about how to enhance one, then you're off the hook for this chapter. Skip it. Spend your time learning one of the other Norton Utilities that can do you some real good.

If, however, you have some sort of morbid curiosity about batch files — which are a sort of macro program for the computer — then stick around. We're going to do a simple introductory session to batch files and enhancing batch files. Nothing very heavy.

Well, nothing very heavy relatively speaking, of course. Considering that there are fat books out about using batch files and learned people can work up a passionate discussion regarding schools of approaches, a couple of pages here is lightweight. On the other hand, just because we're keeping it simple doesn't mean what we're about to learn is insubstantial. This is definitely serious stuff that you'll be able to use as long as there's a DOS.

Not All BATs Live in Caves

First of all, a batch file is a lot like any other document you might create using your favorite word processor. However, there are four important ways in which a batch file is different from that letter you just dispatched to the President:

- ✔ A batch file contains a series of actions — commands that the computer should perform. It's sort of a list of things to do for the machine.

- ✔ Each action to be performed must be on its own separate line.

- ✔ Batch files must be text-only files created by DOS's EDIT command or your word processor, as long as it's saved as a text or ASCII File. (WordPerfect users can use the Text Out function, and Word users can use the Save As command.)

- ✔ All batch files end in the letters BAT — short for Batch, natch.

Once you've typed several commands into a batch file, saved it, and exited your word processor, you can tell the computer to *do everything in the file* and it will perform each of the commands in turn, as though you had typed them individually yourself at the system prompt. The way you tell the computer to *do everything in the file* is just by typing the file's name and pressing Enter. You see, it's built into the operating system of the computer that files ending in BAT contain commands that must be carried out.

Let's try a real live example.

The first thing to do is look at what you do every day. What commands are you repeating all the time? Let's say that every day you turn on the computer, go to a certain directory, and then start your word processing program. If your keystrokes were recorded, you would see that you're doing a whole lot of this:

CD \WP51

WP

These two steps — 10 keystrokes (12 if you count the Enters at the end of each line) — can be put in a batch file called W.BAT. Then, every morning you type just **W** — no BAT — and press Enter.

When you type **W** and press Enter, the computer says to itself, "W? Oh, there's a file called W.BAT, that must be what my human wants me to do. I'll just look inside and see what I'm supposed to do." And then the computer does what the first line says, then the second line, and so forth.

Boom. In 2 keystrokes, you end up where it used to take you 12 keystrokes. Plus — and this is a big plus — the batch file never makes typos. Once you've got the commands in there correctly, it'll pop 'em out perfectly every time.

Although batch files can be incredibly complicated, you don't have to do anything more complex with a batch file than the previous example. There's nothing shameful about learning no more than how to create a simple two-line batch file to facilitate moving all over your computer.

After all, the point of the computer is to make life easier — not to make you feel like you should be learning a bunch of stuff that doesn't apply.

Creating Your First Batch File

We're going to step through creating a two-line batch file. You can use the previous two-line batch file, think of one of your own, or follow the next example, where we try something a little different. But don't worry, we're keeping the batch file down to two lines.

This new batch file could be helpful for Word for Windows users. Instead of starting up Windows and then opening Word for Windows, the batch file offers another approach.

There are eighty million batch files in the Naked City. Here are two ways to make one of them.

Using DOS's EDIT command — or your own word processor

We've edited files before (like in Chapter 5, for example). Also, we covered this in some detail in DOS Boot Camp. Editing probably won't be brand new to you now, and you can concentrate on the batch file experience.

1. At the system prompt, type **EDIT WW.BAT** and press Enter.

   Because this is a Word for Windows batch file, WW.BAT seemed appropriate. You can name it whatever you want, as long as it ends in BAT. One hint, though: Don't name it the same thing as the actual program you're trying to start. It doesn't hurt anything to do that, but if you name the batch file WINWORD.BAT, for example, the computer will ignore the batch file and start the WinWord program itself. (In the the computer's pecking order, batch files go last.)

   • If your DOS EDIT command isn't working, use your own word processor instead, but pay careful attention to saving instructions at the end.

2. Type the two lines of the batch file:

CD \WINDOWS

WIN \WINWORD\WINWORD

This batch file goes to the Windows directory and then starts Word for Windows. If your Windows or Word for Windows directories are different, then be sure to substitute your own.

3. Save the file and exit.

If you're using the DOS EDIT command, press Alt+File⇨**Save**, and then Alt+File⇨Exit. If you're using a word processing program, make sure to save it as a text or ASCII file. In WordPerfect, use the Text Out, Save as DOS file function. In Word, use Save As and choose Text File with Line Breaks.

Something from nothing

The second way to create a batch file — which works best with very simple files — is kind of strange. Did you know you can actually create a batch file using no word processor software — with just your own two little hands. It requires $3,000 worth of computer equipment, of course!

The advantage of using this method is that it's quick. The disadvantage is that editing capabilities are extremely limited. Actually, there are none. So get it right.

1. At the system prompt, type **COPY CON WW.BAT** and press Enter.

2. Type the two lines of the batch file:

CD \WINDOWS

WIN \WINWORD\WINWORD

3. Press the F6 function key and then press Enter.

The F6 key produces ^Z on the screen, which is what we want. After you press Enter, you see 1 File (s) copied, which is also what we want to see.

If you do screw up, press Ctrl+C to cancel the whole thing, and then start again. Maybe you want to give the editing with the word processing a shot.

That's it.

Using the batch file

Once you've got the thing created, using whatever method, exit to the system prompt. Then just type the filename — without the BAT — and press Enter.

To use the WW.BAT file:

1. Get to the system prompt.
2. Type **WW** and press Enter.

Variation on a theme

One of the handiest features in batch-file programming is the *variable*. A variable is an unknown factor that changes. For example, one thing that's a constant is that you use Word for Windows every day. That's why that WW.BAT file is helpful.

However, when you use Word for Windows, the file you edit or create changes every day. Because the file varies, it's a variable!

With a variable command, you can tell the computer to load a file that won't be specified until the moment the WW.BAT file is invoked.

Suppose that today you need to work on a file called REPORT. You type **WW REPORT** — instead of just **WW** — and press Enter. Whatever filename you type after the WW opens for you automatically.

The only trick is that you have to tell the batch file to expect a filename and an instruction about what to do with it. This is what such a batch file looks like:

CD \WINDOWS

WIN \WINWORD\WINWORD %1

That weird-looking **%1** is the variable command. All that is, is a little ol' percent sign (hold down the Shift key and press the number 5) and the number 1. Because a batch file can have tons of variables, they have to be numbered so that the computer can keep them all straight.

Anyway, if you type **WW REPORT**, the computer sees the word REPORT and assumes correctly that it's the first variable and it pretends REPORT was always in the spot where the %1 is and carries out the command.

Tomorrow, you may want to write a letter to Bob, so you would type **WW BOB** and press Enter to start your day. ·

The next day, you may not have even the slightest clue as to what you'll work on once you get into Word for Windows, so you just type **WW** and press Enter — with no variable at all. The computer goes with the flow and just starts the program for you.

If you use another program — Excel, for example — you could create an E.BAT file to start *that* program:

CD \WINDOWS

WIN C:\EXCEL\EXCEL %1

Now you can start every day with either **WW** or **E**!

Introducing Norton's Batch Enhancers

The Batch Enhancer command, also known as the Frank Sinatra command, adds even more functionality to creating batch files.

Okay, so far we've created a couple of simple batch files and even used a variable. I've also mentioned 6 or 12 times that there are lots of other commands out there, in addition to variables, that you can use to create sophisticated batch files. However, the batch enhancers make it possible to:

- ✔ Do really complicated things easily
- ✔ Perform some functions that aren't possible at all in normal batch-file programming

Just as there are lots of commands in creating batch files, there are also lots of batch enhancer commands. We'll dash through a few of them here — and then end up with an example that puts everything together.

If you really want to know more about the batch enhancers, consult the manual — or, at the system prompt, type **BE /?** and press Enter. You get Figure 28-1, which reminds you of the various commands available and how to use them. More is in the manual of course.

```
New commands to enhance batch files.

BE command [parameters] [/DEBUG]
  BE pathname [ [GOTO] label]

  commands are:
    ASK           GOTO          SA
    BEEP          JUMP          SHIFTSTATE
    BOX           MONTHDAY      TRIGGER
    CLS           PRINTCHAR     WEEKDAY
    DELAY         REBOOT        WINDOW
    EXIT          ROWCOL

  /DEBUG          Display the ERRORLEVEL code.

  pathname        Name of a BE command file.
  label           Label in file to start execution.

For more help on a specific command type:
     BE command ?
```

Figure 28-1:
Batch help for the asking? For more help on a specific command, type BE <the command> /? and press Enter.

Employing batch enhancers

In Figures 28-2 and 28-3 are two examples of more complicated batch files that put several of Norton's Batch Enhancer commands to work. Granted, these batch files look pretty nasty right now, but the whole point of the next few pages is to give you the language skills necessary to read and write batch files like these. Who knows, you may come to enjoy life in the batch lane.

BE Beep Beep

Anyone who's ever made an error has heard a computer beep. Once you start making your own miniprograms — which is what a batch file is — you may discover what fun it is to make a computer beep on purpose. Adding a beep to a batch file can notify you that something's all finished or that your attention is required.

Suppose that you made a batch file that copies all document files to drive A. When the computer's finished, you'd like to hear a beep so that you know the job is done. Here's what that batch file should look like:

    COPY *.DOC A:

    BE BEEP

The last line says, "Use the Batch Enhancing command of Beep."

If you want four beeps, you can type **BE BEEP/R4** — /R means repeat. In addition to the number of beeps, you also can specify the tone and more. The Roadrunner never knew Beep Beep could be so complicated.

Remember I said that the Batch Enhancer commands are known as the Frank Sinatra commands? That's because all the Batch Enhancer commands start out with BE. As in BE BEEP, or, as we'll see momentarily, BE ASK — but especially as in do BE do BE do!

Inquiring minds want to know

Another BE command is ASK. Using ASK is a way of making a batch file more general purpose. Instead of lots of little batch files for this or that situation, ASK lets you choose an option on the fly.

ASK is a kind of an extension on the variable idea. It's a way of putting a question in the batch file to determine "Do you want X or Y?" If you answer X, the batch file carries out one set of commands in the batch file. If you answer Y, another set of instructions is performed.

In more concrete terms, you could have a single batch file that asks every morning, "Do you want to use Word for Windows or Excel?" Based on your reply, you get either Word or Excel.

Using an ASK command in a batch file means you're not only responsible for the question — but all the answers as well. The instructions for using Word and the instructions for using Excel have to be in the same file. As you might surmise, using ASK immediately puts us several notches up on the batch-file food chain.

An example of an ASK batch file is in Figure 28-2 — where there are definitely a few more vocabulary words to deal with.

A DOS Errorlevel isn't the same as a golf handicap

In our ASK batch file in Figure 28-2, the question posed is whether you want to use Word or Excel. Your answer is either to press W to choose Word or E to opt for Excel. Whether you press E or W, that response is called an errorlevel. Even though there's no error in an errorlevel, that's what it's called. They should've called it a response, but it's called errorlevel, so what can you do?

The first possible response to an ASK question is called errorlevel 1, the second response is called errorlevel 2, and so on. In our example, the first possible response is W, and it becomes errorlevel 1. The second response, E, is errorlevel 2. Once an errorlevel has been generated, that's the computer's cue to use a specified set of commands.

The "IF" statements must be in descending order   Possible responses

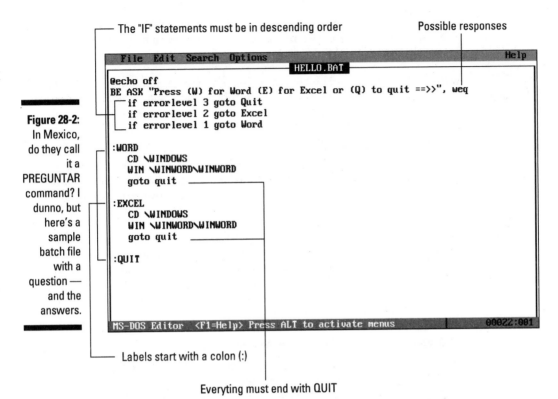

Figure 28-2:
In Mexico,
do they call
it a
PREGUNTAR
command? I
dunno, but
here's a
sample
batch file
with a
question —
and the
answers.

```
 File  Edit  Search  Options                          Help
                        HELLO.BAT
@echo off
BE ASK "Press (W) for Word (E) for Excel or (Q) to quit ==>>", weq
  ┌ if errorlevel 3 goto Quit
  │ if errorlevel 2 goto Excel
  └ if errorlevel 1 goto Word

:WORD
   CD \WINDOWS
   WIN \WINWORD\WINWORD
   goto quit ─────────

:EXCEL
   CD \WINDOWS
   WIN \WINWORD\WINWORD
   goto quit ─────────

:QUIT


 MS-DOS Editor  <F1=Help> Press ALT to activate menus      00022:001
```

Labels start with a colon (:)

Everyting must end with QUIT

Using labels

A *label* identifies each different set of options in the batch file. When an errorlevel number is produced, the computer is sent to the set of instructions for that number, based on its label. There's a line in the batch file that says that if a certain errorlevel exists, then the computer needs to GOTO the appropriate label. Follow the yellow brick road.

You can always spot a label in a batch file because it's the only thing that starts with a colon. It's easier to see than explain. In Figure 28-2, the label that identifies the commands to start Word for Windows is :WORD. The label name shouldn't be complex — it just has to start with a colon.

Asking politely

The actual text of the ASK question — the words that will show up on the computer screen — goes in quotes. After the quotes, type a comma and the possible responses to the ASK question. In Figure 28-2, the possible responses include W, E, and Q (for QUIT — always important to be able to quit). There's nothing magic about W, E, or Q. We could've used 1, 2, and 3, or even A, B, and C.

Because we're putting our own text up on the screen, we need to tell the computer to shut up while we're talking. The shut up command is **@echo off**. It is placed at the top of the file.

At this point, you should be able to decipher and understand the contents of Figure 28-2. Make sure that you're comfortable with it before moving on to more commands.

If it's Tuesday, it must be "3"

Another very cool BE command is the WEEKDAY command. The WEEKDAY command can actually figure out what day of the week it is, assuming that your computer's clock is okay. Every day of the week has its own errorlevel. Sunday is 1, Monday is 2, Tuesday is 3, and so on.

The WEEKDAY command is kind of like an ASK command, but it answers its own question. Once BE WEEKDAY determines the day of the week and returns an errorlevel, the decision is made as to what kind of commands need to be carried out. The WEEKDAY command gives you the opportunity to schedule an event or a reminder once a week, or twice a week — once on Tuesday, the second on Friday. It's your batch file!

Even Tom Cruise could use some screen attributes

Okay, the Screen Attributes command is definitely getting into the range of fancy. But if you're going to run a batch file, why not go all the way and have gaudy red letters — blinking — against a white background? And what's wrong with a little fun, anyway? The range of colors you can use in your batch files won't give Technicolor any cause for concern — but you can choose anything from magenta to cyan. They're all listed in the manual.

An example of the Screen Attributes (SA) command that will produce the blinking red letters on a white background is:

BE SA BLINKING RED ON WHITE /BOLD

You can see that the command to put "blinking red letters on a white background — bold, please" is pretty much in English, and not that hard to do.

However, you don't want red blinking letters all the time, so it's a good idea to use a "put it back" command in there, too. To make normal screen attributes:

BE SA NORMAL /CLS

The /CLS at the end means "clear the screen," which is a polite way to leave the screen after a batch file.

If you start experimenting with blinking characters and different colors, don't worry that what you're doing is permanent. If worse comes to worst, just reboot the computer and everything is put back to normal. So have fun!

Putting it all together

In the dreaded Figure 28-3, we got a very busy batch file.

✔ It starts out by determining the day of the week and producing an errorlevel.

You can see that unless there's an errorlevel of 2, the batch file quits without so much as a single BE BEEP.

✔ If it's Monday and the errorlevel is 2, you'll be asked if you want to run Speed Disk (covered in Chapter 12) — which is a good thing to run once a week and which you might forget to do.

✔ If you reply affirmatively, that produces another errorlevel that results in the files being defragged.

If you don't want to run Speed Disk, you can just say no, and the program quits.

By the way, you could add the batch file in Figure 28-3 to the end of your AUTOEXEC.BAT file so that it'll automatically run every day and remind you to run Speed Disk once a week. You don't have to, but you could.

AUTOEXEC.BAT — the world's most famous batch file

Yes, the AUTOEXEC.BAT file is just another batch file. The only thing that makes it special is its name. Since it's called AUTOEXEC, the computer knows to *auto*matically *exec*ute the batch file every time the computer is turned on.

That way, the things that must be done to make your machine work properly are all handled while you're drinking your morning coffee. If something happens to your AUTOEXEC.BAT file, all sorts of things stop working. It's very bad. And since every batch file is a little snowflake — no two exactly the same — lose yours and you've got a problem.

Always, always make sure that you have a copy of your AUTOEXEC.BAT file on a floppy disk — at

the system prompt, type **COPY \AUTOEXEC.BAT A:** and press Enter.

As a secondary backup, print out the file and put it someplace safe. You can even use Norton's own SYSINFO command (discussed in Chapter 13) to call up the AUTOEXEC.BAT file and print it out.

By the way, I can't resist telling this joke. I don't remember where I heard it originally, but — What do you get when you cross Lee Iacocca with Count Dracula?

Give up?

An AUTOEXEC.BAT, of course.

Wild and crazy screen attributes

We have an "IF" statement
for every day of the week

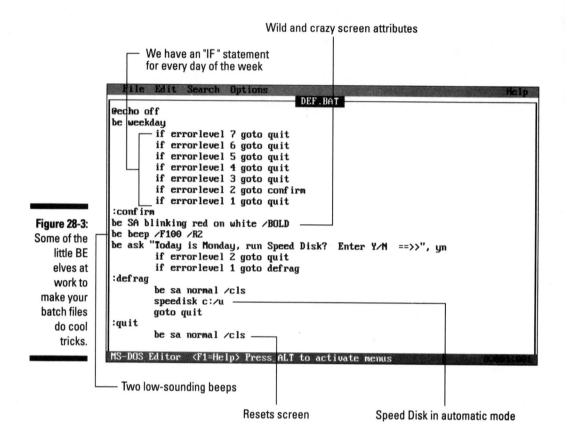

```
File  Edit  Search  Options                   DEF.BAT                      Help

@echo off
be weekday
        if errorlevel 7 goto quit
        if errorlevel 6 goto quit
        if errorlevel 5 goto quit
        if errorlevel 4 goto quit
        if errorlevel 3 goto quit
        if errorlevel 2 goto confirm
        if errorlevel 1 goto quit
:confirm
be SA blinking red on white /BOLD
be beep /F100 /R2
be ask "Today is Monday, run Speed Disk?  Enter Y/N  ==>>", yn
        if errorlevel 2 goto quit
        if errorlevel 1 goto defrag
:defrag
        be sa normal /cls
        speedisk c:/u
        goto quit
:quit
        be sa normal /cls

MS-DOS Editor  <F1=Help> Press ALT to activate menus          00:001:001
```

Figure 28-3:
Some of the
little BE
elves at
work to
make your
batch files
do cool
tricks.

Two low-sounding beeps

Resets screen

Speed Disk in automatic mode

Chapter 29
Disk Monitor

● ●

In This Chapter

▶ The Virus Detective

▶ The disk light at the end of the tunnel

▶ Disk Park and Jurassic Park

● ●

Disk Monitor — or Diskmon, as we say in Jamaica — is a bodyguard program that hovers around in the background. As you go about your normal computer business, Disk Monitor is ever watchful, waiting to spring into action the moment anything happens that may indicate the presence of a computer virus. When Disk Monitor spots any suspicious behavior, he blocks it, and asks what you want to do about it.

Because the M.O. of many viruses is to change the system files that run your computer, carefully watching them for unexpected access is a logical *preventive* approach.

Although being able to detect the possibility of a virus is helpful, Disk Monitor is just a dumb brute. He doesn't have a clue as to how to clean up the virus. For that, you need to buy another program or use Microsoft's Anti-Virus, which comes with DOS 6.0 or later. If you're hearing from Disk Monitor often, you should investigate such fumigation software.

Disk Monitor's other assigned duties — Disk Light and Disk Park — have nothing to do with viruses or file protection and aren't going to change your life. We'll give them a quick nod later in this chapter.

Installing Disk Monitor

Although *you* can manually turn on Disk Monitor every time you start the computer, it's much easier to have *the computer* turn on Disk Monitor every time you start the computer. Besides, the computer will never forget to turn it on — you might.

Before installing Disk Monitor, you may need to know that as long as it sits around in the background, it's consuming about 8K of memory. Generally speaking, 8K is a tiny drop in the memory bucket — but you'll find other memory-resident Norton Utilities while rummaging through the Norton Grab Bag and if you install all of them, they begin to add up.

If you start to receive not enough memory messages, then it's time to start uninstalling some of these background programs. You may never have memory problems, so don't be shy about adding things in. I'm just letting you know that if — that's *if* — you do get an error message, it's no biggie. All these programs are easy to uninstall.

But first, here's how to install the Disk Monitor:

1. From the Norton Utilities menu, press Alt+Configuration ⇨ **Startup Programs** to end up with Figure 29-1.

Highlight and click (or press the spacebar)
to put a check mark next to the option

Norton watches your memory for you!

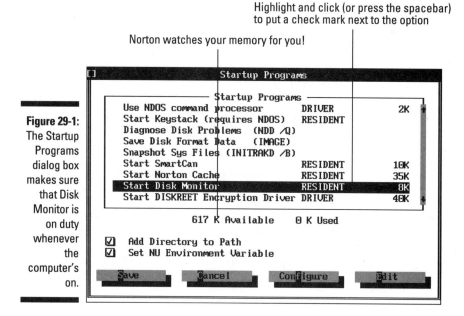

Figure 29-1:
The Startup
Programs
dialog box
makes sure
that Disk
Monitor is
on duty
whenever
the
computer's
on.

2. Highlight Start Disk Monitor and click (or press the spacebar), and you get a little dialog box like the one in Figure 29-2.

This is the one you want for virus protection

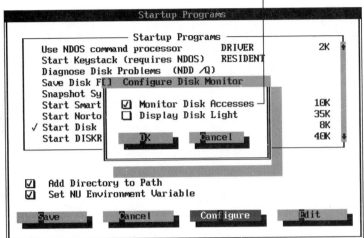

Figure 29-2:
This is
where you
give Disk
Monitor its
job
description.

3. Select Monitor Disk Accesses.

   That's the virus-checking part of the program. The other option, about the disk light, we'll pass on for now. You can always come back later and add it if you want.

4. Press Alt+**O**K.

5. Press Alt+**S**ave.

6. Press Enter or click OK when a box appears telling you the changes won't take place until the computer is rebooted.

Before moving on to the next step, be sure to reboot the computer so that Disk Monitor is in gear.

Disk Monitor at Work

Once Disk Monitor is installed, it will be invisible to you, for the most part. If, however, something does try to move in on those system files, you get a little message from Disk Monitor, as in Figure 29-3.

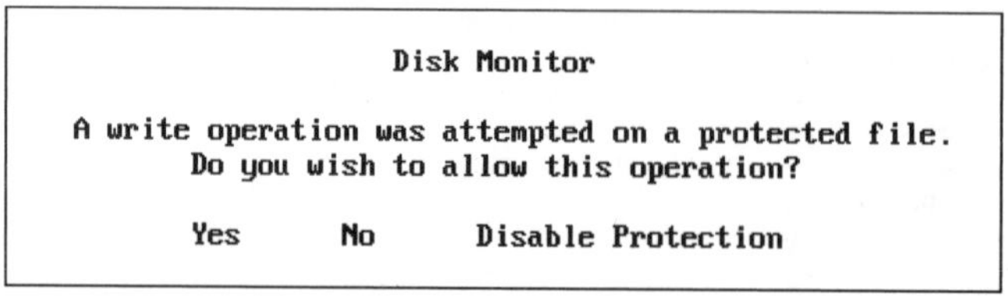

Figure 29-3:
The Hall
Monitor of
your
computer
lets you
know
whether
someone is
out of class
without a
pass.

```
                     Disk Monitor

     A write operation was attempted on a protected file.
            Do you wish to allow this operation?

         Yes        No        Disable Protection
```

Disk Monitor will accept one of three answers to his query:

- Press **Y** to allow whatever's going on to go on. This assumes you know *why* your protected files are being accessed and you think it's fine, chiefly because you're the one who just ordered a save or an update.

- Press **N** to throw a force-field around your system files. If you suspect a problem, run an antivirus program to be sure.

- Press **D** to turn off the Disk Monitor altogether — or at least until you turn on the computer again.

Creating a Battle Plan

Unless you have a special mission for Disk Monitor, you don't have to fool around with configuring it. The defaults are just fine the way they are. Move on to something else.

However, if you're that person that's got to have special treatment . . .

To get to the Disk Monitor dialog box in Figure 29-4, use one of the following methods:

- From the Norton Utilities menu, highlight Disk Monitor and press Enter, or

- From a system prompt, type **DISKMON** and press Enter.

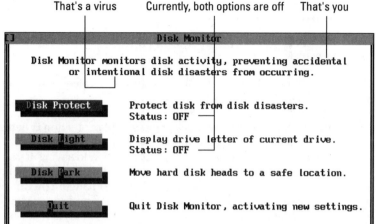

That's a virus   Currently, both options are off   That's you

Figure 29-4:
Disk
Monitor's
central
control —
where you
tell Disk
Monitor
what to do.

Disk Protect

Disk Protect is the main thing Disk Monitor does. It protects the hard drive from an unauthorized access that may lead to the downfall of civilization as we know it.

Press Alt+Disk Protect if you want to specify different files to protect, and you end up with Figure 29-5.

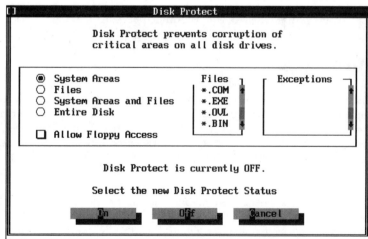

Figure 29-5:
You may
add or
remove
items from
Disk
Monitor's
watchful
eye.

✔ Normal setup should have System Areas and Allow Floppy Access selected.

The Floppy Access option deals only with making it possible to format a floppy disk.

When you're finished, press Alt+**O**n to make your choices active. You can figure out what Alt+**O**ff and Alt+**C**ancel do.

Don't think that if some protection is good, lots of protection is better. Protecting your system files is probably all you need. Many files — especially those you're using — are constantly changing, updating, and saving. If you put a Disk Protect on them, then every time a file is saved, Disk Protect pops up, as in Figure 29-3, asking whether you want to allow the change. You can see that selecting something like Entire Disk will prevent you from saving *anything* without seeing Figure 29-3. If you protect just your data, then when you try to save those files, you also get Figure 29-3. If you protect your programs, you may get Figure 29-3 constantly. Don't protect files unless you know the consequences.

If you're going to do it anyway, here are a few hints:

✔ If you want to select only certain files for protection, but *not* the system files, choose Files.

Disk Protect allows you to protect a group of files — like all EXE files — by selecting them from the Files list. Scroll to the end of the list to add your own.

You also can exclude specific files in the Exception box.

✔ When you're finished, exit as outlined earlier.

Disk Light

Disk Light applies to you *only* if your hard disk light is either not working or you can't see it because the computer's in another room or under the desk — and you want to see it. So if your hard disk light needs are not being met, select this option. Then, when a drive is accessed, its letter appears in the upper right corner of your screen — as long as you're not using a program with graphics (like Windows).

You probably don't need this capability because either your hard disk light works just fine or you don't care. In any case, pressing Alt+Disk Light (from Figure 29-4) produces a message telling you whether you're a candidate for this option.

To make the message go away, press Alt+**O**n, Alt+**O**ff, or Alt+**C**ancel.

Disk Park

First there was Jurassic Park — now there's Disk Park. The only thing the two have in common is that they're both about dinosaurs.

You see, in the early days of computers, hard disks were kind of klutzy and dumb in comparison to current models. In those dark ages of hard disks, when you turned off the computer, wherever the *head* happened to be was where the head stayed — the head being the thing that plays and records stuff on the drive, like a head on an audio or video tape player. Sometimes the head ended up sitting right on the hard disk. This was a bad thing.

So they came up with software to *park* — or move to a safe spot — the hard drive heads before turning off the computer. And it eventually came to pass that hard disk manufacturers got wise and made self-parking drives.

I only go into this whole long-winded explanation as a way of telling you that you don't need this program. If your drive is such a dinosaur that it needs this program, your system probably isn't able to run Norton Utilities 8.

And, finally, no, it doesn't hurt anything to run the Park software if you want the thrill. If you choose Disk Park from Figure 29-4, the heads are parked. Party.

Disk Monitor Shortcuts

Step right up, one and all, for our Disk Monitor command-line shortcuts. Type these at the system prompt and press Enter.

- **DISKMON /STATUS**

  Lets you know what parts of Disk Monitor are at work.

- **DISKMON /PROTECT+**

  This turns on the Disk Protect mode. If you replace the plus with a minus, it turns off Protect Mode. If you don't want the computer to automatically turn on Disk Monitor, then use Startup Programs to uninstall it. If you're feeling particularly adventurous, you can edit your AUTOEXEC.BAT and remove this line.

- **DISKMON /UNINSTALL**

  Turns off both Disk Monitor and Disk Light.

Take two aspirin . . .

With all the publicity about computer viruses, most people are at least acquainted with the notion that a computer virus is a little program that *infects* a computer and then ruins it. The way a virus works is that it attaches itself to the files that run the computer — called the *system files* — and then corrupts them or makes them do bad things, with the end result always the same — trashed data.

Viruses are very insidious because they don't just show up and start deleting files — which is certainly bad enough. Computer viruses, like their biological counterparts, have an incubation period. First they spend time coiled up inside the system files, infecting every file that comes into contact with the system files. The idea is that one of these infected files will be passed on to someone else and the virus will continue to prosper. Only after allowing time for maximum distribution does the virus kick into high gear and wipe you out. Or, sometimes a virus is programmed to go off on a certain date — like Friday the 13th.

The more sophisticated viruses also display a nasty message on the computer monitor, taking credit for your heartbreak.

Why people spend their time creating viruses is a mystery to me. Maybe we need Norton to come up with a HuMonitor.

Anyway, you needn't be overly concerned about viruses if you don't swap disks with other people and don't use a modem to download files. The more contact your computer has with the outside world, however, the more you should be aware.

Also, Disk Monitor is not exactly the most sophisticated virus detector in the world — nor does it know how to remove a virus. There are many programs out there, including one from Symantec called Norton Anti Virus and Microsoft Anti-Virus that comes with DOS version 6 that take a more aggressive approach. Just to give you an idea, the Microsoft Anti-Virus comes with more than 800 virus *signatures* — and you can update the list via a modem, as new ones appear almost daily. (Details on this are in the back of Microsoft's upgrade manual.)

All in all, if you feel your risk factor is low, Norton's Disk Protect feature is good enough.

Chapter 30

Diskreet

● ●

In This Chapter

▶ Encrypting and decrypting your files

▶ Introducing . . . the shortcut!

● ●

Do you have a computer that anyone has access to? Is there data on your drive that you'd just as soon not share with everyone in the office? One way to protect what's on your drive is to use Norton's Diskreet.

You can use Diskreet to protect your data in several ways.

We're going to concentrate on Diskreet's password-protection system, which allows one-file-at-time protection. Only those with the correct password — and who know how to run Diskreet — will have access to your sensitive material.

You also can set up Diskreet so that your entire system is password-protected, and, what's more, you can cordon off sections of your hard drive as secret scrambled-protected zones. However, we're going to just stick with the simple password protection for now, because all the other stuff gets too weird too quickly.

If you set up a file with a password and then forget the password, there is no way to recover the file. Use passwords with care.

Encrypting and Decrypting a File

Okay, it takes a bit more than a decoder ring to make this work, but after you've been through it once, you'll find that it's much easier than drinking enough Ovaltine to qualify for the ring.

For this example, I thought I'd protect a file that I've cleverly named TESTFILE.DOC. When you try out Diskreet, use your own real-live filenames instead. Away we go:

1. To start Diskreet, use one of the following methods:

   - From the Norton Utilities menu, highlight Diskreet and press Enter, or

   - From a system prompt, type **DISKREET** and press Enter, or

   - From Windows, in the Norton Utilities DOS Programs group, click the Diskreet icon

2. Click on Disable this message when you're told that the Diskreet driver has not been loaded. Then press Alt+**OK**.

   The other parts of Diskreet that we're not using require the Diskreet driver. Since we're not going to use it, we don't want to be told we don't have it — because we don't have it on purpose. You will see something like Figure 30-1.

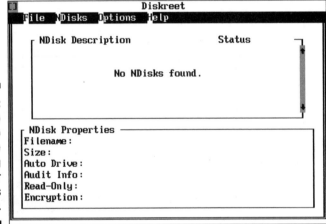

Figure 30-1:
There's no way to describe this dialog box other than it's Diskreet.

3. Press Alt+File ⇨ Encrypt.

   This gives you Figure 30-2.

4. In the File text box, type the name of the file to encrypt.

   Remember, you don't have to exhaust your fingertips by typing a filename — you can point to and click a file in the Files list box.

5. Click **OK** when you're ready.

6. Type a password twice, making sure that it's at least six characters long.

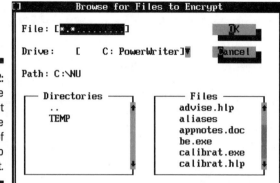

Figure 30-2:
It's the
Diskreet
Zone! Type
the name of
the file to
encrypt.

Because you won't be able to see the password as you type, entering it twice is how the computer knows for sure that you didn't make a typo. Try not to get either too simple-minded (like using 000000 as your password) or too complex (like using SUPERCALIFRAGILISTICEXPIALIDOCIOUS — which is a guaranteed trip to typo hell — as a password). And, if you're Sylvester Stallone, for example, you'd avoid using YOADRIANE as your password. And don't choose the word password as your password. It's been done.

Notice that the computer is giving the encrypted file a new name with the extension SEC — for *security*.

7. Click **OK** when you're finished.

8. You are told that the file was successfully encrypted. Press Enter to acknowledge.

9. Press Alt+**D**elete when the computer asks you about deleting the original file, as in Figure 30-3. After all, what's the point of encrypting a file if there's still an original DOC file lying around unprotected?

10. To exit Diskreet, press Esc.

Figure 30-3:
The rules of
safe
computing
suggest
deleting the
original
unprotected
file.

To work on a file that's been encrypted, you must first decrypt it. It's the same process except in Step 3, use **Alt+File** ⇨ **Decrypt**. Oh, and you won't have to type the password twice.

While you're in the Diskreet program, press **Alt+Options** ⇨ **File** to view the settings opportunities. Once you're in there, reverse the first two check marks so that you won't be pestered by so many questions (see Figure 30-4). Turn on item number one and turn off item number two, and then press **Alt+Save** to make the change permanent.

Figure 30-4:
Change your
options to
Delete
Original
Files After
Encryption
(_oui_) and
Ask
Whether to
Delete
Original
Files (_nyet_).

Introducing . . . the Shortcut!

If you're planning to become a Diskreet demon, then you should consider learning the command-line approach to this program and start building some batch files (see Chapter 28 for more about batch files). All that dialog box stuff becomes tedious every time you want to get into and out of a file!

Here's how to Encrypt and Decrypt from the command line, using the TESTFILE.DOC example from the preceding section.

✔ **DISKREET /E:testfile.doc /P:DUMMIES /T:testfile.sec**

This command encrypts the file with the password DUMMIES. The E in front of the file name is what tells Diskreet it's an encrypt job. The last item is what we want to name the encrypted file. It's called the target file — hence the T.

✔ **DISKREET /D:testfile.sec /P:DUMMIES**

This command decrypts the file, using our DUMMIES password.

TIP

You may already be protected

Did you know that many computer programs have password protection built into their system? Word for Windows, Excel, and even a few DOS-based programs give you the option to password-protect your files. Use the program's Help system — search for PASSWORD — to find out how to do it.

Also, many computers give you the option to ask for a password at the time of boot up. No password, no boot. If you can't negotiate your computer's manual to find the goods on passwords, call the manufacturer or salesperson and ask about it.

Virtually all desktop models come with keys that will lock out the keyboard input and make it very difficult to remove the casing. Using a key is very simple — and there's pretty much no learning curve involved.

Chapter 31

File Attributes

*O*ne fun thing about computer software is that sometimes it solves problems you didn't even know you had. The File Attributes program is such a program. It can meet all your File Attributes needs — even though you didn't know you had any.

File Attributes (FA) starts out working a little bit like the DIR command (or the File Size command, if you read Chapter 6 — or even if you didn't). When you type **FA** and press Enter, you get a list of files in the current directory. Rather than the normal size or date information, the FA list includes the file's *attributes*.

Seeing Beyond a Pretty Face

A file's attributes aren't "has a good sense of humor," "likes kids," "is a Sagittarius," or whatever. This is DOS, after all, and DOS's idea of an attribute is predictably dull, as in Figure 31-1, where File Attributes has been at work.

The four attributes are not John, Paul, George, and Ringo. They are:

✔ **Archive.** A file with this attribute hasn't been backed up since it was last changed.

✔ **Hidden.** A file with this attribute is an invisible file.

✔ **System.** A file with this attribute runs the computer.

✔ **Read-only.** A file with this attribute can't be erased or changed — just looked at.

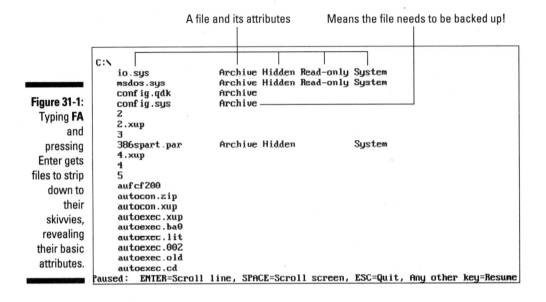

A file and its attributes   Means the file needs to be backed up!

```
C:\
      io.sys              Archive Hidden Read-only System
      msdos.sys           Archive Hidden Read-only System
      config.qdk          Archive
      config.sys          Archive
      2
      2.xup
      3
      386spart.par        Archive Hidden          System
      4.xup
      4
      5
      aufcf200
      autocon.zip
      autocon.xup
      autoexec.xup
      autoexec.ba0
      autoexec.lit
      autoexec.002
      autoexec.old
      autoexec.cd
Paused:   ENTER=Scroll line, SPACE=Scroll screen, ESC=Quit, Any other key=Resume
```

Figure 31-1: Typing **FA** and pressing Enter gets files to strip down to their skivvies, revealing their basic attributes.

For all practical purposes, the Archive attribute, which tells us whether a file has been backed up, is of the most day-to-day benefit to us humans. The Archive attribute can be a reminder to carry out that all-important bit of housekeeping.

Table 31-1 shows how you can demand to see the status of your attributes.

Table 31-1	The Inside Story
To See Files	*Type*
All files and attributes	FA and press Enter
Files not backed up	FA /A and press Enter
Files that cannot be erased or changed	FA /R and press Enter
Invisible files	FA /HID and press Enter
System files	FA /SYS and press Enter

You can use the usual /P switch to see only one screenful of files at a time. For example, typing **FA /A/P** shows all the unbacked up files, one screen at a time.

If you want, you can print out the list FA produces with DOS's built-in PRN command. It works like this: Type **FA /A > PRN** and press Enter. Easier, though, is to use File Find to print out lists, as described in "Getting Serious about Attributes," later on in the chapter.

Getting a New Attribute

If all File Attributes did was show you file attributes, we could say, "Jolly good," go home, and relax. However, FA is not quite the wimp it seems to be. It can also *change* the file's attributes. And this can get you in trouble.

A rule of thumb is not to change a file's attributes unless you know exactly what you're doing. Specifically, that you understand *why* the file's attributes were set that way in the first place and the full consequences of changing the attribute. Especially *never, ever* change the attributes on files with names like IO.SYS and MSDOS.SYS unless you enjoy the adrenaline rush of having your computer stop working. Make this another time to put a plug in for creating a rescue disk (see Chapter 15).

When It's Safe to Change Attributes

There are a few situations where knowing about and changing a file's attributes is a good thing. The message here is not to use the File Attributes command as a fun thing.

Dealing with "Access Denied"

If you've ever tried to delete a file and got an `Access Denied` error message, it was because the file was a read-only file and could not be erased. Sometimes software manufacturers set their files to read-only for your protection. Unfortunately, software manufacturers don't foresee that there may come a day when you want to erase their software from your computer. If you need to erase a file that keeps popping back with `Access Denied`, here's how to turn off the read-only attribute:

1. Get to the system prompt.

2. Type **FA *filename* /R-** and press Enter.

   Don't forget to substitute the file you've been denied access to in the place of *filename* in the command.

   That little minus sign after the **R** removes — subtracts — the read-only attribute. You'll just never guess what a plus sign after that **R** would do.

   All the commands in Table 31-1 work the same way: adding a minus (-) removes an attribute; a plus (+) turns on the attribute.

If you want to use an FA command and need a little command-line boost, type **FA ?** and press Enter to get a list of all your options.

Recovering from a crash

Sometimes when a system suddenly freezes up, you're forced to turn it off and then back on. Sometimes invisible files get left behind as part of your program's back-up system. If you're missing something, run FA in the directory you last saw your files. If FA turns up a hidden file that's got your name on it, you can recover it with the **FA.** *files* **/H-** commands. This removes the hidden attribute.

Hiding out

Let's say you've got a directory on your hard drive containing sensitive information — personnel reports, personal financial data, your diary. You can make the directory invisible with a special FA command.

This keeps the directory hidden from casual observers. Obviously, though, it's not a Fort Knox security method, because anyone using FA or a similar program can detect the directory's existence.

1. Get to the system prompt.

2. Type **FA** *directory* **/DIR+** and press Enter.

   Be sure to substitute the actual pathname for *directory*.

Getting Serious about Attributes

The easiest and best way to use File Attributes is *not to use File Attributes*. File Find (covered in Chapter 5) basically can do all the same things as FA, except File Find has a nice, friendly dialog box to guide you along. Although we didn't cover attributes in Chapter 5 — there was enough to learn about File Find without tossing attributes into the mix — File Find is really the way to go for a little File Attributes action.

Here's how:

1. Get into File Find (usually, type **FILEFIND** and press Enter).

2. Press Alt+**S**earch ⇨ Advanced Search to find files by any or all of the four attributes.

3. Press Alt+**C**ommand ⇨ **S**et Attributes.

Don't forget that File Find makes and prints out lists, as well as creates batch files to carry out commands (like COPY).

XCOPY is Archive attribute-aware

Want to back up the files that haven't been backed up? XCOPY is your command! Type **XCOPY *.* /M A:** and press Enter. This copies all files in the current directory that have not been backed up since they were last used, to the floppy disk in drive A. The /M switch not only recognizes the Archive attribute, but also removes it from the file once it's been copied. You can add your own twists to the command, of course. To copy only the document files, for example, you type **XCOPY *.DOC /M A:**.

Chapter 32

File Date

In This Chapter

▶ Changing a file's date and time stamp

*W*hen incoming mail is received, it is a custom in many offices to stamp the material with the date and often the time received. DOS does the same with files when they are received — a.k.a saved — by the system. Anytime you use DIR or many of the Norton Utilities, you see a date and time stamped to the right of the filename.

Of course, the stamp is only as accurate as the person who runs the clock. DOS makes the assumption that the date and time information on your system's clock is accurate. It's not uncommon to find all files dated January 1, 1980, because that's the date the computer uses if your system clock has gone cuckoo.

If, for whatever reason, you're disappointed with the date and time stamped on your files, Norton's File Date command can rectify the situation. And that's about all File Date does. Think of it as a time machine for your files.

I'll tell you right up front that File Find (discussed in Chapter 5) makes it easier to change the date and time of files. So my recommendation is to check out the Alt+Commands menu in File Find.

Breaking a Date

Unlike some of the other throw-back commands, like File Attributes and the others, typing just plain old **FD** and pressing Enter doesn't give you a directory listing with the date and time of each file. No.

Typing **FD** and pressing Enter gives you the File Date command options. That's right, all four of those exciting command options appear right on your very own screen.

To get something real happening with FD, you've got to name names — a specific file has to be involved.

To change a file's date to the current one, or at least the one your computer thinks is the current one, type **FD** *file.doc* and press Enter. Be sure to substitute your actual file name for *FILE.DOC*.

Clocking In and Out

If you don't want to use the current date for the time stamp, you can specify whatever date you like — if you're willing to mess with eccentric command-line switches.

To dicker with the date, use the **/D** option. To tamper with the time, it's the **/T** option. Here are two examples that use these switches:

✔ Type **FD** *file.doc* **/D10-4-94 /T12:00** and press Enter.

This changes the date stamp on FILE.DOC to October 4, 1994, noon. You can change just the date or just the time — you are not required by law to change both. So many choices, so little time.

✔ Type **FD *.DOC /D10-4-94** and press Enter.

This changes all the DOC files in the current directory to the October 4, 1994, date. And, yes, Virginia, you can use wildcards to change a bunch of files in one fell swoop, if you so desire.

Why would you want to change a file's date and time stamp? I don't have a clue. My best guess is that it's a way to identify one group of files, like a first draft of something, from another set of files that represent the second draft. Or, if you're getting files from someone whose system clock is dead and you want to keep track of the actual date of the files. FD is easy to use in a batch file if you're constantly changing dates on files.

Who knows? I'm sure there are a million and one great ways to use File Date. But don't worry about it very much if you can't think of any.

Does anyone really know what time it is?

Well, in fact, someone does. The U.S. Naval Observatory has the exact time — via an atomic clock, thank you very much — that everyone sets their clocks by. And, if you've got a modem, your computer can call their computer and get the exact time straight from the horse's mouth, so to speak. The way I do it is via a piece of software that knows how to ring up the Observatory, get the time, and then reset my system clock. You can get the same software, or others like it, on CompuServe. One such program is called TSET60.ZIP and can be found in the MSDOS/Shareware library, or NAVTIM.ZIP in the Zenith/DOS Utilities library. Also, check with the manufacturer of your normal communications software. They may have a special script or macro that will do the same job.

Chapter 33

File Locate

In This Chapter

▶ File locating locomotion

*B*ack in Chapter 5, we talked about the incredible File Find — the luxurious superjet of a program that has dialog boxes in all the finest theaters, limousine transport to the found file, batch files to do all the work, and more!

Far more humble is File Locate, known as the little engine that could locate. Although it's an option in the Norton Utilities menu — as all the utilities are — it has no fancy options or dialog boxes. It just tells you where a file is.

The only advantage File Locate has over its fat-cat brother is the fact that File Locate is only about 13K big. If you're using a laptop and space is an issue, take note that File Find is about 96K and requires the Norton Run Time Library to function, which takes another 200K. Even a math genius like myself can see that 13K is a lot less than 300K.

Quick find

Since there are no dialog boxes to get in our way, File Locate is amazingly speedy. However, since there are no dialog boxes to help us out, we have to apply a little wetware — a.k.a. brain power — to File Locate.

1. Get to the system prompt.

2. Type **FL *file.doc*** and press Enter.

   File Locate automatically searches all directories on the current hard drive for your designated file and reports back something like Figure 33-1.

   As usual, supply the filename you're looking for in place of the generic *file.doc* used in the example.

   You can use wildcards with File Locate. For example, **FL REP*.*** finds all files that begin with the letters REP. Or, **FL *.XLS** finds all Excel spreadsheet files. It's fun, it's easy — you try one!

Here's a command to locate
all DOC files — with a pause

```
C:\DOS >fl *.doc /p
C:\CSERVE
      cmos.doc              1,989 bytes      8:11pm   Mon Sep  4  1989
      cts.doc             76,288 bytes     11:58am   Fri Nov  5  1993
      feed.doc               198 bytes      1:04am   Sat May 12  1990

C:\NU
      ncache.doc           9,383 bytes      3:00am   Tue Feb 15  1994
      ndos.doc           816,825 bytes      3:00am   Tue Feb 15  1994
      appnotes.doc        48,485 bytes      3:00am   Tue Feb 15  1994

C:\DOS
      bat2exec.doc         3,067 bytes     11:30am   Tue Jul  3  1990
      capsrlse.doc        10,880 bytes     12:00pm   Sun Apr 16  1989

C:\DU
      comman.doc           9,067 bytes      4:07pm   Fri May 24  1991

C:\EXPRESS
      parser.doc          17,020 bytes     11:10pm   Wed May 23  1990

C:\EZTAPE
      test.doc               119 bytes      4:26pm   Wed Jan 12  1994

Paused:  ENTER=Scroll line, SPACE=Scroll screen, ESC=Quit, Any other key=Resume
```

Figure 33-1:
Crude, but
effective.
File Locate
is a plain
vanilla way
to find a file
on the hard
disk

First page of DOC files   Press spacebar to see next screen!

✔ If you have scrolling problems — in other words, if the results of your *locate* are scrolling off the screen in that typically irritating way DOS has — then add a pause switch. You know, **FL** *file.doc* **/P**. That'll make the scroll stop after every screen, allowing you to read what's been found at your own pace.

✔ If you can't remember FL, you can always fall back on the Norton Utilities menu — that's what it's there for. Just type **NORTON** and press Enter to get in, highlight File Locate, type the name of the file to be found, and then press Enter.

A quick-and-dirty way to get a printed list of files located is to add > **PRN** to your command. For example, typing **FL** *file.doc* > **PRN** prints a list of where that file is found. Of course, make sure that your printer's turned on before you try this command at home, kids.

Switching the Line

You can take File Locate off the main track with a few switches.

✔ If you have more than one drive to search, add the /A switch — **FL *file.doc* /A** — and FL looks for your file on all your drives automatically.

✔ To list files in the wide mode, add a /W switch — **FL *file.doc* /W**.

✔ To search for files only in directories named in your path statement — **FL *file.doc* /T**. In case you were wondering, the T represents the T in Path, I think, since the P was taken for Pause and the A for All. They were stuck with the T. I think it was a good choice. H would've been much worse.

If you don't know what's in your path statement, you can, at any system prompt, type **PATH** and press Enter. The computer shows you the current path.

Chapter 34
Line Print

*E*ven though Line Print is called *Line* Print, it has nothing to do with printing lines or creating graph paper. That would make far too much sense.

Line Print was created as an alternative to DOS's own rudimentary PRINT command. The idea is that using Line Print to print text files is quicker than calling up your word processor, loading the file, and then printing.

Notice that I said Line Print prints *text files*. That means you can't use Line Print to print files created with your word processor. Line Print works well only with ASCII and text files — we talked about those in DOS Boot Camp (Chapter 1).

Examples of text files include the infamous AUTOEXEC.BAT and CONFIG.SYS files. Or you can finally print the secret README.TXT file that comes with many programs. You can even print the enticing WHATS.NEW file that came with Norton Utilities.

Line Printing — The Basic Steps

Once Line Printing catches on, I'm sure it'll be the natural successor to Country Line Dancing. No doubt about it. It's a simple dance, only a few basic steps and very few options. To make your first stab at it, all you need to do is

1. Get to the system prompt.

   It's helpful to be in the directory that contains the file you want to print. If you want to print Norton Utilities' very own WHATS.NEW text file, you should shuffle over to the Norton Utilities directory by typing **CD \NU** and pressing Enter.

2. Type **LP** *file.doc* and press Enter.

   To print the legendary WHATS.NEW file, substitute that filename for the generic *file.doc*. In other words, type **LP WHATS.NEW** and then press Enter. Figure 34-1 shows the riveting graphic that's displayed when you invoke Line Printer.

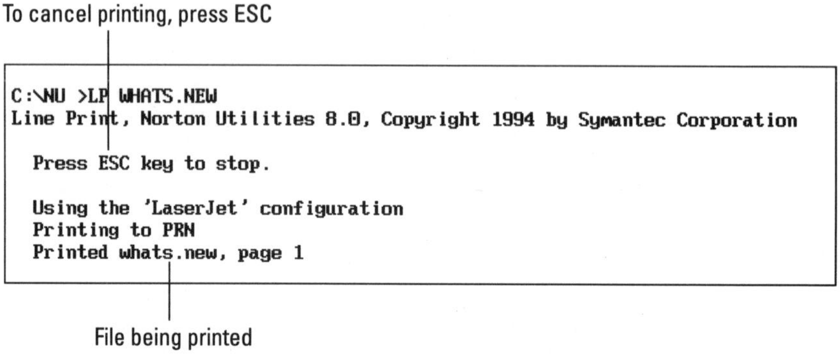

Figure 34-1:
Oooh, I love a little two-step! Typing **LP** *file.doc* and pressing Enter is all you need do to print a text file.

To cancel printing, press ESC

```
C:\NU >LP WHATS.NEW
Line Print, Norton Utilities 8.0, Copyright 1994 by Symantec Corporation

  Press ESC key to stop.

  Using the 'LaserJet' configuration
  Printing to PRN
  Printed whats.new, page 1
```

File being printed

- If you're printing something longer than a page or two, pressing Esc while printing cancels the job.

- Line Print prints the file by using the printer defined in the NUCONFIG program (covered in Chapter 2). If you haven't defined your printer, it'll probably work anyway. Line Print is forgiving.

When the page comes out of the printer, you'll see that LP has thoughtfully added a header to the top of the document. The header contains helpful information like the name of the file, the current date and time, the page numbers, and the number of shopping days until Christmas — information much more than DOS's Print command provides.

Line Printing — Between the Lines

There are lots of ways to change how the material appears on the page, but they requires using switches, making the whole operation change from very simple to kind of complex in the blink of an eye. However, here are the switches you *may* have enough interest in to actually use.

Keeping your header

What's that saying about keeping your header when all about you are losing theirs? You can lose the header or add to it with the following commands:

> ✓ /HEADER0 forces LP not to print at header.
>
> Example: **LP *file.doc*/HEADER0**
>
> ✓ /HEADER2 adds the file's date and time stamp to the header, which makes it a two-line header. I'm sure you know what a two-line header looks like from all those attack of the two-header monster movies they made in the 50s.
>
> Example: **LP *file.doc*/HEADER2**

The default is /HEADER1 — the one-line header. If you want that one-line header, you don't have to lift a finger because you get it automatically.

By the way, did you notice that putting a 0 (zero) after the header command made no headers, a 1 (one) made a one-line header, and a 2 made a two-line header? Sometimes, there's a little logic to all this.

Spacing — The final frontier   .

You can tease Line Print into double- or triple-spacing the printout if you want.

> ✓ /SP# sets the linespacing for whatever number you stick in place of the # sign.
>
> Example: **LP *file.doc*/SP2** double-spaces the file.

Twinkle, twinkle little WordStar

If you're using an older version of WordStar — like version 3 or 4 — then you'll be keen to hear that Line Print can actually print out files created with that old klunker — er, uh, — venerable progenitor of modern-day programs.

> ✓ /WS tells Line Print that the file to be printed isn't a text file but rather a WordStar file.
>
> Example: **LP *file.doc*/WS**

DOS printing

There are a number of ways to print text files in DOS. One is DOS's very own lame PRINT command. Just type **PRINT** *file.doc*. When you are asked about an output device, press Enter, and out the file comes.

An alternative printing technique is via DOS's EDIT command. Typing **EDIT** and pressing Enter gets you into the Edit mode. Press Alt+File⇨Open to load the file to be printed. Then, when the file's on-screen, press Alt+File⇨Print. You get an option that enables you to print either the whole document or just whatever's highlighted. Make your selection and click OK.

Of course — sniff, sniff — neither PRINT nor EDIT adds headers or page numbers or allows adjustment of line spacing. Clearly, Line Print is far more civilized.

Chapter 35

SmartCan

● ●

In This Chapter

▶ Installing SmartCan

▶ Configuring SmartCan

▶ Turning off SmartCan

● ●

*1*s SmartCan the follow-up product to Suzanne Somers's incredible Thigh Master? Hardly. SmartCan is the defender of deleted files.

Basically, once SmartCan is set up, it patiently records the location of files as they are deleted and prevents DOS from recording over that particular space.

SmartCan's activities are automatic and mostly academic until it's time to UnErase a file. Since SmartCan has been protecting the deleted file's space, it's still possible to UnErase a file even if days have passed and you've used Speed Disk. When SmartCan and UnErase work together, it can save *your* can. In fact, SmartCan only works with UnErase — it never talks to people.

Which is fine with me.

The last time I wanted anything to do with a trash can was when Oscar was using one as an apartment. Of course, after all these years as a regular on Sesame Street, I hope he can afford to spend the winters in a dumpster in the South of France.

Okay, now that we know how wonderful SmartCan is, let's trash it for a few seconds. The downside of SmartCan is that, when installed, it grabs hard disk space (for its Endangered Files Preserve) and memory (so that it can hang around in the background all the time).

The bottom line: If you're always erasing things by mistake, SmartCan is a necessity. On the other hand, if a lack of hard disk space is a bigger problem, you may not want to install SmartCan. You'll have to make your own judgment. Don't you hate that?

Installing SmartCan

To be of much benefit, SmartCan must be working invisibly in the background at all times. That means you have to put some sort of command in the AUTOEXEC.BAT file to make sure that SmartCan is activated every time the computer is turned on.

Don't run away just because the topic of editing your AUTOEXEC.BAT file has been broached: Norton Utilities will do all the dirty work if you just ask. In fact, we don't even have to ask — you can rudely point and click.

To install SmartCan in the AUTOEXEC.BAT

1. From the Norton Utilities menu, press Alt+**C**onfiguration ⇨ **S**tartup Programs to end up with Figure 35-1.

Figure 35-1:
The safest way to use SmartCan is to install it as one of your start-up programs. C'mon — it only takes 10K!

```
[]                         Startup Programs                        []
      ┌──────────────── Startup Programs ─────────────────┐
      │ Use NDOS command processor        DRIVER      2K ▲│
      │ Start Keystack (requires NDOS)    RESIDENT      │ │
      │ Diagnose Disk Problems   (NDD /Q)               │ │
      │ Save Disk Format Data    (IMAGE)                │ │
      │ Snapshot Sys Files (INITRAKD /B)                │ │
      │√ Start SmartCan                   RESIDENT    10K│ │
      │ Start Norton Cache                RESIDENT    35K│ │
      │ Start Disk Monitor                RESIDENT     8K│ │
      │ Start DISKREET Encryption Driver  DRIVER     40K▼│
      └───────────────────────────────────────────────────┘
              607 K Available    10 K Used

      ☑  Add Directory to Path
      ☑  Set NU Environment Variable

      ┌─ Save ─┐  ┌─ Cancel ─┐  ┌ Configure ┐  ┌─ Edit ─┐
```

2. Highlight SmartCan and click (or press the spacebar), and you should see a check mark, as in Figure 35-1.

   Remember, if you accidentally check the wrong thing, just check it again to uncheck it.

3. Press Alt+**S**ave.

4. Press Enter or click OK when a box appears telling you the changes won't take place until the computer is rebooted.

Once SmartCan is installed in the AUTOEXEC.BAT file, it's time to start fine-tuning what, exactly, SmartCan will be protecting. Figure 35-2 shows the default SmartCan configuration. You may need to change it.

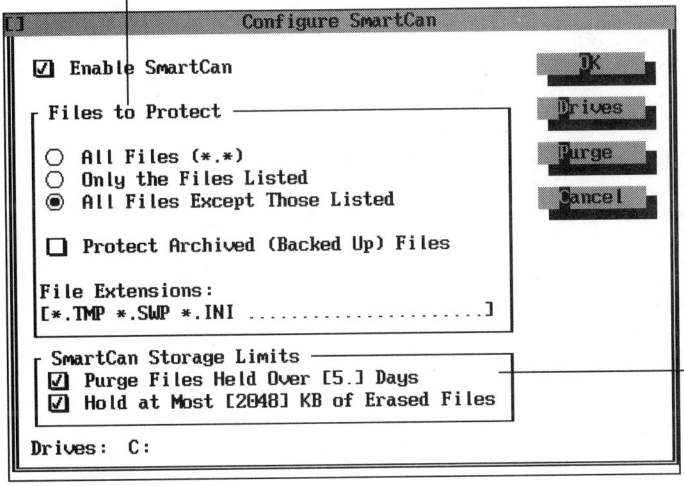

Not all files should be or
have to be protected

```
┌─────────────────── Configure SmartCan ───────────────────┐
│ ☑ Enable SmartCan                              ▐ OK     ▌ │
│ ┌─ Files to Protect ──────────────────┐       ▐ Drives ▌ │
│ │ ○ All Files (*.*)                   │       ▐ Purge  ▌ │
│ │ ○ Only the Files Listed             │       ▐ Cancel ▌ │
│ │ ◉ All Files Except Those Listed     │                  │
│ │ ☐ Protect Archived (Backed Up) Files│                  │
│ │ File Extensions:                    │                  │
│ │ [*.TMP *.SWP *.INI ..............]  │                  │
│ └─────────────────────────────────────┘                  │
│ ┌─ SmartCan Storage Limits ──────────────────┐           │
│ │ ☑ Purge Files Held Over [5.] Days          │           │
│ │ ☑ Hold at Most [2048] KB of Erased Files   │           │
│ └─────────────────────────────────────────────┘          │
│ Drives:  C:                                               │
└───────────────────────────────────────────────────────────┘
```

Figure 35-2: You can put a lid on SmartCan's activities by configuring it to protect only the files you care about.

Choose how many days before trash day and the amount of hard disk space to allocate

For the most part, the default settings in the Configure SmartCan dialog box are satisfactory and there's no pressing need to go changing them all. However, if you just love to get into mischief:

1. Get to the system prompt.

2. Type **SMARTCAN** and press Enter.

   Once in Figure 35-2, you must define what files will fall under SmartCan's purview and how big a landfill you're willing to live with.

3. Select your options.

   - At the upper left of the Configure SmartCan dialog box is the option Enable SmartCan. First, this isn't the same as installing or uninstalling. SmartCan can be installed but turned off if it's getting in the way. For now, leave it enabled, okay?

   - The default Files to Protect setting is that everything is protected except a couple of temporary files and your INI files. If you want to protect only your document files, select the Only the Files Listed button and type ***.DOC** in the File Extensions box.

   The Protect Archived (Backed Up) Files option refers to the BAK files that are often automatically generated by word processing programs. Leave the box unchecked.

   - The SmartCan Storage Limits section is where you dictate how long the files remain protected after deletion. The default is five days. Is that enough for you?

The second issue is the maximum size of your stockpile, as in "Do you want to put a cap on the maximum amount of hard disk space to be reserved for deleted files?" The default is 2MB. You can make it larger or smaller or let SmartCan take as much space as it needs.

If you have more than one drive that needs deletion insurance, press Alt+**Drives** and select your favorite drives for protection.

4. When you're finished, press Alt+**OK**.

Once SmartCan has been installed into the AUTOEXEC.BAT file and all your options set, be sure to reboot the computer to get the thing going!

Whenever you boot the computer, SmartCan provides a report on what's in the can (see Figure 35-3).

Figure 35-3:
A field report from SmartCan, issued automatically when the computer is booted — or anytime you type **SMARTCAN /STATUS** and press Enter at the system prompt.

```
SmartCan, Norton Utilities 8.0, Copyright 1994 by Symantec Corporation

SmartCan Status:      Enabled
Drives Protected:     C: (SmartCan contains 336K in 16 files)
Files Protected:      All files except those with these extensions
                      TMP, SWP, INI
Archive Files:        Not Protected
Files Deleted After:  5 days
```

Taking Out the Trash

One of the nice things about SmartCan is that it empties itself every now and again. After a certain number of days, a deleted file is removed from SmartCan's protection and left to fend for itself. Or if the volume of files being saved exceeds SmartCan's capacity, the older files are tossed even if they haven't quite expired. You have to learn to juggle the two.

Sometimes, *you* may want to take out the trash yourself — especially if you've let SmartCan use as much hard disk space as it wants. When you delete files from SmartCan, it's called *purging*. To see what's in the SmartCan so you can make a judgment about what's to be kept and thrown out, do the following:

1. Get to the system prompt.

2. Type **SMARTCAN** and press Enter.

   Once again, you'll find yourself in something like Figure 35-2.

3. Press Alt+**P**urge to end up with something akin to Figure 35-4.

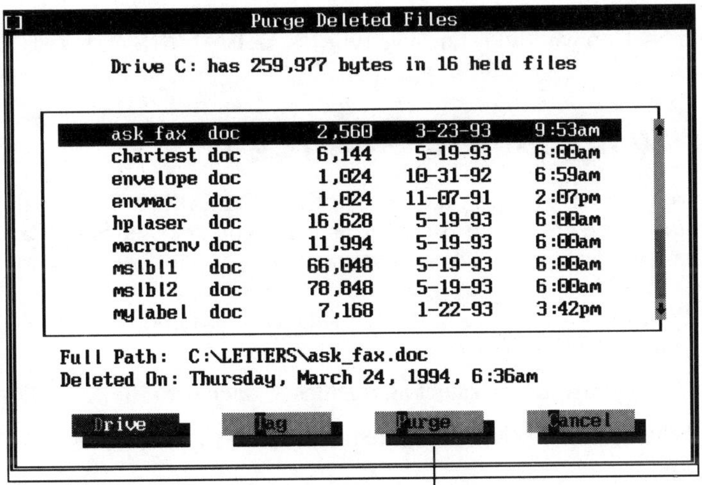

Figure 35-4:
To manually empty the trash can, access the Purge Deleted Files window.

Select files to be purged with
mouse or spacebar — then

4. Select the files to be deleted.

   Highlight each file to be removed and then tag the file by a double-clicking or pressing the spacebar. To select a group of files with a wildcard, use the **T**ag button.

   As you select files, a running total is computed above the filename box.

5. Choose **P**urge to delete the selected files.

6. Choose **C**ancel to exit the Purge dialog box.

7. Press Esc to exit the Configure box and get back to normal.

Recycling

If you decide you want to dump SmartCan and let your deleted files be auto-matically recycled by DOS, then you have two options. Either turn off SmartCan for a little while or forever.

Temporarily disable SmartCan

There are times when you may want to turn SmartCan off for a little while. For example, suppose that you're going to be removing old software and installing new or doing a huge backup followed by wholesale deleting.

The easiest way to temporarily turn off SmartCan is by typing **SMARTCAN /OFF** and pressing Enter. It'll stay off until you reboot your computer. If you want to turn it back on without rebooting, type **SMARTCAN /ON** and press Enter.

Throwing out the SmartCan

To throw out SmartCan, you must edit the AUTOEXEC.BAT file — the instructions for which are *exactly* the same as when you installed SmartCan in the first section. However, you do have to do some cleanup before you start.

1. Purge all the files in SmartCan, using the instructions in the section "Taking Out the Trash."

   You can use **T**ag to select all the files at once with the ***.*** option.

2. When you're back at the system prompt, type **RD \SMARTCAN** and press Enter.

   It should look like nothing happened. But if all went properly, you've just removed the empty SmartCan directory.

3. Follow the Installing SmartCan instructions at the beginning of this chapter to uninstall SmartCan.

   When you get into the Startup Programs dialog box, you'll find SmartCan already checked. When you tag it again, you'll untag it.

4. When you quit the Startup Programs dialog box, if Norton kindly offers to reboot the computer for you, accept the invitation.

   When the computer reboots, you'll be out of the refuse collection business.

If you're not using SmartCan, maybe I can use the name for a Buns of Steel video. Eat your heart out, Suzanne!

Can the can

Since we're on the subject of trash cans, here's our bid for environmentally sound behavior. Actually, this is the only Public Service Announcement you'll find in this book. Did you know that each of us generates 4.5 pounds of trash every day? So, are you doing your bit for the cause? Are you recycling your laser toner cartridges? Are you taking used computer paper to the local recycling center? If we all can the can, our planet will start doing the can can. Otherwise it'll kick the can.

Chapter 36
Text Search

In This Chapter
▶ Finding lost text
▶ Finding erased text

*T*he Text Search (TS) command is the missing link between the bare-bones macho command-line programs and the spiffy dialog box programs. Although Text Search isn't much to look at, it does provide a little dialog box-like assistance to make it easier to find text on a disk. Or if you're a rough-and-tumble kind of person who doesn't like help from anyone, you can still revert to the primitive command-line approach covered at the end of this chapter.

What the heck does Text Search do, exactly? I'm glad you asked. Text Search can tell you in which file — or files — a particular word or phrase is embedded. In plain English, if you've got a bunch of REPORT files, for example, and you can't remember which one had that pithy quote from Albert Einstein, you can get Text Search to zip in and out of all those REPORT files and tell you which one has the quote. Basically, Text Search gives new meaning to the phrase "looking for the right word."

Another Text Search talent is the capability to track down text in *erased space*. This is helpful if you're desperately searching for any bit of text from a file that got obliterated somehow.

Keep in mind also that UnErase (see Chapter 14) can find text in erased space and File Find (covered in Chapter 5) also performs text search operations — and both programs employ all the trappings of civilized life, like dialog boxes and pretty screens.

The one advantage Text Search has over File Find is that it's a small, self-contained file that can be put on a laptop if you're watching your calories. If you're assembling a lean, mean, fighting machine, you may want to go with the minimalist Text Search rather than the larger File Find.

TS, I Love You

Carrying out a basic Text Search is easy. It makes it easier to find text when you have some vague notion of where it is. The more specific you can be in framing your Text Search, the quicker the text will be found. If you don't have a clue, that's okay, too; TS isn't afraid of hard work.

1. At the system prompt, type **TS /T** and press Enter.

   As always, you can opt to start the program via the Norton Utilities menu by highlighting Text Search and pressing Enter.

   The /T switch tells Text Search just to give the names of the files containing the text. If you don't use the /T option, TS stops after every text hit and asks whether it is what you want. This is a real drag unless you're really unsure about what you're looking for or when you're looking for material in erased space. More about un-/T later.

2. Press F when asked to Select search within FILES, all of DISK, or ERASED file space.

   Norton reflects your answer with a Searching contents of files announcement.

   In this first example, you'll just search for text that's in one or more files, which is usually what you do. You can try out the other options in a momentito.

3. When you get the Enter file specification for the files to search prompt, that's your cue to spell out to TS the locale of the suspect files. After you input that information, press Enter.

   If you don't know the path- or filenames, that's okay, just press Enter, and TS sticks in ***.*** — which means "everything" — for you.

   If I were looking for text in my document files in the WORD directory, I'd type **\WORD*.DOC**. If all I knew for sure was that the file was in the WORD directory, I'd use **\WORD** by itself.

4. Next, you are asked to Enter the specific text to search for. Type it in and press Enter.

   In my case, I'm looking for the word *jargon*, so I typed **jargon** — sans quotes — and pressed Enter.

5. Stuff flashes on-screen, and then you should get a list of files telling you where text is, as in Figure 36-1.

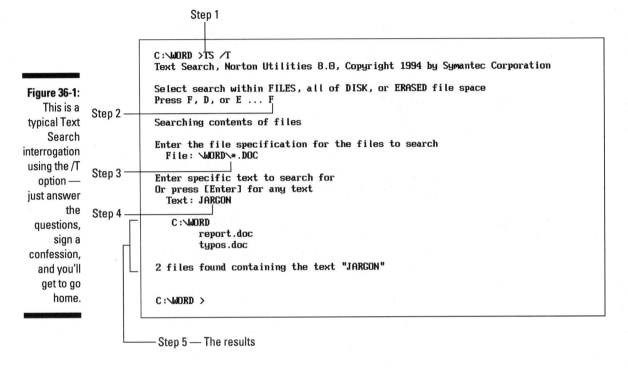

Figure 36-1: This is a typical Text Search interrogation using the /T option — just answer the questions, sign a confession, and you'll get to go home.

Step 1

```
C:\WORD >TS /T
Text Search, Norton Utilities 8.0, Copyright 1994 by Symantec Corporation

Select search within FILES, all of DISK, or ERASED file space
Press F, D, or E ... F

Searching contents of files

Enter the file specification for the files to search
   File: \WORD\*.DOC

Enter specific text to search for
Or press [Enter] for any text
   Text: JARGON

      C:\WORD
            report.doc
            typos.doc

2 files found containing the text "JARGON"


C:\WORD >
```

Step 2

Step 3

Step 4

Step 5 — The results

If you opt not to use the /T option, your search results in something like Figure 36-2, where you must respond Y or N to say whether you want to continue the search, if you're thirsty for more.

Figure 36-2: Without the /T option, Text Search slips into an interactive mode, stopping to ask if you want to continue the hunt or if you've had enough.

```
Searching C:\word\old.doc

Found at line 1, file offset 145

Jargon?
Jargon pervades software documentation.  Manuals seem unable to esacep jargon b
cause computers fascienate those who work around them and because the people wh
 work with and write about computers are not afraid of computers or the jargon
hat goes with them.


Search for more (Y/N) ?
```

To send the results of the search into a file that can be read or printed, add **/LOG > file.log** at the end of the command. The command line should look like this: **TS /T /LOG > *file.log***. Remember, File Find does stuff like this automatically, so if you're feeling overwhelmed, just stick with File Find.

At any time during the Text Search, press Esc to bring the whole operation to a screeching halt. You can also Esc if you give a wrong answer or make a typo when you give the search parameters to TS. Doesn't *search parameters* sound impressive?

Transcendental Searching

In the basic search example, you exercised a search for text in Files. That's not the only place to find text. At your fingertips is the capability to search the entire disk or to narrow the search to just Erased file space. Either way, the process is — almost identical.

1. At the system prompt, type **TS /T** and press Enter.

2. When asked to `Select search within FILES, all of DISK, or ERASED file space`, press E for Erased or, you guessed it, D for Disk.

   Norton confirms your answer by reporting that it's either `Searching unused data space` or `Searching entire disk`.

3. Next, `Press the letter of the drive to search` — usually that's C.

   TS sets you up for success by telling you the name of the drive you're using before asking this question. When in doubt, go along.

4. Next, press Enter to avoid copying `text into file`.

   This option is used if you're trying to rebuild a file rather than merely attempting to locate some misplaced words. If your goal is to resurrect a file, use UnErase. Don't use this option.

5. Next, you are asked to `Enter the specific text to search for.` Type it in and press Enter.

   This is the one thing you should know: what is it you're looking for?

6. Stuff flashes on-screen, and then you get a list of files telling you where text is, as in Figure 36-3.

Figure 36-3:
It's 10:00 —
do you know
what text
has
engaged
your
clusters?
Press Y if
you want to
continue the
search.

```
Searching C: cluster number 168, sectors 3,017 - 3,032

Found at byte offset 145

Jargon?
Jargon pervades software documentation.  Manuals seem unable to esacep jargon b
cause computers fascienate those who work around them and because the people wh
 work with and write about computers are not afraid of computers or the jargon
hat goes with them.


Search for more (Y/N) ?
```

Bypassing the Text Search Interrogation

If you know in advance what Text Search options are needed to find your text, then the command-line method lets you cut to the chase. Otherwise, just use the interactive method. (The interactive method is what we just did — where Text Search prompts you for each bit of information.)

The command line syntax for performing the basic search example from the first section is

> **TS pathname text /T**

Substitute your own search directory (if you know it) and search text when you run this command. If you had used a command line search with the example at the beginning of the chapter, it'd be **TS C:\WORD*.DOC JARGON /T**.

Adding an /S to the end of the command requires Text Search to look in the subdirectories under the WORD directory as well.

To do all that and create a file containing the results of the search,

> **TS C:\WORD*.DOC JARGON /T /LOG > file.log**

Whew!

There are lots more switches and options, but I don't know why anyone would want to put themselves through this kind of torture. This program already has more slashes than a Friday the 13th movie. Let's get out of here!

Chapter 37

Wipe Information

· ·

· ·

Wipe Info's raison d'être is to utterly obliterate files on your system. Think of Wipe Info as the Humpty Dumpty of Delete — because once Wipe Info deletes, the files can never be put back together again. Not by King's horses, not by King's men, and not even by Peter Norton. Period and amen.

Why would anyone unleash such a destructive force on a computer? Some people — maybe even you — have a hard drive full of private, ultraconfidential material. If you think deleting that stuff from your computer will keep it from falling into enemy hands, then you haven't read about UnErase (discussed in Chapter 14), which resuscitates deleted files. And if *you* can do it, so can the bad guys.

Wipe Info is prepared to do a Quick Wipe, which deletes information so that normal people cannot UnErase data. However, the government has its own standard for deletion, which takes longer and is more complicated. I know, it's hard to accept that our government came up with something slow and complex, but go with me on this. The government standard deletes information not merely forever, but also for forever *and* ever.

Once you've chosen the wiping method, Wipe Info applies it in one of two ways: to directly delete a particular file or files (sort of as a replacement for DOS's DELETE command) or to dissolve any residual data in currently unused space. Only tech-types could conceive of a program that deletes space.

Unless confidentiality is an important issue for you, don't use Wipe Info as a fun alternative to Delete. A slip of the wrist could wipe out a file you mean to keep or inadvertently block your chances of retrieving something later if you change your mind. Not to mention that Wipe Info can wipe out everything on your hard drive, including the files that make it boot. In short, Wipe Info is not a toy.

Wiping Information

To get to the Wipe Info opening dialog box, shown in Figure 37-1, use one of the following methods:

- ✔ From the Norton Utilities menu, highlight Wipe Information and press Enter, or

- ✔ From a system prompt, type **WIPEINFO** and press Enter

In the opening dialog box, you have four options — including Alt+**Q**uit.

Figure 37-1: The guardian of Wipe Info bids you welcome.

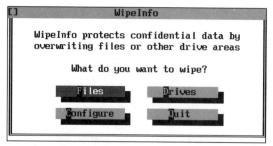

Configuring Wipe Info

You can skip the Configuration step if you just want a normal, totally destructive Wipe. If you need that extra government security, then you have to press Alt+**C**onfigure from the opening dialog box and get into Figure 37-2.

Figure 37-2: The only option missing is Handi-Wipe.

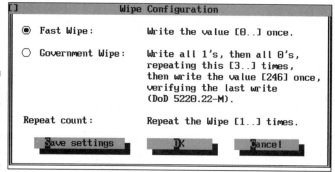

If you need the Government Wipe — which I used to think just happened every April 15 — click the appropriate button. Pressing Alt+**S**ave Settings makes the current type of Wipe the default. Pressing Alt+**OK** makes the current settings active for this session only. No matter which button you select, you end up back at Figure 37-1.

Phasering files

If I haven't scared you off yet, then I guess you really want to wreak some havoc. So, let's party!

The Wipe Files dialog box (see Figure 37-3) gives us plenty of ways to triangulate on material to be wiped out.

Figure 37-3:
The only nondestructive option here is *Wipe unused file slack only.* If you *Confirm each file,* you get one additional chance to retract this decision when Wipe Info asks, "Are you sure you want to do this?"

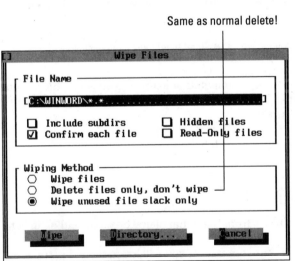

Same as normal delete!

The File Name box lets you specify which file or files to wipe out. If you suddenly can't remember the directory name you want to work with, press Alt+**D**irectory to browse through a directory tree until you find the name you need.

When you've made your choices, press Alt+**W**ipe. You get a warning box repeating that you're about to permanently Wipe whatever you wrote in the File Name box. Press Alt+**W**ipe again if you want to proceed.

If you choose to Confirm each file, you get a dialog box like the one in Figure 37-4, where you have one last chance to make a decision about Wiping or Skipping — not Wiping — files.

Figure 37-4: The Last Stop cafe — press Alt+**A**uto only if you want *all* named files to be Wiped without further ado.

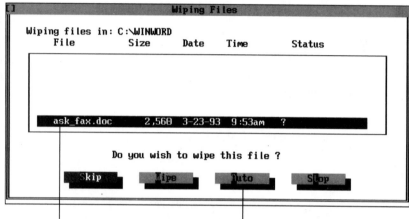

```
[]                          Wiping Files
Wiping files in: C:\WINWORD
       File          Size      Date      Time        Status



    ask_fax.doc     2,560   3-23-93   9:53am      ?


              Do you wish to wipe this file ?

      Skip            Wipe           Auto           Stop
```

The file in question   Auto automatically deletes all files

When all files are either eliminated or skipped, you get a little announcement summarizing what just happened. Press Enter to make the dialog box go away and return to Figure 37-1.

If you're finished, press Alt+**Q**uit.

Disrupting drives

If you press Alt+**D**rives from the initial dialog box, you end up in Figure 37-5.

If you select Wipe entire drive, you will irreparably destroy *everything* on the drive forever.

After you choose a drive and a method, press either Alt+**O**K to continue or Alt+**C**ancel to skedaddle out of there.

Once you're back at Figure 37-1, Alt+**Q**uit gets you out.

Pick a drive to wipe

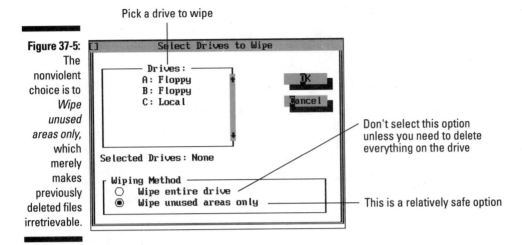

Figure 37-5: The nonviolent choice is to *Wipe unused areas only,* which merely makes previously deleted files irretrievable.

Don't select this option unless you need to delete everything on the drive

This is a relatively safe option

Wipe Out

If you need to, files and drives can be wiped out via our old friend, the command line.

✔ **WIPEINFO** *file.doc* **/BATCH**

This wipes out a file called FILE.DOC — put the name of your victim file in there instead — and doesn't show any dialog boxes (that's what the **/BATCH** is for).

✔ **WIPEINFO** *file.doc* **/GOV /BATCH**

Does the same as the preceding example — except to the Department of Defense standard.

✔ **WIPEINFO /E /BATCH**

Wipes out the erased and unused space.

✔ **WIPEINFO** **.doc* **/K /BATCH**

Wipes the slack space in all the DOC files in the current directory.

Tempest in a computer

If you think this business about a Department of Defense standard for deleting data is over the top, then wait until you hear about *Tempest*—which, if you hold your breath long enough, is an acronym for Transient Electromagnetic Pulse Emanation Standard.

It kind of all started in 1980 with a Dutch engineer name Wim Van Eck, who demonstrated that computers inside a building 100 yards away were broadcasting signals he could pick up.

The government and everyone else with stuff to hide went completely wacko when they realized that computers inside the CIA were merrily transmitting our secrets a bit at a time to any Tom, Dick, or Yuri with the right equipment who might be sitting outside. Thus was spawned the Tempest industry, providing computer companies their patriotic opportunity to overcharge for special computers that don't emanate transient electromagnetic pulses to "Van Eck listeners," as they've since been nicknamed.

Part VI
The Part of Tens

The 5th Wave — By Rich Tennant

"IT'S AMAZING HOW MUCH MORE SOME PEOPLE CAN GET OUT OF A PC THAN OTHERS."

In this part...

Here's a half-dozen helpful lists that summarize some of the stuff in the book, detail where to get more help, and share what's new with Norton Utilities 8.

Chapter 38

Ten Ways to Fake
Your Way Through Norton

· ·

In This Chapter

▶ Use the Norton Utilities menu

▶ First, do no harm

▶ Quick Tips to navigate a dialog box

▶ Cancel a command

▶ Make NuConfig install and remove start-up programs

▶ The Huh? command

▶ File Find is your friend

▶ UnErase

▶ Order up a rescue disk

▶ Learn a few Norton buzzwords

· ·

*H*ave you seen that obnoxious commercial starring two plumbers who are chortling about how they get to charge $65 an hour to fix a problem anyone could solve themselves with a dollar's worth of Drano?

The people wise enough to use Drano don't know anything more about plumbing than the poor schmoes who fork over the $65. All they really need to know is to pour the stuff down the drain.

Computer professionals are a lot more like those plumbers than you think. I don't want to get letters from plumbers or computer consultants on this; my point is that often you can fix your own problems without understanding what the problem is. On the other hand, there are times you need professionals. And they more than earn their $65.

First, however, be smart enough to try the $1 solution.

Here are ten ways you can cluelessly surf through Norton's features.

Use the Norton Utilities Menu

Can't remember any commands? Just type **NORTON** and press Enter, and all of Norton's Utilities are at your fingertips. Once you're in the Norton Utilities menu, you can see the name of each program on the left and an explanation of what it does on the right.

Really impress your friends by instantly reorganizing the utilities programs by name or topic. Alt+N switches to an alphabetical list by name, and Alt+T groups the list by topic.

Need more explanation? Press F1 to get more detail.

First, Do No Harm

Have plenty of floppy disks ready when you go into a Norton recovery situation. Then, whenever Norton offers to make an Undo disk, take advantage of it. That way, if you don't like what Norton did, you can put things back and you'll be no worse off.

Quick Tips to Navigate a Dialog Box

Dazzled by all the options in a dialog box? Just use the mouse to point and click. If you don't have a mouse, pressing Tab moves you from group topic to group topic, and pressing spacebar selects or deselects items. Whenever you see a button with one letter highlighted, pressing Alt plus the highlighted letter activates that option. If you see an Exit button, for example, pressing Alt+X activates that command. Pressing Enter is the same as clicking OK.

Cancel a Command

Anytime you're anyplace you don't like, press Esc to cancel what's going on. Press Esc enough times and you are completely backed out of the program. Note that sometimes it takes a second for Norton to get to a safe stopping place. Be patient.

Make NuConfig Install and Remove Start-Up Programs

A number of Norton Utilities need to be activated every time you turn on the computer. These programs are called *start-up* programs. If you tell Norton which programs you want to use, Norton takes care of the bookkeeping involved in telling your computer to always start the programs. Type **NUCONFIG** and press Enter; then select the Startup Programs option. Once in the NuConfig menu, select the programs you desire, and Norton does the rest! The same method also turns the programs off if they irritate you.

The Huh? Command

You know how when you're in the Norton Utilities menu you automatically get an explanation of the highlighted command and some options on the right? You can get all of those options, plus more, when you're not in the fancy menu. Just type the name of any utility and add a /? before pressing Enter.

Examples: **FILEFIND /?** or **UNERASE /?**.

Use this option if you're not sure whether it's the right command.

Really impress your friends by printing out the information. Type **FILEFIND /? > PRN** and press Enter to get a printout of the instructions.

File Find Is Your Friend

The bottom line is that probably 80 percent of what you do in Norton Utilities involves File Find. Typing **FILEFIND** and pressing Enter is all you have to know to get started. Use the help system as needed. Remember, *missing files* is replacing *financial woes* as the leading cause of divorce in the United States. Don't let it happen to you.

UnErase

When you're not using File Find, you're using UnErase. You don't have to know squat about files, clusters, tracks, and heads to use this program. Just type **UNERASE** and press Enter.

Really impress your friends by typing **UNERASE /LIST** and pressing Enter to produce a quick-and-dirty list of files in the current directory that are available for recovery.

Order Up a Rescue Disk

See Chapter 15 for instructions on how to make a rescue disk, and then do so for all your computers. You'll really impress everyone by coming back from a battery failure or a messed-up File Allocation Table like a pro. Don't let on that you don't know what any of those things are. Just be prepared.

Learn a Few Norton Buzzwords

If you're faking your way through Norton in front of coworkers or the boss, you con add a hint of authority to your actions by saying something in Norton-ese every now and again. For an extra added air of intimidation, add the phrase "I'm sure I don't have to tell *you*, but . . ." to the front of each statement.

If you're using File Find, say something like, "It'll take just a second for File Find to traverse the system's architecture."

If you're using UnErase, try saying, "Our chances for success are enhanced if the files are in contiguous rather than noncontiguous clusters."

If you're using Norton Diagnostics, you can say — with an air of frustration — "Darn! If only we had popped for those loopback plugs, we could test our serial and parallel I/O."

Then, in case of extreme emergency, look thoughtfully at the computer and say, "Well, if we have to, we can rebuild the partition table."

Chapter 39
Ten Ways to Get Out of Trouble

● ●

In This Chapter

▶ Take a deep breath

▶ Don't copy anything to your hard disk

▶ Review Part IV — Rescue Me!

▶ Review help options

▶ Follow data recovery procedures in the Norton manual

▶ Use Rescue Disk

▶ Locating lost files and text

▶ Fouled-up floppies

▶ Handling `Seek Error` messages

▶ If all else fails, use backed up files

● ●

*T*here's nothing worse than that helpless feeling when your computer betrays you by failing to perform as expected — as *needed*. Nobody knows that better than the people who created Norton Utilities in the first place. Sometimes having a problem presents another problem — how to get enough information to solve the first problem. Here are a few signposts and tips to point you in the right direction.

Take a Deep Breath

Frankly, this is key to everything. Granted, if anything can drive someone to the brink, it's the disappearance from the computer of the proposal that's due in ten minutes. Besides, freaking out doesn't bring anything back. Also, while freaking out, you may make a mistake that can jeopardize the whole rescue. Use that adrenaline for heavy celebrating after the rescue.

If something goes wrong, take a deep breath — take a walk if you have to — but don't start troubleshooting in an agitated state of mind.

Don't Copy Anything to Your Hard Disk

First, don't copy any programs — even Norton's — to the hard disk when you're in the middle of a disaster. As long as you have hopes for repairs, also don't copy the back-up copy of the file or create a new file with the same name as the lost file. The message here is simple — the fewer changes to the hard drive, the greater the chance for your recovery procedure.

Review Part IV — Rescue Me!

Part IV of this book is about recovering from a disaster and the various Norton programs designed expressly for that purpose. Go through those chapters and see whether your problem matches any of the solutions. At the very least, you'll know what your problem isn't.

Review Help Options

Chapter 43 reviews 10 ways to get help with Norton Utilities 8. Is your problem covered by the Norton Advisor or any of the Help systems? You can search by topic in both DOS and Windows Help. Give it a shot.

Follow Data Recovery Procedures in the Norton Manual

Another approach to the Rescue Me! section in this book is the "Emergency Data Recovery Procedures" section in the Norton manual itself. In an emergency, don't leave any stone unturned — or cliché unused.

Use Rescue Disk

Did you make a rescue disk? If you did, now's the time to drag it out. It will help restore your system's configuration if you're getting Invalid `Settings` messages or you've just changed the battery. It can also restore your computer's index system so that files are properly cataloged.

Locating Lost Files and Text

If the trouble you're in has to do with missing files or text, then try File Find (covered in Chapter 5) and UnErase (discussed in Chapter 14) to search the hard drive to pinpoint and recover the material.

Fouled-Up Floppies

If you're having problems with floppy disks, then run Norton Disk Doctor (see Chapter 26) or Disk Tools (covered in Chapter 22).

Handling Seek Error Messages

If Norton Disk Doctor doesn't help with this, be sure to give Calibrate a try, which is discussed in Chapter 17. Calibrate is another way to fine-tune — and perhaps repair — your disk.

If All Else Fails, Restore Backed-Up Files

This is another plug for backing up. There's a law of computer usage that says the probability of disaster increases geometrically with the importance of the file. In other words, if you're working on the most critical file of your entire life — odds are that something untoward will befall it. If it's a big deadline, a big project, there's no law against backing up several times a day. It makes moments of disaster a little easier to bear, knowing that you've got a fresh backup to fall back on.

Chapter 40

Ten Ways to Compute Defensively

In This Chapter

▶ Review Part III — An Ounce of Prevention

▶ Learn what directories you use

▶ Back up frequently

▶ Use Safe Format and Speed Disk

▶ Keep an eye on your resources

▶ Keep things neat and tidy

▶ Make copies of your key files

▶ Learn a little DOS

▶ Watch drive lights

▶ Use caution when driving or operating machinery

*I*f you're a high-wire act, it's unprofessional to work *with* a net. For everyone else, though, working without a net is foolhardy at best. If your data is your career, then do everything you can to protect them both. This chapter is a checklist for your internal safety net.

Review Part III — An Ounce of Prevention

It's all there in Part III. Do that stuff and you'll be prepared for darn near anything that can happen to you.

Learn What Directories You Use

DOS Boot Camp (in Chapter 1) contains a chart in which you write the names and places — directories and files — that are important to you on the hard drive. Sometimes you take a wrong turn on the drive, but if you don't know where you're supposed to be, how can you tell whether you're lost? The more you get a clear picture of what is *normal* for you, the easier it is to spot a problem and solve it.

Back Up Frequently

Make copies of files you've created and changed. Every day. Who can predict what will happen tomorrow? If you have back-up copies, then even if the computer gets flooded, frozen, or earthquaked, you can always recover.

Use Safe Format and Speed Disk

Two easy-to-use programs that help keep you out of trouble — Safe Format (discussed in Chapter 11) and Speed Disk (discussed in Chapter 12). Don't forget to dust them off and use them now and again.

Keep an Eye on Your Resources

Although Windows has sort of preempted the word *resources*, I'm not just referring to Windows here. How much space is left on your hard disk? How big is the file you're working on? How much memory does your computer have? Unlike the government, we can't use more than what we've got. Once the limit of the system has been exceeded, it crashes. So pay attention.

Keep Things Neat and Tidy

Delete what you don't need. The less extraneous matter on the computer, the more likely you'll be able to find what's important in the event of disaster.

Make Copies of Your Key Files

There are only about eight thousand ways to make copies of your key files like AUTOEXEC.BAT, CONFIG.SYS, WIN.INI, and the other INIs. Take advantage of Norton's Rescue Disk or many of the other programs that provide quick and easy ways to make copies of these files. It's so much easier to recover when you've got a backup of the file rather than trying to create it from scratch.

Learn a Little DOS

The more DOS you know, the more you'll be able to interpret what's going on. At least make sure that you understand the material from the DOS Boot Camp in Chapter 1. Remember, information is power.

Watch Drive Lights

These are on the floppy drives. When you save to or copy from a floppy drive, watch those little drive lights. Wait until they go out before removing disks from the drives. Even though the screen says "all done," it's not really finished until the drive light goes out. There is a severe penalty for early withdrawal. Mainly, the file or even the whole disk can become scrambled.

Use Caution When Driving or Operating Machinery

This is a problem for people who work at home. Your back is out, or you're recovering from some illness and you don't feel well enough to work. So you're sitting around all numbed up on Vicodin or TheraFlu and you've had enough of the talk shows and you see that computer sitting there and you start thinking, "Hey, I'll do that system backup on the computer I've been putting off." So far, so good.

But then it happens.

"It" is the brilliant idea that "while you're in there" you'll first delete some things on the computer — which gives way to the notion that you really ought to reorganize — overhaul — turn years of accumulated clutter into a model of sleek efficiency! Yeah.

Wrong!

What happens next is the typical sick-day disaster. You delete something that you shouldn't have or start messing with something you don't understand and suddenly you're in a fix. The same stuff that made you too stupid to drive also makes you too spaced out to handle anything complicated on your computer. Of course, trying to get out of trouble while ill is also a special treat not to be missed.

The backup was a good idea. Stick to that. Save the Home Improvement for another day.

Chapter 41

Ten Most Commonly Asked Technical Support Questions

by Wes Santee

● ●

● ●

Why should I use Norton Disk Doctor (NDD) when I already have Check Disk (CHKDSK)?

NDD does everything CHKDSK does, and much more. For example, NDD explains every step that it performs before making any changes, and it allows you to create *undo* files to reverse those actions on the rare occasion that you don't like how things got fixed. On the other hand, once you run CHKDSK/F, there's no stopping it and no turning back.

Also, at the end of NDD's diagnosis and repair process, you can generate reports containing technical information about your hard drive so you can impress your friends. Try *that* with CHKDSK!

Overall, NDD provides a much safer diagnostic and repair environment than CHKDSK. And finally, the *real* reason you should use NDD instead of CHKDSK is because it looks neat.

Whenever I try to install Norton Utilities from Windows, it never works! What's the deal? It says "Compatible with Windows" on the box!

Although Norton Utilities will work in conjunction with Windows, it's still predominantly a DOS program and the install program is not designed to work in Windows or any other multitasking environment. During the installation process, several tests are performed on the drive to determine whether there is any reason the installation program shouldn't be allowed to continue. Successful testing involves probing around on your drive in a lot places that Windows doesn't like.

Once the installation program finishes, it automatically sets up your program groups and icons so that you can use The Norton Utilities from within Windows. It's just the installation program that you can't use in Windows.

Speed Disk is giving me too many optimization choices! Which one should I use?

Unless you're a nerd, you'll probably want to use Unfragment Files Only on a daily basis and Full Optimization once a week. For a full explanation of the various options, see Chapter 12.

What are all these X'd out files in Speed Disk?

Before Speed Disk begins the defragmentation process, it scans your drive to check for files that shouldn't be moved. For example, if you run Windows, chances are there's a big file sitting on your hard drive that Windows uses as its swap file. Windows expects that file to be in a specific place on the drive. Windows will not be your friend if Norton moves the swap file and it's not there when Windows tries to find it.

To avoid such unpleasantries, Speed Disk marks these files as *unmovable*. Unless you're a nerd, you probably don't want to know what constitutes a file being marked as unmovable.

Okay, if you really want to know how Speed Disk knows which files not to move, here's the lowdown. Speed Disk examines each file on your drive and determines what attributes are set for those files. If Speed Disk finds a file with the System and Hidden attributes set, Speed Disk marks that file as unmovable. That's right, if you want to allow Speed Disk to move those files, take those attributes off (see Chapter 31 for more information on attributes and the FA command, which can remove or edit attributes). Remember, though, that System and Hidden attributes are set for a reason and you should not tamper with them unless you're a certified genius.

My copy of Norton Utilities doesn't work! Why can't I use it on my old IBM PC or PC XT?

Beginning with version 7 of The Norton Utilities, specific instructions in the programs are being used that keep Norton Utilities from being used on anything less than an IBM AT computer (commonly referred to as a 286 machine). If you have an original PC, PC XT, or PS/2 Model 30 (commonly referred to as an 8088 or 8086 machine), Norton Utilities versions 7 and above will not work on your machine.

I don't understand all these terms that Norton Disk Doctor (NDD) is using! Should I say "yes" or "no" to correcting the problems?

In general, you should say "yes." Make sure, however, that you create an undo disk just in case — and this is rare — the fix is worse than the problem.

For a brief discussion of the different terms that NDD might use, see the "Disk Companion" section of your Norton Utilities manual.

If you don't have your manual handy, here are a couple of the most frequent problems you probably will encounter, what they mean, and how they usually happen:

- *Lost Clusters.* These are lonely chunks of data on your drive that are suffering from an identity crisis. Whenever you create and save a file to your drive, a link ties the data contained in that file to the filename you specify. If a program you are running crashes, that link may be broken. Thus, you end up with a file that doesn't know where its data is and data that doesn't know to whom it belongs. This is a lost cluster. NDD reestablishes the link to the data, albeit without its correct filename (which is now lost), and saves it on your drive. See Chapter 26 for the details on how this all works.

- *Cross-Linked Files.* Cross-linked files are like two trains on the same track. They both shouldn't be there and there will be problems when they meet — the laws of physics being what they are. When two or more files become cross-linked, each thinks it owns the same space on the drive. NDD determines which file has the right of way and moves the other files(s) elsewhere.

Why does Norton Utilities leave behind the text that was on the screen before I ran it?

Starting with version 7, most programs that make up The Norton Utilities act like *pop-up* applications. This includes leaving behind all the stuff at the DOS prompt. If you ran Norton Utilities hoping to hide what you just typed about your boss, then you ran the wrong program.

If you really want to clear the screen before executing the Norton Utilities, write a batch file to clear the screen and then run the Norton program you desire. Don't know how to write a batch file? It's time to make a blatant plug. Go get *More DOS For Dummies*. It can help you learn how to create your own little batch files and tell you lots of other neat stuff, too.

I want to run Norton Utilities on my NetWare, OS/2 HPFS, or other non-DOS partitions. Why won't it let me?

The Norton Utilities is a DOS product. It understands the intricacies of how the DOS file system is implemented. Other file systems like NetWare and OS/2 use vastly different structures to store data on your drive. The Norton Utilities does not understand these structures.

What I'm trying to say here is that you're right: You can't run Norton Utilities on non-DOS partitions. That's why it's called Norton Utilities for DOS (and Windows).

Norton Disk Doctor (NDD) keeps crashing when I try to run it! What's going on?

Usually when NDD crashes, it's due to another program conflicting with NDD's operation.

In general, NDD is designed to be used as a maintenance and repair program. It's generally not a good idea to allow other DOS/Windows programs to run while a maintenance/repair program is being used. You wouldn't try to fix the engine of your car while it's running, would you? Same principle, different setting. The only exception is NDD for Windows, which is created to run in the background.

If NDD or other Norton Utilities applications crash even when there is nothing else running in your system, contact Symantec Technical Support for assistance.

I'm seeing all sorts of weird characters on my screen! I want them gone! How do I do it?

Actually, I think they're kinda cool. But if you want to use standard ASCII characters (what all those *other* DOS applications use) instead of these cool graphic ones, then go to Chapter 2, which covers the issue in hideous detail. For now, here's how to do it:

1. At the system prompt, type **NUCONFIG** and press Enter to pop into the configuration program.

2. Choose Video and Mouse — the first option.

3. Press Alt+Display **M**ode to select graphical controls.

4. Press Alt+down arrow to display options.

5. Highlight Standard and press Enter.

6. Press Enter to accept the change.

7. Choose **Q**uit to exit NUCONFIG.

Chapter 42

Ten New Features in Norton Utilities 8

*W*hat's more exciting than the arrival of a new phone book, more anticipated than the Fall Preview Issue of *TV Guide*, more fun than the annual *Sports Illustrated* swimsuit issue? Yes, folks, it's the list of what's new with Norton Utilities 8, and where to find — in this very book — more about those new features!

Norton Disk Doctor for Windows

Similar to Norton Disk Doctor for DOS, the new Norton Disk Doctor for Windows is very cute. Its main attraction is that it runs in Windows — and in the background. You can be running tests on your disks while working. Norton Disk Doctor for Windows is covered in Chapter 26.

Speed Disk for Windows

Although both Speed Disk for DOS and Speed Disk for Windows are very similar, Speed Disk for Windows also has the unique capability to run in the background. It also knows how to work in conjunction with Norton Disk Doctor for Windows. Speed Disk for Windows is covered in Chapter 12.

Updated File Fix

File Fix continues to keep pace with new versions of software, including WordPerfect version 6. File Fix is covered in Chapter 24.

More Norton Diagnostics

More technical things have been added. Specifically, Norton can produce an IRQ status report to let you know what is where. If you don't know what an IRQ status is, then you don't need to worry about it now. The IRQs become important once you start buying attachments for your computer. Oh, and the diags can now detect a joystick. Norton Diagnostics is covered in Chapter 25.

File Compare for Windows

Compares, side-by-side, two text files. Mostly it's there to let you contrast two versions of AUTOEXEC.BAT or two versions of WIN.INI, for example. File Compare is covered in Chapter 7.

Windows Configuration Management

An exciting addition to the Norton Family are the INI Tools — INI Advisor, INI Tuner, and INI Editor. The trio of programs provides options, explanations, and easier ways to fine-tune your Windows system. Even if you feel uncomfortable touching anything having to do with the inner workings of Windows — if it ain't broke, don't fix it — there are some fun things to play with as well. They are all covered in Chapter 20.

INI Tracker for DOS and Windows

Even though it's called INI Tracker, it also keeps an audit *trail* of your AUTOEXEC.BAT and CONFIG.SYS files. This allows you to reinstate a previous — presumably functional — version of those important files if something accidentally gums up the works. INI Tracker for DOS and Windows is covered in Chapter 19.

More Info in System Information (SI)

The oft-referred to SI — or System Information, covered in Chapter 13 — now compares your system to a Pentium muscle machine, just in case you weren't feeling inadequate enough already.

Enhanced WipeInfo

Wipe Information now includes support for compressed drives. Wipe Information is covered in Chapter 37.

System Watch for Windows

System Watcher is a sort of super "About." You know how you can see the status of your memory and other system resources by using the About command? Well, System Watcher lets you not only see more about the inner workings of your system than you really want to know, but it also has an alarm system to notify you when resources dip below a certain level. This lets you avoid crashes and other unpleasant moments. System Watcher is covered in Chapter 18.

Chapter 43

Ten Free (Mostly) Ways to Get Help with Norton Utilities 8

In This Chapter

▶ Use on-line help

▶ Use the Question mark switch

▶ Use the Norton Integrator

▶ Use the Advisors

▶ Use a modem

▶ Call or fax Symantec Technical Support

▶ Call Symantec Customer Service

▶ Use Symantec's Fax Retrieval System

▶ Dialing for dollars

▶ Look at the Manual

Use On-Line Help

While using the Norton Utilities, DOS or Windows, you can always press F1 or Alt+Help to receive context-sensitive help. Yes, believe it or not, software can be sensitive to your needs. What sensitivity for software means is that if Help is summoned while you're puzzling over Optimization Methods, for example, Norton knows where you are and provides help on that exact topic. The new QuickHelp in Windows provides instant guidance for the major features of the utility you're in.

Use the Question Mark Switch

Almost all the Norton Utilities for DOS have more switches than a politician and it's hard to keep them all straight — the switches, not the politicians. Whenever you find yourself staring at the system prompt wondering whether you need to use **/T** or **/D**, type the main command with a **/?**, and you get a quick list of clues. For example, typing **SFORMAT /?** and pressing Enter gives you all the command line options for Safe Format.

Use the Norton Integrator

Because you may not use a number of the Norton programs on a daily basis, it's easy to forget the name of the program you need to use. Type **NORTON** and press Enter to call up the Norton Utilities Menu, also known as the Norton Integrator, which displays the names of all the Norton programs on the left and what they do on the right. Scroll through the programs until you bump into the one you're searching for.

Get Some Good Advice

Ever wish you could have Peter Norton sitting with you — like a friendly angel — guiding you when you falter? Well, you already do (almost) with DOS's Norton Advisor and Windows' INI Advisor.

If you run across a problem while in the Norton Utilities menu, go to the Help menu and call up the Norton Advisor. Problems, error messages, and other difficulties you may encounter with Norton Utilities are listed there along with possible solutions. Maybe your question is amongst 'em.

While in Windows, you can get into the INI Advisor by double-clicking on its icon or selecting it from the toolbar in the INI Editor and INI Tuner. Again, excellent advice is available to cover many situations.

Use a Modem

If you own a modem, there are a number of additional options for not only making contact with tech support geniuses at Symantec, but also tapping into the wealth of information that people in the trenches have accumulated. Who knows, maybe you can help someone who has less experience than you.

- America Online

  While online, use the Keyword **SYMANTEC**.

  To join America Online, call 800-227-6364.

- CompuServe

  While online, use **GO SYMUTIL**.

  To join CompuServe, call 800-848-8199.

- Symantec's BBS (free!)

  9600 baud, call 503-484-6669.

  2400 baud, call 503-484-6699.

Call Symantec Technical Support

You can call or fax a question to Symantec's Technical Support team. You get free support from them for your first call and for 90 days thereafter. So try to have all your emergencies within a three-month span.

- Voice: 503-334-7470
- Fax: 503-334-7470

International Technical Support and Customer Service

United Kingdom

Symantec UK Limited
Sygnus Court
Market Street
Maidenhead
Berkshire
SL6 4AD
United Kingdom
0628 59 222 (voice)
0628 592 287 (fax)

Europe (all countries except UK)

Symantec Europe
Kanaalpark 145
Postbus 1143
2321 JV Leiden
The Netherlands
31 71 353 111 (voice)
31 71 353 150 (fax)

Australia

Symantec Pty. Ltd.
Upper Level
408 Victoria Road
Gladesville, NSW 2111
Australia
61 2 879 6577 (voice)
61 2 879 6805 (fax)

All other countries

Symantec Corp.
10201 Torre Ave.
Cupertino, CA 95014
U.S.A.
408-252-3570 (voice)
408-253-4992 (fax)

Call Symantec Customer Service

The customer service department can refer you to consultants or otherwise make suggestions about where you can get more help.

▮ ✔ 800-441-7234

Use Symantec's Fax Retrieval System

Symantec provides technical notes on all its programs 24 hours a day via its Facsimile Retrieval System. The first thing to do when you ring up the service via a Touch-Tone phone is to order the 12-page Index of Technical Documents.

Once you've got the index, you can call again and select the topic you need help with. Someone else may have suffered the same problem and there may be a solution for you.

▌ ✔ 800-554-4403

Dialing for Dollars

Once your initial 90 days of free support has expired, Symantec offers all sorts of priority and premium care technical support services for $25 per *incident* (via credit card) or $2 a minute (via a 900 number). Alternatively, you can pay an annual fee of $149. To find out more about these extended services, call 800-441-7234.

Look at the Manual

If you need any incentive for giving the manual a try, read the preceding section.

Although we've all had problems with instruction manuals, every now and then they're worth picking up — if for no other reason than they need to be dusted. Maybe you gave up on the manual, and for good reason, when you first purchased Norton Utilities. However, with a bit more Norton experience under your belt, you may discover that the manual suddenly makes a lot more sense. You actually understand what it's saying and — shock upon shock — it is actually helpful. It could happen. Maybe you can get help in the manual after all.

Also, the manual contains more advanced information that you may become interested in once you've conquered the basics. The scope of this book is to get you using Norton Utilities. The manual will guide you to total global domination.

Not quite ready for global domination? That's okay, too. In the beginning of the manual are several chapters labeled as *Tutorials*.

They really aren't tutorials in the way that you might think of tutorials — you know, like lessons in school. They are in fact the basic step-by-step instructions required to use the software. You might try running through them if you're having problems.

Index

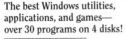

Order Form

Order Center: (800) 762-2974 (8 a.m.-5 p.m., PST, weekdays) or (415) 312-0650

For Fastest Service: Photocopy This Order Form and FAX it to: (415) 358-1260

Quantity	ISBN	Title	Price	Total

Shipping & Handling Charges

Subtotal	U.S.	Canada & International	International Air Mail
Up to $20.00	Add $3.00	Add $4.00	Add $10.00
$20.01-40.00	$4.00	$5.00	$20.00
$40.01-60.00	$5.00	$6.00	$25.00
$60.01-80.00	$6.00	$8.00	$35.00
Over $80.00	$7.00	$10.00	$50.00

In U.S. and Canada, shipping is UPS ground or equivalent.
For Rush shipping call (800) 762-2974.

Subtotal _____

CA residents add applicable sales tax _____

IN and MA residents add 5% sales tax _____

IL residents add 6.25% sales tax _____

RI residents add 7% sales tax _____

Shipping _____

Total _____

Ship to:

Name _____

Company _____

Address _____

City/State/Zip_____

Daytime Phone _____

Payment: ❑Check to IDG Books (US Funds Only)   ❑Visa   ❑Mastercard   ❑American Express

Card# _____ Exp._____ Signature_____

Please send this order form to: IDG Books, 155 Bovet Road, Suite 310, San Mateo, CA 94402.

Allow up to 3 weeks for delivery. Thank you!

IDG BOOKS WORLDWIDE REGISTRATION CARD

RETURN THIS REGISTRATION CARD FOR FREE CATALOG

Title of this book: Norton Utilities 8 For Dummies

My overall rating of this book: ❏ Very good [1] ❏ Good [2] ❏ Satisfactory [3] ❏ Fair [4] ❏ Poor [5]

How I first heard about this book:

❏ Found in bookstore; name: [6] _____

❏ Advertisement: [8]

❏ Word of mouth; heard about book from friend, co-worker, etc.: [10]

❏ Book review: [7]

❏ Catalog: [9]

❏ Other: [11]

What I liked most about this book:

_____

_____

What I would change, add, delete, etc., in future editions of this book:

_____

_____

Other comments: _____

_____

Number of computer books I purchase in a year: ❏ 1 [12] ❏ 2-5 [13] ❏ 6-10 [14] ❏ More than 10 [15]

I would characterize my computer skills as: ❏ Beginner [16] ❏ Intermediate [17] ❏ Advanced [18] ❏ Professional [19]

I use ❏ DOS [20] ❏ Windows [21] ❏ OS/2 [22] ❏ Unix [23] ❏ Macintosh [24] ❏ Other: [25]_____

(please specify)

I would be interested in new books on the following subjects:

(please check all that apply, and use the spaces provided to identify specific software)

❏ Word processing: [26]

❏ Data bases: [28]

❏ File Utilities: [30]

❏ Networking: [32]

❏ Other: [34]

❏ Spreadsheets: [27]

❏ Desktop publishing: [29]

❏ Money management: [31]

❏ Programming languages: [33]

I use a PC at (please check all that apply): ❏ home [35] ❏ work [36] ❏ school [37] ❏ other: [38] _____

The disks I prefer to use are ❏ 5.25 [39] ❏ 3.5 [40] ❏ other: [41]_____

I have a CD ROM: ❏ yes [42] ❏ no [43]

I plan to buy or upgrade computer hardware this year: ❏ yes [44] ❏ no [45]

I plan to buy or upgrade computer software this year: ❏ yes [46] ❏ no [47]

Name: _____ Business title: [48] _____ Type of Business: [49] _____

Address (❏ home [50] ❏ work [51]/Company name: _____)

Street/Suite# _____

City [52]/State [53]/Zipcode [54]: _____ Country [55] _____

❏ **I liked this book!** You may quote me by name in future
IDG Books Worldwide promotional materials.

My daytime phone number is _____

IDG BOOKS

THE WORLD OF COMPUTER KNOWLEDGE

❏ YES!

Please keep me informed about IDG's World of Computer Knowledge.
Send me the latest IDG Books catalog.